The New
GERMAN SHORTHAIRED
POINTER

by C. BEDE MAXWELL

Third Edition
ILLUSTRATED

with line drawings
by Phyllis Kjerulff

1979 — Fifth Printing
HOWELL BOOK HOUSE INC.
230 PARK AVENUE
NEW YORK, N.Y. 10017

Dr. Charles Thornton, in 1961, handed over his records and photos to the author. These are now in the American Kennel Club Library in New York City. *Photo: Shirley Miner.*

To the Great Pioneers,
DR. CHARLES R. THORNTON,
MR. JOSEPH BURKHART,
MR. WALTER MANGOLD,
MR. ERNEST ROJEM
whose breed strains dominate
the background of our best American dogs,
this NEW GERMAN SHORTHAIRED POINTER
is most respectfully dedicated.

Intensity, the mark of a keen hunting dog: Dual Ch. Sager v. Gardsburg.

Field Ch. GREIF V. HUNDSHEIMERKOGEL (imp. Austria)
Amazingly versatile, this great stud of modern times died in 1958.
He is shown here with his trainer, Stanley Head of California.

Contents

Acknowledgments vii

1. Origin and Early Development 10
2. 20th Century German Breed Pillars 30
3. Modern-Day Strains in Germany 46
4. The Early American Scene 63
5. Progress in American Breeding 79
6. German Shorthaired Pointers in the West Coast 94
7. From the 1960s into the 1970s 112
8. The Danish Strains 124
9. The German Shorthaired Pointer in Britain 131
10. The Field Trial Dog 147
    The Shorthair in Obedience 169
11. Field Trials for German Shorthaired Pointers in America 171
12. Physical Constitution of the German Shorthaired Pointer 189
13. Showing Your German Shorthaired Pointer 192
14. The Standard 207
15. Breeding Your German Shorthaired Pointer 239
16. Picking Shorthair Pups 282
17. Gait 287
18. German Titles, Vocabulary, Etc. 295
    Bibliography 304

History maker Am. & Can. Ch. Gretchenhof Columbia River, only GSP to ever win Best in Show at Westminster (1974). "Traveler's" AKC record includes 29 BIS, 102 G1, 44 other Group placings and 182 BOBs including 3 independent Specialties. Bred by L. V. McGilbrey, owned by Dr. Richard Smith, and handled by Joyce Shellenbarger.—*Ludwig*

Am. & Can. Ch. Jillard of Whispering Pines, C.D., a foremost winning bitch, with record of 75 BOBs, 7 G1, 19 other Group placings, and win of 3 Specialties including the Eastern GSPC over entry of 265. Owned and handled by Patrick and Sally Nannola.

Acknowledgments

SINCERE thanks are due to the many breeders who so generously made their cherished records available towards the compilation of this book. Far too many to be named individually, their contributions are made plain within the body of the text, for lacking these contributions there could have been, of course, no book at all.

In particular, though, our indebtedness must be acknowledged in respect to the contributions of the great pioneers. Dr. Charles R. Thornton, of Washington, made available his complete kennel records, pedigrees, photographs, journals. Mr. Walter Mangold, of Nebraska, also forwarded his German pedigrees and much information on pioneering experience with the breed. Mr. Joseph Burkhart, of Minnesota, went to a great deal of trouble to clarify historical puzzles, as did Mr. Rudolph Hirschnitz, of California. German Shorthaired Pointer breeders of the present day should never underestimate their indebtedness to these pioneers, in both the practical and the historical sense.

Thanks are due, also, to the several breeders of our time who were history-minded enough to keep informative files, and generous enough to make them available. Here we owe to Mr. Donald Miner, of California, Miss Irene Pauly and Mr. Thomas Witcher, also of California. For practical help and encouragement, thanks also to Mr. and Mrs. J. Deiss and Mr. and Mrs. Don Sandberg, of Minnesota. We are indebted to Dr. Lewis L. Kline, of Florida, and Dr. Wm. Hartnell, of Utah, for information concerning the background of the Danish imports, and to Mrs. Earle Dapper, of Sacramento, and Mrs. K. Metcalf Allen, of Carmel, for many kindnesses.

From overseas, help was very extensively given. From the amazing historical records of The Kennel Club (England) came the matter on which is based the first part of the chapter on the German Shorthaired Pointer in Britain, this through the courtesy of the Assistant-Secretary, Mr. C. A. Binney. The German Shorthaired Pointer Club (England) also made much historical matter available through the kindness of the Secretary, Mr. Arthur W. Mongor, and through many individual members, especially Mr. Michael Brander, of Scotland. The newly-formed German Shorthaired Pointer Club in Ireland also was helpful, through the President, Mrs. W. L. G. Dean.

The Osterreichischer Kurzhaar Klub (Vienna, Austria) provided valuable information and cherished historical photographs, this through the untiring interest of the Secretary, Dr. Otto Fischer. Klub Kurzhaar Berlin (Stammklub DK) also helped, officially as a body and individually through members. Here our debt is especially great with respect to the compilation of the Kleeman-Auslese-Prüfung placings in the years since competition was resumed in this most important event following World War II. For this we are indebted to the interest of Herr F. Böllhoff, of Münster. Herr Carl Seidler, of Südwestdeutscher Klub Kurzhaar, its President, is also a contributor as is, in a most special way, Frau Maria Seydel, of Recklingshausen-Süd. This famous breeder made generous loan of many priceless basic breed monographs and historical matter, including a copy of the breed's definitive work, by Dr. Paul Kleeman and Herr v. Otto, which is so frequently referred to in the text of this book. Opportunity to peruse this in the original language has clarified much that had until now been lost to us through the confusions of translation. In addition, Frau Seydel forwarded back issues of sports and hunting magazines that presented aspects of modern German Shorthaired Pointer development in post-war Germany, enabling us to take an objective look at the present-day status there of her beloved breed.

For historical photographs and engravings culled from his library, one of the world's great collections of canine bibliography, we owe thanks to the keen sporting dog enthusiast, judge and breeder, Leonard L. de Groen, President of the Gundog Society of Australia.

To all these helpers specifically, as well as to the hundreds besides who have contributed in the individual sense, the thanks of the publishers, the compiler, and the German Shorthaired Pointer breeders of the present and the future, are hereby gratefully extended.

C. Bede Maxwell

Ch. Gretchenhof Moonshine, retiring at the age of 4, compiled 15 BIS and 50 G1, a record in the breed. Top Sporting for 1963 (Phillips system), she was owned by Gretchenhof Kennels, California.   *Photo: Mrs. C. B. Maxwell*

1

Origin and
Early Development

THE popular modern utility sporting breed known as the German Shorthaired Pointer was brought into being over a term of years to suit the rapidly changing needs of 19th century German hunting sport. Hunting privileges, long reserved for the wealthy nobles, had become available to lesser men who owned or rented their game preserves. Such men did not want to maintain big kennels of specialized breeds, even had a saying that a man who went hunting with three dogs had NO dog!

Yet it was clear that to enjoy sport with only one dog along it would need to be capable in every sphere. It must point the game its good nose had first allowed it to find, do this at reasonable distance for a man hunting afoot. It must retrieve fur or feather, from land or water. It must have the will and courage to destroy predators, and tracking instinct to trail a blood spoor of a wounded animal if necessary. No humane hunter would wish to leave touched game to die miserably.

The intention to breed all these qualities into one dog demanded work, time, breeder co-operation. The latter, of course, proved the hardest to get, humans being humans. While all concerned agreed upon the qualities a versatile hunting dog would need, from the first there was widest disagreement as to how these could be secured and fixed in a true-breeding strain.

Breeders could use only material available—flesh-and-blood dogs that actually existed in the country. Mere pre-vision of some dreamed-of ideal paid no dividends in any practical sense. That some widely variant sources were co-opted is made clear by old records and pictures, the historically recorded and unrecorded experiments of such enterprising men as Hofjaeger Isermann, of Nordhausen, and many others.

Nowadays, Klub Kurzhaar (Berlin) admits frankly that early experimental German Shorthaired Pointer breeding produced stock that little resembled the breed type as fixed today, either shapewise, temperamentwise, even coatwise. In a letter of 1961, the Klub spokesman pointed out that early types bore about the same resemblance to present dogs as did Man's ancestor, the ape, to human beings of our time. Dr. Paul Kleeman, long time *Vorsitzender* (President) of Klub Kurzhaar, the third to hold the honor in the life of the Klub, the most knowledgeable authority to write of the German Shorthaired Pointer development, makes many references to pioneer activities—and squabbling!

The more practical breeders recognized that the dogs would most likely be produced by breeding selectively to performance, possibly the reason so many different strains, types, even breeds, were used. As a practical measure, the services of dogs that were actually available in the country were used. One group held to firm belief that Germany had once possessed an ancient sporting dog of all possible virtues and dedicated itself to reproducing its like. This group clung to outward physical indications believed to indicate inherited working qualities. They held these to be mainly long, rounded ears, a stopless profile. Dr. Kleeman's belief, as published, was that the historical paragon belonged to the realm of fairytale—a *Märchen*, he described it. He also reminded all that clamored for "such a dog as our fathers hunted with" that most of their fathers had been only thwarted onlookers. Their "social betters" had kept the hunting privileges jealously to themselves.

Germany's ancient dogs, as those of Europe, including England, were, by the old-time writings, endless variations on the theme of

11

the Old Spanish Pointer and the Hounds of St. Hubert. "Old Spanish" had fanned out first from Mediterranean lands at civilization's heels. St. Hubert's are believed to have reached the famed French monastery with the Crusaders returned from the East, these bringing to Europe not only new kinds of dogs, horses, modes of architecture, but even modes of thought, an everlasting influence. "Old Spanish" was much valued. Basic of all sporting breeds that stand to game, his instinct to hesitate momentarily before springing has, down the centuries, been sharply honed by sporting men to their finest tool. The St. Hubert's brought cold-trailing abilities. They stand as the progenitors of all scenting hounds now known to us, either in modern or historical representation.

Many ancient writers, artists, have left descriptions of "Old Spanish." The engravers show him with heavy head, jowl, deep flews, large sunken eyes, upthrust nose with a cleft "double" nostril. His bone was huge, his coat a little rough, but never enough to fuzz his outline. His tail was docked. His liver-and-white color scheme was also his gift to sporting breeds. Surely no beauty, he was nevertheless the pride of kings in his day, hunting to hawk or net. Pointing was his virtue, slow gait his vice. When firearms developed, were improved, when men could shoot down birds where they flew dark against the sky, sportsmen everywhere set out to liven "Old Spanish" with some cross-breeding.

The English went to Foxhound, gaining elegance and speed to make their new specialized Pointer a national pride. Foxhound colors prettied the sober liver-and-white, the lemon, orange, black fleckings and patchings, and even solid blacks and full livers. The solids, in our time, are extremely rare. The Germans long ago used the black to form one type of German Shorthaired Pointers, and Scandinavian countries still have some true-type solid blacks, while Australia's best known Pointer breeder of today also has such a bitch. That America has had solid livers is to be proved by an historical painting in the De Young Museum, San Francisco, in which such a one is running with the turnout of Mr. Ogden Mills, of California.

The French also livened "Old Spanish," securing stepped-up elegance in the production of beautiful pack hounds, especially, with diverse variation of St. Hubert stock. Widely distributed, these became basics of other breed developments. Those who think

THE OLD SPANISH POINTER, painted Stubbs (1724–1806).

Photo lent by L. L. de Groen, Australia.

Early German Pointers—the breed in transitional stage.

Photo lent by L. L. de Groen, Australia.

of scent hounds only in terms of Bloodhound or Basset heaviness and wrinkle should check historical pictures of the Talbots and other vanished tall French hounds—the Gascons, Normandys, etc., and even the Kerry Beagles (Ireland), pure French Talbot in origin and so maintained, a century and more, standing to 24″, with wrinkle-free heads—to prove how type could be changed and maintained. Kerry Beagles, as their photos show, had even that round ear the German pioneers craved, and straight profiles as well. The superb Talbot brace in the famed painting (now in Christchurch Museum, New Zealand) of the great British colonizer, Edward Gibbon Wakefield, a notable dog fancier in his day, also shows what could be done in terms of beautiful-headed tall hounds.

The 19th century French were well ahead of the Germans in breeding up good-looking, balanced hunting dogs from original clumsy material. Comparison of the 1871 experimental German Shorthaired Pointer, Feldmann I, with the 1865 prize-winning Gascon Hound, Genereaux, at the Paris Exhibition is in this respect interesting. This Genereaux will not look *too* strange to German Shorthaired Pointer folk, apart from his ears and tail. Balance-wise, he leaves Feldmann I for dead! E. v. Otto describes Feldmann I, bred by the Prince Albrecht zu Solms-Brauenfels, as *dreifarbig* (tricolor). Genereaux, following true to the Gascon Hounds, was blue-mottled. As it turned out, French breeders of the 19th century backed the wrong horse. Hunting with pack hounds went out of style in the practical sense with changing ways of life, fencing of properties, but the German Shorthaired Pointer's dog-of-all-work status has been upheld in popularity even to the present day.

Some among modern-day breeders here still argue strenuously from the firm, if wishful, belief within their own hearts that the background of the German Shorthaired Pointer is to be found only as "Old Spanish." *No* English Pointer, no, sir! No Hound, no! Some "authorities" have even engaged themselves with confidence in compartmentizing the breed heritage—so much percent Pointer, so much percent Bloodhound, etc. etc. Anyone could be so definite!

Dr. Kleeman points out that early-day German breeders had access to several types of pointing dogs, often as developed first in other countries. There was also a little native German "bracken," considered of little merit and hard to train. However, the hunting fraternity (*Jägerei*), the Hanoverian especially, had long favored

"Généreaux," a Gascon Hound, won First Prize, Paris Exhibition, 1865. The French were first with tall, wrinkle-free sporting dogs.

Photo lent by L. L. de Groen, Australia.

Feldmann I, not reg., wh. 1871. An early experimental dog, owned by Prince zu Solms-Braunenfels of the Royal House of Hannover.

infusion of English Pointer to improve the noses of their dogs. As Dr. Kleeman clarifies the squabbling for us, the opposition interest, obsessed with patriotic aspirations, wanted nothing English—not even dogs. These people could not be persuaded that to the required qualities of Pointer nose and style could also be added the utility qualities the Pointer admittedly did not have. Serious breeders admitted the deficiency of the Pointer in utility respects, but clung to a belief that weldings could be contrived. One faction, then, would seem to have argued along positive lines, the other along negative.

By 1879, when some widely divergent breed types had already appeared, the patriotic believers in an ancient German utility dog held strength enough in Committee to enforce their views. They denied the Stud Book to any dog lacking round ears, a stopless profile. All right, present-day "Old Spanish" fans, look away from *him* as the sole breed founder—his profile was anything *but* stopless! Look rather to inheritance from St. Hubert—say, such a browed profile as the now-vanished Talbots showed—along with other hound badges, such as that short roughness under the tail, and the slightly longer hair in back of the thighs, as these are still asked for by the American breed standard for the German Shorthaired Pointer.

Argument has long ranged as to whether the German Shorthaired Pointer does or does not owe to the Bloodhound. It must be accepted that modern German authority rejects any such notion entirely. The Germans have tried their best to kill the stubborn belief that was fostered first by English-writing "historians" of the breed. It has been officially spelled out for us. First, in 1951, in answer to California pioneer breeder, Rudolph Hirschnitz, Herr Rommeswinkel, long-term President of Klub Kurzhaar (Berlin) spelled it out all the way. NO BLOODHOUND! This breed had *nothing* to do with Kurzhaar inheritance! In 1961, the present writer enquired from Klub Kurzhaar whether there had been any change of thought. A spokesman for the Parent Club (Herr Rommeswinkel being now dead) was just as emphatic: *"There has never been any connection between our breed and the hound known in English as the Bloodhound.* True, the Kurzhaar in his work is set upon the *Schweiss-spur* (the blood trail) of wounded game. From this, doubtless, we hear so often that fairy tale of Bloodhound origin prevailing in America especially." (*Letter to the author, June 28, 1961.*)

16

The Talbot Hound of the 1700's (from "Cynographic Brittanica," 1800), prototype of many breeds of European Scent hounds. The Talbot is now extinct but lives on in many a present-day modification.

Photo lent by L. L. de Groen, Australia.

In the shape and make of Wodan Hektor II v. Lemgo, 1276, wh. 1888, may be seen the legacy of the Talbot Hound inheritance used by pioneer breeders. His body proportions, length in relation to height, and distinctly ram-nose profile, constitute the proof of it. Wodan Hektor II is an all-time breed basic; many of the best German Shorthaired Pointer pedigrees are founded upon him. Owner: Professor Engler, Lemgo.

The misconception has, however, been so often repeated it is now held by most to be truth. Wherever interested folk have written of the German Shorthaired Pointer in English they seem to have culled from the same limited sources, each one repeating the other's error. Actually, the original mistake seems to have turned on one of those traps that lurk in translating language.

The German name for the Bloodhound as a separate breed IS *Schweisshund*. German writers on the German Shorthaired Pointer *do* specifically say that the foresters' working dogs were *Schweisshunde,* and that these were incorporated into the developing utility breed. However, dictionary definition of *Schweiss* is "scent, sweat, moisture, perspiration, exudation, and the blood-trail, as in hunting." *Any* dog that will follow *Schweiss* (scent in any form) is therefore a *Schweisshund*—even a police-tracking Doberman or German Shepherd. *Hund* means "dog," not necessarily "hound." If he works a trail, presto—he's a *Schweisshund.* But by no manner of means is he necessarily a *Bloodhound.* If the German language were written in the same way as English, the use of the capital letter would clarify the point—Bloodhound, as a separate breed, spelled with a capital *B,* and bloodhound, as a tracking dog, with a small *b.* The German language capitalizes all nouns.

However, if the Germans are firm in repudiating the heavy, wrinkled hound that the English know as a Bloodhound, they would never doubt that, as all Scent Hounds trace to the same St. Hubert origin, the Bloodhound shares with their own lighter-bodied, trail-keeping types of that earlier day the qualities inherited from their mutual ancestors. For this we may look in passing at a description of the *English* Bloodhound of the very time the Germans were making their new breed. It comes from one of the best of 19th century dog writers, "Idstone."

"They (the Bloodhounds) are for the most part—for tempers vary in dogs as in Christians—amiable, sagacious, faithful, obedient, docile. They are tremendously clever at tracking wounded deer and are, additionally, as a breed, tremendously fond of water. Theirs, too, is the gift of bell-like baying that distinguishes all hounds gifted with keen discrimination and delicate powers of scenting, holding to the line. They can retrieve most tenderly, and decidedly they propagate good scenting power, mate them to what you will." (*THE DOG,* "*Idstone,*" *p. 59.*)

18

In that easily-recognizable catalog are counted out the exact qualities that the Germans wanted for their new dog; that came with the universal heritage of Scent Hounds through the ancient endowment. All over Europe, in one bodily shape or another, were good, nice-natured, working scenthounds (SCHWEISSHUNDE, yet!) with these virtues. All over Europe, they were being combined with this and with that. None of these virtues belonged to "Old Spanish," said to have been a surly fellow even at his temperamental best. As they were incorporated into the developing German utility dog they did not come from him. One thing, though, the *Schweisshunde* of the German foresters must have been spryer on their legs than the English Bloodhound of the time. "Idstone" writes that the Bloodhounds were so slow they were carried on horseback to where a trail began!

In compiling the history of any breed—or of anything!—there is always danger in following unquestioningly the tracks of the Other Guy. This is vividly stressed in other aspects of German Short-haired Pointer history besides that of the trap in translation that the Bloodhound belief represents. One rather startling example, long overdue for revision, was that discoverable in the unlikely location of the A.K.C. official publication, *The Complete Dog Book*. It would have electrified the German authorities, with their rigid breed control, strict stud books, to have read in the 1961 edition that "...about fifty years ago, German and Austrian sportsmen, looking with envy on the speed and dash of our American pointers, straightway started to cross their heavy German Pointer with our American or English pointer."

In newer editions of the A.K.C. book the statement has been removed. Nothing in the breed history, in fact, suggests that at any stage the German Shorthaired Pointer in his homeland was subjected to irregular cross-breeding with the American Pointer, nor that foreign breeders envied any of that breed's qualities, speed, dash or whatever. Parallel claim, made in 1942, in *How To Train Hunting Dogs*, by Wm. F. Brown, may have been drawn from this A.K.C. source (or the other way around!). On p. 21, Mr. Brown claims: "With the growth of popularity of (American) Field Trials, there was an infusion of the agile American Pointer to streamline the conformation of the Shorthair."

Both statements, unfortunately, appear to endorse officially a prac-

19

tice that, where provable, is of such irregularity as to render the produce of such cross-mating unregisterable, in Europe or here. As these books tend to fall into the hands of novices, it is not at all impossible that the dangerous mis-directions may be taken for gospel, inspiring like experimentation. In truth, though the Pointer *was* originally combined with other breeds to form the German Shorthaired Pointer a century ago, the latter has long, long since developed into a separate breed. Any belief that the re-introduction of Pointer (or any other basic breed) is merely "in the family" procedure is quite erroneous. To breed together a Pointer and a German Shorthaired Pointer in this age is to bring about a cross-breeding, a mongrelization.

In early years of importation here, hunting men buying from pioneer breeders such as Dr. Thornton, not understanding they were buying purebreds, sometimes did ignorantly crossbreed their German Shorthaired Pointers not only to "the agile American Pointer" but to the agile Springer, Setter, Coonhound, even to the agile Heinz in his many varieties. Dr. Thornton often received photos of mongrelized produce of his stock—to his horror! However, such dogs were unregisterable, dropped from sight. If, later, "with the growth of popularity of Field Trials" there *has* been "infusion of the agile American Pointer" it must of necessity have been secretly done. Registration of resulting stock could only be secured by fraudulent misrepresentation. The A.K.C. does not knowingly register German Shorthaired Pointers with American Pointer sires or dams. For that reason, and for the danger that novices may gain a wrong impression of what is or is not permissible or even wise, it is good that the serious error in the official Book and Standards has been withdrawn.

Back to the 1870's . . . Early experimentation in Germany produced at first some very undesirable, often awkward dogs, heavy-bodied, stumpy-legged. Progress, as in all the undertakings of man, had to be by trial and error. The stubborn patriots lost themselves entirely, chasing head and ear shape, though the more malleable saw merit in the direction given by their early-day patron, Prince Albrecht zu Solms-Brauenfels, of the Royal House of Hanover. He gave the breeders a direction best now to be translated into the familiar "Form Follows Function." He told them that the only way to develop the wished-for utility dog-of-all-virtues was to take and use only the dogs best performed in these requirements, not to worry at this early stage about outward appearances. These would with time take care of themselves. He gave a practical lead by his own experiments in breeding, producing some truly extraordinary-looking dogs, with what future influence on the breed we do not now know. Doubtless they too were basics.

Time proved the Prince's direction valid. Form *did* follow Function, eventually producing the dog known to us today. All manner of plums went into the pudding: hound, pointer, braque, with a dash of setter. All elements were eventually blended skilfully, culled, reblended to produce a competely new breed. It was then no longer—*nor is it now*—possible to re-introduce any of these components in the "raw" state without the irregularity screaming out for all to recognize, be the introduction sporting dog or hound.

The stubborn continued to ignore the Prince's direction. When the performance of the early-registered dogs, chosen by the appearance pattern, the head-and-ear deal, matched his worst forebodings, His Highness bowed out of the breed interest. Dr. Kleeman, in his famed breed monograph, *Deutsch Kurzhaar,* also shrugs off the early approvals of the Stud Book, including Hektor I, the first entry.

"Unenergetic, cold-blooded clods," he held them, and "anciently German" only wherein they in part resembled "Old Spanish." Their performance was as clumsy as their looks. He quotes a contemporary who held there was as much sport to be had hunting fleas across the back of a German poodle as in hunting birds with a German dog. Of the deliberations of the Klub he reports sourly: "Nature errs never—committees very often!" This, by the way, is as true now as then.

Prince zu Solms' directive, though, had not gone for nothing. There were breeders choosing their stock on grounds of ability, and there was much use of the English Pointer to improve that most important tool of all, the nose. From among such appeared, in 1881, Herr Julius Mehlich, of Berlin, working the first really well performed German Shorthaired Pointer, Nero 66. At a Pointer/Setter trial at Buckow, this brown, tick-chested, strong, fast, good-nosed dog made a fine showing, though the traditionalists took after him, full cry, for his lack of a "German head," calling him an English Pointer. Herr Mehlich seems to have given no argument, but in later years Dr. Kleeman specifically named Mehlich's strain

Meisterzuchter Julius Mehlich with his foundation dog, Nero 66 (Hoppenrade), in 1883.

Photo: Courtesy, Kurzhaar Blätter, *Germany*.

as Pointer-endowed, but for more than merely the evidence of Nero's head.

In 1883, Mehlich's Nero 66 was in the news again, tying first in the German Derby with the brown dog, Treff, always identified by two numbers, 1010 in the German all-breed registration, and 56 in the new Kurzhaar Stud book. The tie-placing is interesting, for these two brown dogs are the all-time breed pillars.

After that Derby, Herr Mehlich and Nero were guests at the hunting preserve of "Hoppenrade." A charming story, told in several places, German and Danish, tells of Nero taking off under the eyes of the host, Herr Smidt, after a touched hare. The dog was so long gone the party thought he had met with accident. Then—suddenly! —there was Nero, on the far side of a swift stream, the hare heavy in his jaws. Despite what had been a long, weary carry, Nero plunged into the swift water, battled across to bring the hare to Herr Mehlich. Herr Smidt was loud in admiration. "From this time on, you are no longer merely Nero 66—you are Nero v. *Hoppenrade!* And the name shall be given to all your descendants as well."

So was the famous strain name gained. Nero's descendants lent it luster, and it is paramount in early-day breeding, with Nero's granddaughter, Erra Hoppenrade, 382, having the honor to count No. 1 in the Gebrauchshunde-Stammbuch (the German Working Dog stud book) after her 1892 competition wins. Erra's dam, Cora 40, was litter sister to Sally, the dam of Treff 1010, and she shared Treff's sire, Boncoeur 30.

(Note. In some publications, Erra's name is erroneously given as Gora. Matching historical sources prove the No. 1 registration went to an Erra, *382; it may be that the mistake is based on confusion with the name of her dam—Cora.)*

Nero 66 was dead within the year, a bitter 1884 loss to Herr Mehlich. That same year, his daughter Flora produced three browns to Hektor 64 (Treff ex Diana, wh. 1880). They were Waldin, 175, Waldo, 174, Hertha, 188. Dr. Kleeman sees the true turn of breed fortune in these, especially when Waldin made his mark against Pointer/Setter competition in an English-style field trial at Buckow. This best Nero grandson was known as "Kranzler's Waldin," an honor to his owner, A. Kranzler, of Berlin. Waldin won the admiration of the German Emperor, who enjoyed the dog's work on pheasant to such an extent that he commissioned a famed German artist, Sperling, to paint Waldin's picture.

In those years, Hoppenrade dogs placed a mortgage on Derby competition especially. Many of the names gained fame; Harras and Morell, Maitrank, were all great names in early breed history. Much credit seems to rest with the introduction Herr Mehlich made from the breeding of Herr Koch, of Bohnenwald, the bitch Holla (later Hoppenrade). She was the first full-ticked introduction to this strain of chest-ticked solid brown (liver), and is identified as being by Caro from Cora 180. Her quality must have been excellent, and this is luckily provable in the comments of a judge who put her up in London (England) as B.O.B. in 1887. Her sons, Morell (brown, ticked chest) and Maitrank (ticked and patched), are her memorials within the breed.

Photographs show a tremendous difference, typewise, between Morell and Maitrank—much, much more than one would expect from half-brothers whose sires were father and son, Morell being by Waldin, 175, and Maitrank by Waldin's son, Balsam Hoppenrade. However, some interesting scuttlebutt is recorded by Herr Sahre, in the 1962 Winter issue of *Kurzhaar Blätter,* the Klub Kurzhaar breed paper. He tells how the breed-master of Hoppenrade, one morning, when Holla was in full flush of season, found in her kennel the brown Pointer, Donner, who had chewed his way through the fence to reach her. On the same day, she was mated to Balsam. However, Herr Sahre points out that to expect that she entertained her enterprising caller all night without results is to expect rather much, though, actually, nothing had been witnessed. From this mating mix-up came the useful and prepotent derby-winning Maitrank Hoppenrade, wh. 1890, who resembles no other Hoppenraden dogs as their photographs come down to us, but who is recognized as a breed pillar of worth. In this early stage of breed formation, the irregularity (if any) could be absorbed, though many breeders noted Maitrank's virtues as only Derby.

Herr Mehlich died in 1893, his strain woven through the developing breed. Meanwhile, it is necessary to backtrack to Treff 1010. No great beauty in modern sight, this dog is the most solid taproot of all. He set his name all over, and most dogs trace to him. Not to be confused with all the other Treffs to be located in early pedigrees, he is always identified by his double numerical endowment.

Saul-Fuhrberg (reg.), Schweisshunde, a recognized European breed, much used by foresters modernly. Prinz zu Solms-Brauenfels owned many good ones. Saul bears close resemblance to GSP taproot, Treff 1010 (below).

Juno 192, wh. 1882, bred and owned by Hofjaeger F. Isermann of Nordhausen. This is the earliest photo so far found of a registered German Shorthaired Pointer bitch. She is in many basic pedigrees.

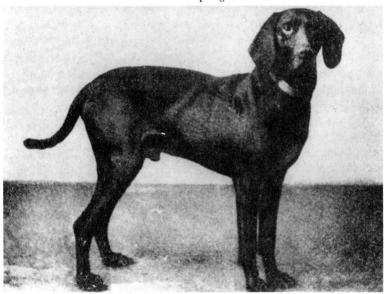

Treff 1010, ZK 56, wh. 1881. Most pedigrees in the breed trace to Treff (Wodan Hektor II was his grandson). Diversity of pioneer breed type is made plain in comparison of Treff with Cora.

His parents, Boncoeur 30 and Sally, the sister of Cora 40, are described for us also by Herr Sahre—Boncoeur 30, wh. 1878, as mostly brown, strong, but not inelegant, and of Cora 40 only her whelping date of 1879. Their location was in Thüringia.

Treff is everywhere to be found, but strongest perhaps in his v. Lemgo get. Founded by Professor Julius Engler, of Lemgo, based on his brown-ticked Juno v. Lemgo, 1315 (ex Wanda Brokemeier by Treu 93, a brown whose dam, Wanda 80, had a double cross of Hektor I), the most useful history of this strain so far encountered was that written (in Danish) in 1915 by Stationsforstander N.B. Buchwald, of Viborg, Denmark, published in the 1933 issue of the Danish Kurzhaar Klub magazine. Nor are v. Lemgo and Hoppenrade the only strains clarified in these history-rich publications of so much merit in compilation.

From a ticked son of Treff 1010, acquired by Prof. Engler, Wodan Hektor I v. Lemgo, 1275, wh. 1883, ex Diana v. Bünau, came Wodan Hektor II v. Lemgo, 1276, wh. 1888. This dog, of visible improvement in appearance, drew from Herr Richard v. Schmiederberg, judge, that this strain was "too handsome to be German!" But it was actually still a time when Form lagged behind Function. Registration numbers suggest many may have been bred, few retained. Such cull wastage attends upon the formation of any new breed, screening out unwanted characteristics. (As the Australians wrote of forming their cattle dog from radical crossing: "We bred a lot and we drowned a lot!")

Problems of experimental breeders can be visualized by comparing Treff's photo with that of Juno 192. Whelped 1882 to Treff's 1881, Juno is the earliest-dated bitch whose photo we have found. By an unidentified Feldmann from an unidentified Diana, owned by the bravely experimental breeder, Hofjaeger Isermann of Nordhausen, she shows as thick-headed, clumsy, Hektor-One-ish, the type that displeased Dr. Kleeman. Yet her mating to Treff 1010 underpins much contemporary breeding, and history knows her as the ancestress of Rubin Hoppenrade and the fine Hektor v. Pirna. The Danish breeding, where we first picked up her track, owes to her daughter, Bessie v. Jagerhaus, 254, mated to Marki, 322, the son of Waldin, 175, doubtless explaining breed-type improvement. Her great-grandson, Larron v. Sonderhausen, is one of Denmark's most important basics.

With Herr Mehlich's death in 1893, new names come to view—
v. Lemgo, v. Freudenthal, Holzweiler, Altenau, v. Freithof, Alten-
bach, v.d. goldenen Mark. The ear-and-head party saw its clumsy
dogs outclassed. The zu Solms direction began to make sense. It
became clear that Pointer nose *could* be kept, separated from unwanted Pointer characteristics such as aversion to trailing, dislike
of water, jam-tail flight from, instead of at, predators. Utility
qualities were secured from the good working dogs of the foresters,
the *Schweisshunde*—but NOT bloodhounds!

Most good early-day dogs were brown (liver). It was long held
the only permissable Kurzhaar color. Many were chest-ticked, as
Waldin, 175, his son Morell, 444, and daughters; as Graf Hoyer v.
Mansfeld, 867, as Trumpf Otto, 2129, a most distinguished one.
The v. Lemgos, mostly ticked, carried the brown of Juno's sire,
Treu, 93, as in the Wodan Hektor II v. Lemgo son, Nidung, 1288,
and his good great-grandson, Waldo Waldheim, 178 B, ex Tellus
v. Freudenthal's daughter, Hertha v.d. Maylust, 4622, a fine dam
force, both these latter being ticked and patched.

Behind Nidung, wh. 1890, seems also to lie experiment. Stationsforstander Buchwald, in his v. Lemgo history, intimates that Nidung's solid-color dam, Frigga v. Berry, 1338, wh. 1886, owes to
Irish Setter! In detail he describes her coat, rough and coarse, her
body longish, standing over a lot of ground: "as an Irish hunter," as
Herr Buchwald translates the familiar phrase. Frigga was owned
and used as a matron by Professor Engler, but Hofjaeger Isermann
bred her, her parentage given as Wanda, 149, and yet another unidentified Hektor, who may have been *it*. As long coat is recessive to
short, and Frigga v. Berry, as pictured, is out of tune with accepted
Kurzhaar shape, maybe Herr Buchwald has the right of it. However, her son, Nidung, proved a strong breed pillar.

The setter incross proved fairly persistent, lingering along the
generations to pop up every so often with some longish-haired
whelps, as Herr Sahre, in his fine breed summary of 1962, also notes
(p. 573, *Kurzhaar Blätter,* Winter 1962). This proved to be especially the case in connection with the descendants of Golo Holzweiler, whom we will presently meet. So much so, that breeders
often took care to advertise proudly that *their* stock was *"Golo-frei,"*
that is, lacked Golo.

Waldo Waldheim, 178 B, wh. January 1900, links the centuries,

Tellus v. Freudenthal, wh. 1893, a son of Wodan Hektor II v. Lemgo, was known as "The Medal Dog." He is also a famed breed basic.

especially with his brown son, Caro Latferde, 245 D, wh. 1902. Caro sired roman-nosed Tell aus der Wolfsschlucht, 358 H, wh. 1907. Tell showed all desired virtues, including docility and style. Interestingly, the Germans rate docility high. Rightly, for lacking it, other qualities can be water over the dam. Tell is remembered too for long life, a familiar good in this breed. German Shorthaired Pointers well into their teens are not unusual. Since molding a good sporting dog takes time and money, longevity is a useful bonus.

From Tell we have K.S. Michel v.d. goldenen Mark, 422 M, wh. 1911. His name backstops many American strains. His color, brown, came not only from Tell, but from his dam, Beye's Vilja v.d. goldenen Mark, 542 K, whose brother, Beyes Stopp, 683 K, channeled solid color on and down. By the 1920's, though, fashion was losing solid color. Old Jagdjunker v. Bassewitz, of Schwerin-Mecklenburg, his strain founded on Trumpf Otto, was asking sadly: *"Wo sind sie hin, die guten braunen Gebrauchshunde auf die wir mit Recht stolz waren? Sie sind verschwunden und vergessen!"* ("What has become of them, the good brown utility dogs of which we were rightly so proud? They are vanished and forgotten!")

Dr. Kleeman said, not so! In the Kurzhaar issue of *Deutschen Jager-Zeitung* of 1921, he points out that the good brown utility dogs of Schwerin, Trumpf Otto blood strong within them, were still a breed force. What the breeders had once in these still flourished. Color may have dwindled, but the qualities were there. Work must be done to restore the solids to their place in the breed. Dog breeds, as the world we live in, require all kinds to produce harmony and balance.

With K. S. Michel v.d. Goldenen Mark, we look directly back to Treff 1010. From brave experimentation of the 1870's/1880's, to the goodlooking, well-performed Sieger of 1911, thirty years had seen the new breed established. True to Prince Solms' forecast, Form had faithfully followed Function.

2

20th Century
German Breed Pillars

As important as it is interesting, is the chain of inheritance, among the many examined in these pages with relation to the influence exerted on American breeding, anchored on Golo Holzweiler, 123 c.

Wh. 1902, bred by Th. Rings, of Holzweiler, an active pioneer breeder, this dog's name soon becomes familiar to serious breed students. Historians seem unable to make up their minds whether to praise or damn him. His background is full of question marks, his utility qualities were about minus, and yet he is behind so many of the breed's best dogs! Dr. Kleeman said his blood was so mixed (heterogeneous) as to be difficult to blend into existing strains. Herr v. Otto saw him as less desirable as a type than as a means to secure it. Later historians repeat these opinions (often as their own!).

Some breed writers claim him to be Pointer-sired. His pedigree does not say so, but there he was, with his big head and his dished face that matches poorly with that roman-nosed profile of Wodan Hektor II v. Lemgo, to whom he carried back along several lines.

Golo Holzweiler, 123 c., wh. 1902. He was a most controversial stud, but to be found behind great dogs. His dishface may explain his ability to endow his get with wonderful scenting power.

K.S. Michel v.d. goldenen Mark, 422 M, wh. 1911, in strength behind many of the best dogs, German, Danish, and American. A powerful source of solid color. Note the "hound" signature of his ram's nose. Comparison with Golo (above) emphasizes the diversity of inheritance incorporated by pioneer breeders, weldings fixed in all the best dogs.

He tended to throw a percentage of stock with longish coats, which ties up with the Nidung line behind him. Yet he had good qualities —his nose, his constitution, his easy-keeper habit, maybe his setter-gentlemanly temperament. These things he gave his stock. His owner used him, and some of his friends, and with success. Some other breeders, strong in utility-bred stock, tried too, and though many failed with Golo, some had great success. For American interest, the most successful was Herr Gschwindt, whose famed Südwest line contributed much on this side of the Atlantic. It was founded on his Trudel Südwest, 226, wh. 1918, with eight crosses to Golo!

For specific step-by-step information on Golo's breeding we are again in debt to the Danish Kurzhaar Klub compilations. These take us to Wodan Hektor II v. Lemgo, and to Nidung. Golo's grand-dams (maternal and paternal) were German-registered Kurzhaar—Mary Holzweiler, 5349, and Spinne, 2499. His sire, Nimrod II Otzenrath (ex Spinne), was also fully registered in Germany. He, in turn, was by the brown, Nimrod Otzenrath, 3799, a Tellus v. Freudenthal son ex Morna v. Mansfeld, she a brown of brown parentage, Graf Hoyer v. Mansfeld and Janka v. Jägerhaus (granddaughter of brown Treff 1010). Golo's dam, Senta Holzweiler, 73 C (ex Mary Holzweiler) was by Greif Nidung Rheydt, 1367 (Nidung ex Erna v. Lemgo, 1320). With Erna we are right back to the pioneering spirit and experimental kennel of Professor Engler, where we might possibly expect to find some explanation for the dished face of Golo Holzweiler, 123 c. But too many years have gone by, dogs and people are dead, and the answers to our question can never now be given. So we must accept Golo, with whatever he carried, for he certainly cannot be ignored. Not only American dogs, but German and Danish are in his debt. The Danish take from him mostly through Ch. Rolf v. Freithof, sire of Ch. Hassan Freithof. And Südwest is certainly not the only famed German strain he backstops; count in Artus Sand's as well.

The careful extensions of these pedigrees, such as Golo's, available in the double-spread pages of the Danish club compilations, also provide the most valuable information concerning color. This has already been used by geneticists in compiling modern-day scientific color-inheritance research. Further, it constitutes a deep well of truth into which German Shorthaired Pointer researchers of today may dip, establishing the belief that some judges *and* all self-proclaimed galleryside "experts" could be on shaky ground in rejecting, merely out of hand, all clear-white-and-liver, pointer-patterned coats in German Shorthaired Pointers.

Most come down from the close inbreeding practiced by the pioneers. To reject dogs in the showring (or elsewhere) *merely* because of this color might possibly involve the purist in the rejection of some good, time-hallowed strains. In American breeding, show dogs, field champions, hunting companions, even Dual Champions, may well and legitimately, in certain throwback conditions, come up with this color scheme. However, it might also be considered that in some instances color may be trying to tell us of modern-day unpermissable experimentation, clumsily attempted. In that case, other characteristics, notably coat-texture, will be present for the judge to evaluate very carefully.

Early German breeders, especially around the turn of the century, often fussed about the possibility of some breeder having conducted an experiment with a new Pointer incross, knowing it could throw the breed inheritance awry. An interesting point, which needs to be brought to the attention of those few American "breeders" who may feel that further raw infusion of Pointer blood into their German Shorthaired Pointers may help them to win field trials, is that when the Germans used the Pointer in those formative years 'way back, from the first experimental breedings, they used it to gain *nose* and, in some cases, style. Never, at ANY time, did they consider the Pointer cross as useful to them to promote mere ability to *run*. They needed the *high nose,* took some risks to get it, but quickly counterbalanced the infusion to rid their developing breed of Pointer characteristics that did not belong in utility work—and from a so-called "Pointer" with a greyhound tail they would have fled in horror!

It should also be pointed out to optimists who are willing to "take a chance with throwing in a Pointer" (as it is phrased!) that they can use only such stock as is available to them here, and that stock is often, itself—since breed-type split, in the field-running type —at least doubtful in terms of simon-pure, long-term Pointer inheritance. So, in "taking the chance," unless they are VERY sure of what they are using, they could be getting still further from *nose,* for which *running* could prove a poor substitute in a field sport dog. Maybe the experienced breeders *do* know these things, and even which end of a Pointer to look at to gauge its likely status as purebred from all the way back. (*Note:* Writes that most famous of all Pointer men, William Arkwright: "The head is invaluable for showing character . . . but for the certificate of blue blood apply at the other end!") Novices, however, do *not* usually know these things, and as a large percentage of German Shorthaired Pointer ownership is most often novice, the risk needs to be spelled out here —as well as the danger of listening to often-equally-ignorant "old hands who know all about how to breed a good (running) German Shorthaired Pointer!"

By the early years of this century, any German breeders even suspected of "throwing in" a Pointer were subject to disapproval. One who had to weather such gales was Christian Bode, of Altenau, whose business in England interested him in Pointer *nose.* He built his line on Zeche, 2243 (Liebenberg, 694 ex Fauna unreg.), a brown Dr. Kleeman held basic. Her mate, Rolf Giersdorf, 5363, brown and white, was by Hektor-Wotan-Gutland, 1547, ex Toni Hardenstein, 3738. Hektor was a Wodan Hektor II v. Lemgo son ex a Morell Hoppenrade daughter. From Zeche and Rolf came Bessie Altenau, 69 c. When Bode bred his Bessie to his K.S. Flott Altenau, 12 F, who was her son and great-grandson, most historians note the "Pointerlet" look in the issue, Rino Altenau, 31 B, wh. 1907, though he did lack such embarrassment as Golo's dishface. Rino's best son, Rino Weisseritztal v.d. Wessnitz, 131 N (ex Hertha v.d. Burgerweise, 479 K), is behind many early imports here; also Artus Sand stock that came later, through the Artus Sand sire, Yelmos Gotz v. Kauffungen. From Bessie Altenau, too, came Lola Altenau, 642, whom Herr Sahre, in a 1962 *Kurzhaar Blätter,* described amusingly as good in the field, but reluctant to go in water unless the weather was *very* hot! Lola had American influence through her mating to K.S. Blitz v.d. Maylust, 147 J (Hektor v. Gerathal 2 C ex Frigga II v.d. Maylust). From this came Panther v.d. Maylust, making impact through his son, K.S. Edelmann Giftif, 68 Q.

In most breed history written in German, Edelmann Giftig's name sets the fur flying. His dam, Asta Giftig, was ex a litter sister of Rino Altenau. Most historians feel he brought temperamental faults. Herr Sahre considered his influence catastrophic. Yet, he was a Derby, Solms, Gebrauchshund-Prüfungs-Sieger. Sahre holds that this owed mostly to a first-class handler, and describes the dog's temperament as *"hochgradig nervenschwach und schreckhaft . . . vor dem kleinsten Geraüsch oder ungewohnter Erscheinung prallte er seinem Fuhrer zwischen die Füsse!"* ("[he was] extremely weak-nerved and spooky . . . at the slightest clamor or unfamiliar circumstance he dived between his handler's feet!") (*Kurzhaar Blätter*, 1962, p. 575).

Such displays of temperament could not win German tolerance. Yet Edelmann Giftig, whose virtue was staunch, faultless pointing, could pass this virtue on, suggesting it was not merely the efficiency of that good handler. As he is firmly there in back of many great German dogs, and virtually ALL American basics, one wonders at this distance in time if the dog was *over*-trained, *over*-pressured. Over the years, in this and other breeds, one has seen dogs whose nerves had gone to pieces though they could rack up wins and get stock temperamentally healthier than they. Anyway, he is in strength behind such here as the basic imports to Montana, John Neuforsthaus and Seiger's Lore (1928); the 1931 Nebraskans, Claus v. Schleswig-Konigsweg and Jane v. grünen Adler; also the three famed 1932 newcomers to Minnesota, Arta v. Hohreusch, Bob v. Schwarenberg, Feldjager's Grisette. And one wonders of his strain name—*Giftig*. Translated, it means: "poisonous, venomous, pernicious, malignant, spiteful, angry"—words not in tune with breed temperament, as one knows.

Some German historians also point to irregularities behind famed Mars Altenau, through his sire, Hassan Altenau, 712. Whether scuttlebutt or history, it's too long ago to tell. Mars Altenau was a strong prepotent. Konrad Andreas, breed historian, remembers Mars as great-hearted, with grand nose, will to work, clever at trailing, but a fireball, needing strong handling.

Artus Sand, 1839 V, a little younger than Mars, carries the Golden Name in the breed. His dam, Ella Sand, 543 U, was ex Frigga Sand, 104 P, she a K.S. Michel v.d. goldenen Mark daughter. Yelmos Gotz v. Kauffungen, 21 T, sire of Artus Sand, was by a K.S. Michel son, Lump Mauderode, ex Susl v. Kauffungen. That puts much solid brown (liver) behind Artus Sand, as Lump Mauderode was so, and K.S. Michel. It could be that from here stem the calm temperaments for which Artus Sand was famed.

All breed historians agree on the complementary qualities of

Mars Altenau, 69 P, wh. 1914. A famed prepotent with fiery disposition, "Altenaus" leaned towards pointer virtues.

Artus Sand, 1830 V. Breeders found him the perfect complement to the stock of Mars Altenau, by disposition calm and wise, and so endowing his get. His litter sister, Atta Sand, foundation of v.d. Radback, was tricolor, which may indicate the origin of the good "hound" virtues of temperament in this inheritance. He remains the golden name in breed history.

Mars and Artus, the fireball and the calm. Mars produced the sons, Artus the daughters. Dr. Kleeman could never seem to over-praise Artus Sand daughters. We find one, Asta Mauderode-Westerholt, 69 Z, mated with Mars' son, Rino Forst, 1685 U, wh. 1920, to produce great bitches. One, Edda Mauderode-Westerholt, 702 C, wh. 1928, makes almost all pedigrees now through her son, K.S. Kobold Mauderode-Westerholt, 124 F, wh. 1930. Kobold's sire, K.S. Magnet v. Ockerbach, 388 D, wh. 1928, was also Mars-Artus weld. His dam, Eule v. Runenstein, wins from Dr. Kleeman an accolade as the best Artus Sand daughter. His sire, Junker v. Bomlitztal, 1271 Z, came from Mars through Prince v. Schlosshof, 556 Z.

The international influence of K.S. Kobold is enormous. Brought early to America was his son, Donn v. Sulfmeister (ex Willa v. Wilsederberg). Imported by Dr. Thornton, Donn sired Timm v. Altenau (sire of 15 Am. Champions) and Fritz, sire of prepotent winner, Ch. Davy's Jim Dandy—two (only) reasons why Donn v. Sulfmeister could be named sire-most-neglected-by-breed-historians here.

K.S. Kobold's best German son could be K.S. Bodo v.d. Radbach, 190 H, wh. 1932 (ex K.S. Hussa v.d. Radbach), 571 e, by Hasso v. Nibelungenhort, 918 (ex Richa v.d. Radbach). For American interest, Hussa's "B" litter of 1932, including Bodo, was followed by her "C" in 1933. The sire was Kobold's own, K.S. Magnet v. Ockerbach, ex Artus Sand's best daughter, remember? From this litter, Dr. Thornton imported in 1935, Cosak v.d. Radbach, 257 i. This scion of Germany's proudest breeding spent most of his life in Bitter Root Valley, Montana, siring hunting dogs sold for modest prices; that is, when he wasn't thrilling the living daylights out of the doctor with his way of working a pheasant, or retrieving a hare against tough odds.

American breeders missed the chance Cosak represented, maybe because of the error in his FDSB registration, which seemed to get into more hands than his A.K.C. one, which is correct. As 240355, the FDSB registers him as ex a *Russa* v.d. Radbach, a meaningless name. His stemming from the great German Siegerin, status as three-quarter brother to famed Bodo, is lost in a typing error! Yet, consider what he represented, blending K.S. Hussa with Eule v. Runenstein, the best Artus Sand daughter! No wonder Dr. Thornton's reminiscing today dwells on "Old Coxie" (Cosak), the great working heart of him, the retrieves over miles and over mountains. And what a sad little notation in one of the doctor's Kennel Journals when "Coxie" left him for the East where, so far as these records go, the trail fades. Anyone know the end of the story?

Fortunately all his good was not wasted. He is behind Dual Ch. Valbo v. Schlesburg, also behind Sieglinde v. Meihsen, dam of the breed's first B.I.S., Ch. Sportsman's Dream. That the registration error was belatedly caught follows on Dr. Thornton's gift to this compiler of all his records. Perhaps now some breed enthusiasts will look up pedigrees and set an old wrong right.

Exceptionally strong in America is the impact of the Mars Altenau son, Heidi Esterhof, 342 (ex Cora v. Merkenich-Esterhof, 422 S). His get from Vita v. Wienbiet, 152 V (she an Edelmann Giftig granddaughter) included, in 1923, K.S. Tasso, Bob, Zilla—all v. Winterhauch. Tasso sired Seiger's Lore, imported here and represented in many Western pedigrees, especially through her Brickwedde descendants (by imported Artist v.d. Forst Brickwedde). Bob v. Winterhauch literally supports the Minnesota breedings from Joseph Burkhart's three imports. Of these Feldjager's Grisette was a Bob daughter. Arta v. Hohreusch and Bob v. Schwarenberg were half-brother and sister by Bob's son, K.S. Benno v. Schlossgarten. Zilla is the grand-dam of Hallo Mannheimia (K.S. Frei Südwest ex Cita Mannheimia), whose importation to New York and mating with Arta v. Hohreusch resulted in the siring of Treu v. Waldwinkel, one of this country's all-time prepotent sires.

K.S. Benno v. Schlossgarten made himself a great name in Germany. Through his daughter, Arta v. Hohreusch, he made himself a great name here as well. As the dam of Treu v. Waldwinkel, and also of Ch. Fritz v. Schwarenberg, not to mention several fine bitches, and some useful sons who crop up in the pedigrees very nicely, Arta conditions us to expect a good dog wherever she appears in multiple representation in any pedigree. A beautiful bitch sired by a beautiful dog, she is behind some of our very best, including Dual Champions, emphasizing that conformation, after all, is what a dog stands on, runs with and by. It is NOT something to find *here,* while the dog stands over *there,* as some seem to believe. Taken care of, good conformation keeps breeders in business. Permitted to degenerate, it runs them out as surely as rain falls down, not up. So with Arta's good qualities. Taken care of, they still

K.S. Benno v. Schlossgarten, 49 B, wh. 1926, a beautiful German dog that supports pioneer Minnesota breeding through imports.

K.S. Kobold Mauderode-Westerholt, 124 F, wh. 1930, a strong German stud force with great influence in America.

ornament the breed. Where they have been swamped with rubbish, not even she can overcome the wrong done.

Scotland's poet, Robert Burns, was writing of a personal enemy, not of dog-breeding, but it fits, by golly, it fits:

> "Bright ran thy line, O Galloway,
> Thro' many a far-famed sire.
> So ran the far-famed Roman way,
> And ended in a mire."

The years just before World War II saw the full flowering of many great strains of Kurzhaar in Germany. Some were later swamped and lost in the fiery tide, but many survive, and the best have representation here. Südwest, Beckum, Grabenbruch, v.d. Radbach, Waldhausen, Seiger's, v.d. Forst Brickwedde, Jägers, Pöttmes, Seydel's, v.d. Schleppenburg, v. Blitzdorf, were but some among the many supports for the breed edifice built in this country.

Südwest, one of the oldest, influenced many German strains, as well as pioneer establishment here, through the K.S. Frei Südwest son, Hallo Mannheimia, bred and exported through Herr Carl Seidler, still a force in the affairs of Klub Kurzhaar, as well as a well-known international breed judge. In Germany, a long stream of Siegers carried the name of Südwest, and some are intertwined also with the Grabenbruchers of Herr Peter Kraft, another source of Sieger gifting. Herr Seidler also had great success with K.S. Kora v. Grabenbruch, though his greatest breed pride in his life, as he still happily writes us, was his great Flott v. Dubro (Mannheimia). From Grabenbruch's wide acres, too, came America's first Sieger import, little Sepp v. Grabenbruch (K.S. Odin v. Weinbach ex Leda v. Grabenbruch, he a son of the great Reichs-und-Welt Sieger, Heide v.d. Beeke, she a K.S. Frei Südwest daughter).

Beckum is also extremely well known here, and perhaps the more so for the not entirely ethical habit of some American breeders of "borrowing" famous German strain names for locally bred dogs. To trace Beckum to its sources would entail overturning most of German breed history. Max Jürgens, of Munster, obviously established his breeding practice in the 19th century. Old pedigrees tell the story. It is perhaps as well told as anywhere in the pedigree of Lore Beckum, 58 g, wh. 1931, the foundation bitch of the Blitzdorf strain. Herr Böllhoff, the master of Blitzdorf, has made

The foundation bitches (Die Stammütterchen von Blitzdorf), Lore Beckum and Adria v. Blitzdorf.

Photo: Herr R. Bollhoff.

K.S. Zeus v. Blitzdorf, 322 E, wh. 1955, Kleeman-Sieger for 1958. Many of his get found their way to America.

this pedigree available to us here. It takes us back by way of Lore's sire, Horst Beckum, 55 g, generation after generation—Freya Beckum, 379, Diva Beckum, 300 Z, Bessi Beckum, 186 X, Troika Altenau Beckum, 1013 U—right to the far edge of the pedigree paper. Bessi Beckum is graphed in the same line with Golo Holzweiler (wh. 1902). Bessi's dam, Troika, is in the same line with Golo's sire, Nimrod II Otzenrath. It's a long, long way. . . .

Lore Beckum's pedigree teaches us much concerning the German background of other strains here. Her sire, Horst Beckum, was by Zeus v.d. Bode, 720 c. He shares *his* sire, Taps Harrachstal v.d. Bürgerweise, with John Neuforsthaus, the first good stud in the breed to come to America. The dam of Zeus v.d. Bode, was a full sister to Pack v.d. Bode (Edelmann Giftig ex Kitty v.d. Bode), who counts so strongly behind the first imports to Nebraska.

From the old strain of Max Jürgens, we also have imported K.S. Franco Beckum, 1147 W, wh. 1947. Franco's dam, Viktoria Beckum, draws much as does Lore of the Blitzdorfers. Her sire, Monarch Beckum, was by Horst Beckum ex Rita v.d. Radbach. Franco, also an Amerian champion, is sired by a successful dog in K.S. Adel v. Assegrund (Junos v. Heidebrink ex Pierette Roggenstein), one that had great successes under the care of Herr H. F. Seiger. Pierette Roggenstein, a K.S. Markus Freising granddaughter, was by Seiger's Prinz. The Seiger strain has sent several useful dogs here, commencing with the in-whelp bitches, Seiger's Lore and Seiger's Holla II, brought in by Dr. Thornton. K.S. Seiger's Adel (K.S. Franco Beckum ex a sister to K.S. Adel v. Assegrund, Adda) has made more recent contributions. Here came his son, Harro v. Klostermoor (ex the K.S. Axel v.d. Cranger Heide daughter, Wiesal v.d. alten Postweg, 847 A); also the Michigan import of Carl Schnell, his Eros v. Scheperhof, 220 C (ex Delta v. Scheperhof, 292 A, she by K.S. Franco Beckum ex Seiger's Toska). K.S. Adel is well represented in Germany by such good ones as K.S. Duro v. Braumatal that made such an impression recently on the American breeder-judge, Bob Holcomb, who saw him in competition over there, reporting him as excelling in class and style, with drive and nose.

The Seiger strain is still to the fore, even after more than 30 years of active participation in German activities. Seiger's Para, a 1960 Spitz (which means top-rated, by the way, not a representative of quite another breed; *Spitz,* in German, means the apex, the top-dog), proved herself outstanding. Seiger's Tarantella, aunt to Para, was best bitch in the Kurzhaar Zuchtschau in Hannover, 1959. A year earlier, Seiger's Saltus was carrying the flag for this strain that, like the brook, seems likely to go on forever.

Which, in a way, brings us back to Lore Beckum. She whelped a daughter to a fireball, K.S. Don v.d. Schwarzen Kuhle, 209 f. Temperament came to Don honestly through his grandsire, Heidi Esterhof, the son of Mars Altenau. The daughter was most handsome. She was Adria v. Blitzdorf, 1487 m, first to carry this now-famous strain name into the pedigrees, and her breeder was Herr F. Böllhoff, present-day vice president of the Kurzhaar Klub for West and North Germany. Adria is behind all modern Blitzdorfers, including the Kleeman second-place dog of 1953, K.S. Pol v. Blitzdorf, 220 A, wh. 1951. Adria is the grand-dam of Pol's sire, Lux v. Blitzdorf and the dam of Freya v. Blitzdorf, 197 t, who whelped him. The 1958 Kleeman-Sieger, K.S. Zeus v. Blitzdorf, carries a like inheritance, being ex a litter sister to K.S. Pol. Bringing the story further along, the 1961 Kleeman-Sieger was also a Blitzdorfer, K.S. Elch v. Blitzdorf, 90 H, wh. 1958, and behind him in this same exacting competition for that year was K.S. Falk v. Rothenberg, 531 I, wh. 1959, who is by K.S. Zeus v. Blitzdorf ex a very sharp daughter of Ulk v.d. alten Postweg.

Americans know K.S. Pol v. Blitzdorf best as the sire of imported Dual & Nat'l. FT Ch. Kay v.d. Wildburg, 1959 Am. Field National winner and runner up for 1961. Kay was wh. 1956 (ex Cora v. Wesertor, whose background runs K.S. Axel v.d. Cranger Heide ex Fitz v. Tann). K.S. Axel is by a Moritz v.d. Postweg son, and Fitz is a K.S. Quandu v.d. Schleppenburg daughter. K.S. Quandu is also a Kleeman dog, his sire, Seydel's Gin, from a famous strain presently to be discussed. Further of interest is that the v.d. Wildburgs are carried on by one of the few old-time breeders still active in Germany. This is Oberförster Gummer, of Hemsloh-über-Diepholz, who for 30 years and more has bred and campaigned a single litter each year. His greatest may have been the 1953 Kleeman-Sieger, K.S. Eros v.d. Wildburg (K.S. Quandu v.d. Schleppenburg ex Drossel v.d. Wildburg, daughter of K.S. Axel v.d. Cranger Heide).

Kay v.d. Wildburg came to America in his Derby age, which means before he was subjected to any training pressure to conform to the German requirement to drop to shot, game, etc., thereby avoiding the confusion that bedevils mature, trained German dogs that come here and are required to conform to different requirements here— often none too successfully. Kay did very well under the expert handling of Richard S. Johns, of Pennsylvania.

Another K.S. Pol v. Blitzdorf son was the post-war-years star, bred by the famous Herr Bleckmann, K.S. Vito v.d. Radbach, Kleeman-Sieger of 1955. No more famous, long-enduring name than v.d. Radbach exists in the world of the German Shorthaired Pointer, and the tally of champions stemming from this strain is by now beyond count. Only Herr Bleckmann himself could possible say how many times he has swung through and through the alphabet to name his litters bred. K.S. Vito's dam, Resi v.d. Radbach, was a K.S. Adel v. Assegrund daughter, ex Ondra v.d. Radbach. As Bodo made v.d. Radbach history before World War II, so did K.S. Vito in the mid-1950's, when the German breeders were getting into gear again after the loss and frustrations of the terrible years between. It was the worst of fortune that this beautiful dog should have met with death in a hunting field accident soon after sale to a breeder in Austria.

Several Vito descendants are here, perhaps as interesting as any being a quality daughter, the solid liver Centa v. Bornfeld, 477 H, wh. 1958, imported in 1961 by California breeder Don Miner, of Saratoga. In whelp to K.S. Arco v. Niestetal, 181 G, a Kleeman finalist of 1959, Centa had much to give here. Her dam line is a double cross of famed Heide v.d. Beeke, and her grand-dam, Seydel's Senta, 572 y, was a daughter of K.S. Seydel's Hella, the import closely resembling that famed Siegerin in type. Centa brought a sparkle to the eyes of Field Trial buffs as she went strutting by, an elegant, livewire lady, and a credit to Vito, her pa.

Also well-known in America, and usefully proved at stud, is K.S. Ulk v.d. Radbach, ex Ruth v.d. Radbach, full sister to Vito's dam, Resi. Owned by Dr. Kenworthy, of Vermont, Ulk was replaced in Germany by his son. K.S. Benn v.d. Gottesstiege who, in turn, sired Arco v. Niestetal to whom Centa v. Bornfeld (above) was mated before export. K.S. Benn v.d. Gottesstiege is a good dog, as is his son, Arco, who in the Hannover Zuchtschau of 1959 took the Best Male award. Bred by A. Klinge, owned by Frau A. Poggenpohl, of Hannover-Bothfeld, whose late husband was an active pillar of breed interests in Germany, Arco is handled by Oberförster Heinz Burk in all his competitive outings. Heinz Burk, who bred Benn v.d. Gottesstiege, was well-established as a breeder when, in 1945, he was driven from his home by the Russian advance in Germany. As a refugee, all his dogs lost, he reached the West, where he made a fresh start, counting it luck that he managed to secure again a bitch of his former breeding that chanced to be located on the right side of the divided territory line.

Similar fortune did not attend all German Shorthaired Pointer breeders on the "wrong" side of the political wall. The Klub Kurzhaar mourns many good people and many fine strains of pre-war vintage that are lost to it completely.

K.S. Arco v. Niestetal, 181 G, wh. 1957, strongly represented in recent American imports.

Axel v. Wasserschling. This prepotent dominated GSP breeding for almost a decade in Germany. His get and grand-get have been exported worldwide. Owner, Gustav Machetanz, Dortmund.

K.S. Vito v.d. Radback, 1456 C (K.S. Pol v. Blitzdorf ex Resi v.d. Radback), wh. 1953.

Seiger's Para, 1960 Spitz, a worthy representative of this famous strain.

3

Modern-Day Strains
in Germany

A FULL-SCALE history of German breeding is beyond our scope. Here the aim is merely to examine some of the strains that have made major contributions to American bloodlines. It involves a hop-skip-jump technique, strain to strain, year to year. Few are the strain names that do not find some mention, somewhere, in the pedigree of one or another of the many imports.

Waldhausen we know for the impact of Treff v. Waldhausen, 422 Z, wh. 1924. The strain name is much respected, long-established. On January 12, 1962, the German breeders combined to congratulate the master of the v. Waldhausens, Cyriak Grohe, on the occasion of his 90th birthday, wishing him many years of good health. This great dog of his strain, Treff, later in the proud ownership of Herr H. F. Seiger, held a First in the Solms, the Shield of Honor at the International Exhibition at Hannover in 1929. His fame at stud was made through his son, R.S. & W.S. Heide v.d. Beeke, and his direct American influence is through his get from the imports, Seiger's Lore and Seiger's Holla II, brought in whelp to him. Holla's son, Kamerad v. Waldhausen, wh. 1934 in Montana, proved very prepotent, though with limited opportunities of his time. He was sired in Treff v. Waldhausen's last year at stud, the next-to-last litter, to be precise. The last (also in 1934) got Heide v.d. Beeke ex Diana v. Landsherrn, 867 h.

Heide v.d. Beeke must have been extensively used at stud and his batting average, if one may use the term, must have been high. Few extended German pedigrees now will lack his name. That he is still held in high regard there—he and his Waldhausen strain background—is established by the use of his picture in 1959 on the cover of *Kurzhaar Blätter,* the official magazine of Klub Kurzhaar (Berlin). Though many years dead, Heide v.d. Beeke's influence warranted this posthumous distinction.

The late 1930's, too, was the time of K.S. Marko v. Schaumberg, 1639, son of K.S. Kobold Mauderode-Westerholt, ex K.S. Kascha v. Schlossgarten, 1171. Marko interests American breeders through his son, Markus Freising, 1668, ex Juno Freising (by Furst v. Fuchspass). Not only is this dog solidly behind the "A" litter of the Assegrunds, and so behind K.S. Franco Beckum, but he is also the sire of one Berta Spiessinger v. Pfaffenhofen/Ilm DK 1166 (ex Gera v.d. Forst Brickwedde, 613 p). Berta, as all who have taken cramp from writing her name so often well know, is the dam of the fantastically propotent Austrian import, Field Ch. Greif v. Hundsheimerkogel, whose story is for the American chapters rather than for here.

The little ones of the late J. Meyerheim, the Pöttmes, constitute another strain usefully introduced to this country. Rudolph Hirschnitz, of California, and the late Wm. Ehrler, of the Rheinbergs in Michigan, had regard for these, and brought in several. They were all exceptional performers, capable for anything, and their tiny size was in direct opposition to the bulk of their breeder. Inbreeding closely but cleverly, Herr Meyerheim named his bitches along the way in numerical order, *Siebte, Achte, Neunte,* (Seventh, Eighth, Ninth), etc., reaching his apex (Spitz) with the solid liver, K.S. Elfte Pöttmes (the Eleventh). This strain ran strongly to solid liver.

So, too, does the famed strain of Seydel's, established also in the 1930's by Dr. (of medicine) Carl Seydel and his devoted wife, Maria, of Recklingshausen-Süd. The Seydel's strain wields great breed influence in Germany, but dogs sent here have in many cases been prey to exasperating accidental misfortunes. However, it is in terms of sheer human interest, as well, that the strain merits discussion here.

Now the question is, who was that first Herr Seydel to show a German Shorthaired Pointer? The year was 1887, the place was Barns Elms, London, an English K.C. show. The occasion was the only one in which GSHPs have been exhibited in England before the post-World War II years. The dog's name was Adda (Uncas-Aunsel). Frau Maria, nowadays, says she has no idea who the gentleman was—maybe a relative of her late husband. Yet, also coincidentally, Dr. Seydel always wanted a brown German Shorthaired Pointer, and when he acquired one the pick pup of her first litter became Seydel's Adda! The story may never be finished for us. . . .

The dog that Dr. and Frau Seydel first acquired, a puppy, was Hella v. Böhmerwald-Gothnersitz, 186 1 (Aspodlesi 727 ex Flora v. Lindenschlösschen, 185 1). Hella capped a fine show career with a Welt Siegerin title at the Paris Exhibition of 1937. It was a wonderful win for such newcomers to the breed, but then Dr. and Frau Seydel discovered that to make her mark in Germany, Hella must do some winning in the Field. The doctor was professionally too busy to undertake her training. As a pet, she was too precious to be sent to any handler. Frau Maria learned Field Trial training along with the dog. It was tough going at first, but together they made the grade. Hella founded the famous strain, and Frau Maria became a famous handler, still greatly respected today, still working her dogs.

Hella was bred to that same fireball, K.S. Don v.d. Schwarzen Kuhle, 209 f (Wodan Peppenhoven 1222 Z ex Hertana Päpinghausen, 26 Y, she a Mars Altenau granddaughter through Heidi Esterhof), whom we've already met as the sire of Adria v. Blitzdorf. The Seydel litter produced from brown Hella, six ticked, four brown (liver). The four were retained for the kennel. Careful linebreeding from three especially, Adda, Arno, Asta, made a tremendous contribution to the revival of the color of the pioneer basics. Researchers have since had pleasure in tracing back the solid-color inheritance that came strongly into Seydel's strain and has influenced so many great German strains onward till our present time.

The first Hella brought the color in her gift, through her sire line,

K.S. Seydel's Hella, possibly best known of all the "Seydel's" dogs. At age 12, she shared a companionship with Frau Maria Seydel's 85-year-old mother.

Frau Maria Seydel made gift of this picture of her great ones. Old S. Hella is anchor-gal on the right.

through Wallo Eichsfeld, 334 M. Her dam line also goes clear back to brown in Trumpfdame Canzoe, 665, wh. 1889, a daughter of Carokönig, a good one in his day, a son of Waldin, 175, who of course was of the time when all the best dogs were famously brown, all carefully in tune with the model proposed by the important Hoppenraden. Wallo Eichsfeld's background of Beyes Stopp, 683 K, is also famously brown. His sister, Beyes Vilja v.d. goldenen Mark, is often mentioned in these pages when discussing the pre-potency of her son, K.S. Michel v.d. goldenen Mark.

Adda and Asta were mated to a solid-color, 12-year-old K.S. Bill v. Hirschfeld, he by K.S. Wehrwolf v.d. goldenen Mark, 465 Z, ex a K.S. Michel daughter, Frigga Sand, 581 Y, also met already as the grand-dam of Artus Sand. Asta produced Seydel's Betty, 688 o, a very well-performed one. Betty whelped to Jäger's Naso, 1265 (by K.S. Frei Südwest) the famed K.S. Seydel's Hella. Adda, so beauti-ful, and a favorite of Dr. Seydel's, was in her day pronounced by Dr. Kleeman to be a very model of the breed. Her first litter produced a later-successful stud in Seydel's Gin. Of her second, she died whelping under the hail of bombs in a wartime raid in 1943. Coincidentally, the owner whose great pride she had been lost his life the same year. Dr. Seydel, critically injured during a bombing raid on an army train in which he was riding, on New Year's Eve, 1943, sacrificed personal attention to his own hurt to work with the wounded, and this cost him his life.

K.S. Seydel's Hella pleased the critics in her day, and has been described as the embodiment of feminine elegance in movement and deportment, her head with its dark eyes described as ideal. Frau Maria, to whom we are indebted for the background informa-tion on her famed strain, writes that there was great pleasure in handling Hella, who never failed to get her fox at the first sight, and was a clever worker in the trials. "In the forest she searched close, in the field went wide, and solid as a rock on point. All her work was to hand signals. She was also wonderfully man-sharp, a great guard. After my husband's death, she stayed always close by my side, nor would she work for any other hunter. A better hunting companion I never shall have, nor yet one that became a closer member of my family."

Hella lived out the long life of a good German Shorthaired Pointer. From many photos, we have chosen a charming study, taken in her twelfth year, in company with Frau Seydel's 85-year-old mother. *"Die beiden guten Alten,"* Frau Seydel has captioned it. ("The two good old ones.") Both, she added, were *"recht rustig in dem Alter,"* which means both preserved their quality into old age.

Seydel name and fame does not begin or end with the two Hellas. Many good dogs have carried the strain name: Lotti, Claus, Moni; Seydel's Hill (brother to K.S. Hella), who is the grandsire of Moritz v.d. alten Postweg, 263 v, an elegant dog owned by Herr Ludwig Schürholz that sired his K.S. Axel v.d. Cranger Heide, 1994 w. K.S. Seydel's Troll, 1003 y, ex Moni, is a Moritz grandson, also through K.S. Axel, and is himself a Kleeman-Sieger (1951). Seydel's Gin also sired a Kleeman-Sieger, Quandu v.d. Schleppenburg. So it has gone, past and present, with the tireless lady still working her Shorthairs till the year of her death, 1970.

In Germany, the breed ideal never moves away from that of the competent working but elegant dog, of conformation to fit it for the showring if required. A famed German sports writer, Konrad Andreas, has commented: "There is no doubt that some hunters do not care whether a dog is or is not beautiful, so long as it is good at its work. This is no new thing to hear! It is certain that even the most beautiful shell is worthless if the kernel beneath is no good. However, in dogs it is well known that the one quality never does disqualify the other. We find in our Kurzhaar continually that our most beautiful dogs are also our very best to work." (*WALD UND WILD, October 1948*)

No worthwhile German breeder ever thinks that a sporting dog is likely to be better at work for being poorly constructed. Those in this country who proclaim (surely it is a *pose!*) that to breed for good looks in a dog is to cancel out its working qualities may, for all we know, merely be whistling bravely down the long, dark, sad lane of their own inability to breed a dog of good conformation. Their aim, then, may be to make necessity appear a virtue of choice. Unfortunately, such a complex, boldly and brassily expressed, as complexes tend to be, can often become accepted as truth by novices. Such indoctrinated novices can go into breeding ventures believing that there is neither virtue nor health in the breed Standard. Yet the wonderful tally of the German Shorthaired Pointer Dual Champions that keeps on building in our time proves how wrong is any such belief that a good-looking dog cannot work. It is a myth

51

fostered by the ignorant, the frustrated, the unfortunates with only poor-type dogs in their ownership. And how the German breeders would despise such—they, who refuse to breed to even the *best* working dog if it should possess some discernible fault of conformation!

The ultimate ruin that can be imposed by the belief that poor conformation is anything but bad has been demonstrated in other breeds. The law of diminishing returns, operating for a few generations, is what put many one-time Pointer and Setter men into German Shorthaired Pointers in the first place. To a breed they found still unspoiled, some of them brought, however, the exact undesirable scale of values that ran them out of their previous breeds. The Germans, as well as the British, have always been much wiser. The honor of the Championship title, and all the privileges of the breeding pen that go with this, are reserved to dogs that can prove themselves desirable in both the performance and the conformation sense. Truly, as experience has proved to the hilt, and as Konrad Andreas phrases it, there is no reason to believe that one quality will cancel out the other.

As Heide v.d. Beeke in his day, so in his day was K.S. Axel v.d. Cranger Heide, 1994 w, seldom lacking in present-day pedigrees. Owned by Herr Ludwig Schürholz, of Hervest-Dorsten, and campaigned with the careful enthusiasm of this experienced breeder, Axel is ex Dora v. Schloss Dorneburg, 2204 t, wh. 1947. According to the description preserved by those who wrote of him in his prime, K.S. Axel was a somewhat smallish dog, but of great elegance, and possessed of a wonderful front-end flexibility (which, of course, means good shoulders). He was fast, obedient, quick to find, and his manners were excellent. Those who had known Mars Altenau many years earlier often commented that K.S. Axel greatly resembled the earlier breed pillar.

In 1952, the *Deutsche Hund-Zeitung* gave to K.S. Axel the top spot in German Shorthaired Pointers over the earlier two years of competition in Germany. His distinguished get is too numerous to spell right out here, but for American interest he will be found behind many present-day imports. As the sire of K.S. Gernot v.d. Heidehöhe, a Kleeman-placed dog, we have him behind the Illinois-owned import, Mr. R. C. Bauspies' Dual Ch. Alfi v.d. Kronnenmuhle (ex Heide v.d. Emmstadt). Dual Ch. Alfi is happily the dam of a Dual

Ch. bitch in Miss B'Haven v. Winterhauch (by Dual Ch. Captain
v. Winterhauch), for this time a record, a Dual with two Dual
parents. (Where, asks my novice, *do* the good ones come from? Answer: They come from other good ones!) K.S. Axel is also the
grandsire of K.S. Arco v. Niestetal (already mentioned). In Germany,
Axel has sired Drossel v.d. Wildburg, dam of the Kleeman-Sieger,
Eros v.d. Wildburg; K.S. Amor v.d. Beeke; K.S. Seydel's Troll; K.S.
Bosco v.d. Ilenburg—all Kleeman stars, as is seen in the table further
along. This makes plain his great prepotency.

Contemporary with K.S. Axel v.d. Cranger Heide, and indeed
quite often in competition with him in the field, was another very
proud German stud force of those same earlier 1950's. This was
K.S. Quandu v.d. Schleppenburg, 728 x. As the Kleeman-Sieger
for 1950, he was a certain pride for his owner, Apotheker Leueu,
of Lübbecke. Sired by Seydel's Gin ex Here v.d. Schleppenburg,
1108 c, this Sieger carries a name also become familiar here. His
work on birds has been described by a lyrical observer as poetry, his
movement as a song. In America, the strain has his best representation through the solid-colored dog, Field Ch. and National Ch.
of 1959, Oloff v.d. Schleppenburg, owned in Illinois by Roy J.
Thompson. His breeding is by Chick v.d. Schleppenburg ex Gerda
v. Stau.

K.S. Gernot v.d. Heidehöhe, 5887, the K.S. Axel v.d. Cranger
Heide son ex K.S. Bärbel v.d. Heerstrasse, is also of importance, as
just mentioned in connection with Dual Ch. Alfi v.d. Kronnenmuhle. In Germany we find him often in the pedigrees, especially
through his mating with the Diana-Siegerin of 1954, K.S. Aeskulaps Wiesel (by K.S. Widu v. Braumatal). This strain of Aeskulaps
is represented also by many good modern-day dogs in Germany.
The Siegerin's individual reputation is continually enhanced by
her descendants, especially through her 1955 daughter, Aeskulaps
Frigga, the dam of K.S. Arco v. Niestetal, resultant from the above-
mentioned mating with K.S. Gernot v.d. Heidehöhe.

K.S. Widu v. Braumatal, in his own right, was also an excellent
performer, and this strain name is also well-represented in America
nowadays, put forward by imports of the 1960's, sired by such as
Duro v. Braumatal and K.S. Lümmel v. Braumatal. Lümmel, a well-
regarded performer, is one of the stud strengths of the v.d. Steilkuste
establishment of Herr Eggersh, of Bargloy, and has some of his

get already established here in the Pacific Northwest. Also with long association here is the strain of v.d. Forst Brickwedde, of Herr R. Schulte, of Brickwedde über Bersenbrück. The history-minded will immediately think of the pioneer import, Artist v.d. Forst Brickwedde, and Alfred Sause's Ch. Dallo v.d. Forst Brickwedde. In present-day representation there is imp. Ebing v.d. Forst Brickwedde.

Modern German pedigrees also carry the names quite frequently, as Herr Schulte conducts a very extensive operation, and has done so for many years. His K.S. Quandus v.d. Forst Brickwedde is one of the names to catch the eye in any scanning of English pedigrees of the present day, too. Most strongly, the strain seems to be modernly indebted to K.S. Amor v.d. Beeke (K.S. Axel v.d. Cranger Heide ex Toska v.d. Beeke).

The postwar years saw the emergence of new names. The strain name with most impact has been that of Wasserschling. Herr Gustav Machetanz, out of East Germany ahead of the Russians, built up his strain to eminence as out of the Westfalen area and its environs to nationwide, even world-wide recognition. As from the Siegerin Thea v. Wasserschling, who took second place behind K.S. Aeskulaps Wiesel, from another famous strain, in the 1954 Diana Prüfung, to the sturdy solid liver stud, Axel v. Wasserschling, the build-up was tremendous. The German Shorthair scene, in its native land, *needed* in the immediate postwar years, such a dog as Axel. Catching the eye and the interest of the knowledgable Herr Bollhöff of the Blitzdorfers, and actively praised by this breeder-judge, Axel, sound, solid, strong, over a space of several years, and into his old age, came to dominate the breed to such an extent that by the later 1960s, the breeders were made aware of an unexpected difficulty—the scarcity of outcross blood. The search for "Axel-frei" bloodlines became urgent.

Why the need for the services of sound, solid, strong Axel? Mainly, for the circumstance in which postwar German breeders found themselves—the war years had taken away their great dogs of the 1930s, and cessation of breeding had left virtually nothing to replace them. The search for good breeding stock was an agonizing one as the clubs were with all manner of difficulties, political as well as practical, reformed. In 1971 the *Frankfurter Jagdklub* published a magnificent 50-Year Jubilee Journal (1921–1971) in which the history of this body is accurately traced. The portion that deals with the resuscitation of the Jagdklub in the post WWII years illuminates the difficulties. Under Occupation, meetings were prohibited —no trials, no hunting, no permitted ownership of guns. Even the beer lacked; too often *gemütlichkeit* had to be fueled by water—only!

With the lifting of the tightest restrictions, the Frankfurter Klub, as others in the land, began to gather and assess the local dog stock, the survivors. "Das Hundematerial liess allerdings in Form and Gebäude zu wünschen übrig. Die Hunde waren grössenteils zu leicht und hatten kurze spitze Fänge. . . . Zur DK-Sonderschau im Rahmen der Hundeausstellung auf dem Frankfurter Schlachthof am Aug. 1947 waren 35 Hunde (15 Rüden und 20 Hündinnen) erschienen, wovon 4 Rüden und 3 Hundinnen mit 'vorzüglich' ausgezeichnet wurden." (*Ersten Frankfurter Jagdklub* 1971, pp. 23/24.)

(*Trans:* "The dog material left everything in shape and build to be desired. The dogs for the most part were too light-framed and had short, pointed muzzles. . . . At the Shorthair-Specialty in the Frankfurter Schlachthof, Aug. 1947, of 35 entries, 15 males, 20 bitches, only 4 males and 3 bitches gained award of "Excellent.")

The situation in Frankfurt was mirrored across Germany. The search for breeding stock of type and substance was rigorously pursued. Nor, indeed, was Axel the only stud with these qualities to convey, but he was the most promoted, and so the most used. Over the years since 1947, German breeders have labored to build the breed up to required substance and type excellences, and considerable success has attended these efforts, but there remained far too much of the substanceless, short-sharp muzzled rubbish, still being screened out as late as the end of the 1960s. By then, however, the breeder-care had provided increasing stock of good dogs, widening the blood pool so that one-stud dominance has become a thing of the past.

THE KLEEMAN-AUSLESE PRUFUNG

In line with their most admirable intention of perpetuating within the Fancy the names of those who have done their breed great service, the Kurzhaar breeders of Germany named their most exacting Trial for that genial man of great knowledge, Dr. Paul Kleeman, so many years their Klub President. No German dog can carry a title prouder than that of Kleeman-Sieger or Siegerin. The exclusive roll-call of those so endowed may in a very literal sense comprise the roll-call of the modern-day breed's greatest representatives.

First established in 1939, at Aschersleben, the Kleeman-Prüfung was at that time rather less of a working Trial than it is in present-day practice; rather, it was in the form of an exhibition of Stud Dogs in the Field. From 1949 on, however, new rules brought it closer to its present form. These rules have been further revised—in 1953, and since then. Requirements and qualifications continue to tighten, year by year.

No German Sieger—as no English Champion—ever comes by his title easily, or by default when the good dogs stay home; he has to work for it. Since 1953, a Kurzhaar Sieger must qualify in running well in a Kleeman Search. It must also have First Prizes in the Derby and Solms, and at least a Second in a *Verbandsgebrauchsprüfung* (Klub Utility Search), or else a Derby or Solms First, plus a First in the *Verbandsgebrauchsprüfung*. Later, the aspirant must add its *Verlorenbringenprüfung* on the trail of wounded hare (*krankgeschossenen Hasen*) that the dog has not previously seen (*geäugt*). It comprises finding and retrieving such lost game. When a dog has successfully competed so over a required distance of 400 m., under two recognized judges, he gains his award of Vbr. (*Verlorenbringenprüfung*), an endorsement found on many of the German pedigrees that reach here with imported dogs. The exacting tests match oddly with the opinion of some quite prominent American handlers, especially, who claim in print or in correspondence that the German Shorthaired Pointer is by inheritance no worthwhile tracker, retriever, or water dog!

By 1949 it had become possible again to reinstitute the famous Kleeman Suche in the manner of pre-war years. Two dogs of American interest gained their KS in this year of resumption, K.S. Franco Beckum and K.S. Axel v.d. Cranger Heide.

DIE KLEEMAN-SUCHE: (Courtesy, F. Böllhoff)

1949 (Krefeld, Rhineland). (6 gemeldet, von denen 5 bestanden)

1. K.S. QUANDUS V.D. FORST BRICKWEDDE, 5940. Kleeman-Sieger.
2. K.S. AXEL V.D. CRANGER HEIDE, 1994 w
3. JÄGERS WEHRWOLF, 2477 t
4. KEMNAS CHICK, 289 w
5. K.S. FRANCO BECKUM, 1471 w

1950 (Krefeld, Rhineland) (erschienen 10, bestanden 5)

1. K.S. & V.S. QUANDU V.D. SCHLEPPENBURG, 728 x. Kleeman-Sieger.
2. BODO V. HEIMELSBERG, 742 w
3. K.S. AXEL V.D. CRANGER HEIDE, 1994 w
4. ARTUS V.D. WEDELER, 956 w
5. ARKO V.D. WEDELER, 954 w

1951 (Frankfurt a. Main) (erschienen 7, bestanden 4)

1. K.S. SEYDEL'S TROLL, 1003 y. Kleeman-Sieger.
2. TAPS V. ALTEN POSTWEG, 1514 y
3. GREIF V.D. BRUNAU, 766 y
4. XANTIPPE SUDWEST, 1486 y

1952 (Peine) (erschienen 10, bestanden 4)

1. K.S. ARMOR V.D. BEEKE, 1206 z. Kleeman-Sieger.
2. CLAUS V. WEIDENHOF, 1430 x
3. K.S. GERNOT V.D. HEIDEHÖHE, 588 z
4. K.S. LIPPERT'S ARGO, 1893 w

1953 (Frankenthal/Pfalz) (erschienen 18, bestanden 9)

(This year, the bitches were judged separately from the dogs.)

a. *Dogs.*

1. K.S. EROS V.D. WILDBURG, 529 A. Kleeman-Sieger.
2. K.S. POL V. BLITZDORF, 220 A
3. K.S. RAUCK V. ALTEN POSTWEG, 991 y
4. K.S. BILL V. BRAMBERG, 540 z

b. *Bitches.*

1. K.S. BANJA V. GALGENACKER, 34936 (Switzerland). Diana-Siegerin.
2. CARLA V.D. WEDELER, 1216 z
3. K.S. BONA V.D. SCHLEPPENBURG, 837 z
4. JOLANTHE SUDWEST, 1191 y
5. ZILLA V.D. SCHWABENBURG, 611 z

1954 (Bückeburg) (erschienen 12, bestanden 4)

1. K.S. ARCO V. BRAUMATAL, 504 z. Kleeman-Sieger.
2. K.S. BOSCO V. ILENBECK, 449 B
3. SEIGER'S EDLER, 213 C
4. GRIMM V. PAPPELHOF, 396 z

1954 Diana-Prüfung (bitches). (Krefeld) (erschienen 14, bestanden 9)

1. AESKULAPS WIESEL, 625 A. Diana-Siegerin.
2. K.S. THEA V. WASSERSCHLING, 421 A
3. HERTA V.D. MATENA, 243 A
4. JÄGERS FRITZI, 408 A
5. GRILLE V.D. GROSSEN TULLN, ÖHSt.B (Austrian Studbook) 1866
6. BLANKA V.D. SCHWABENBURG, 1855 B
7. ANKA V. SONNENWEG, 899 y
8. XILLI V. ALTEN POSTWEG, 784 B
9. CITA V. DAMMERWALD, 1366 B

1955 (Frankenthal) (erschienen 16, bestanden 6)

1. K.S. VITO V.D. RADBACH, 1456 C. Kleeman-Sieger.
2. K.S. JUCKER V. BIRKENBACH, 679 C
3. ZORN V. WATERKOTTEN, 1417 C
4. FALK V. LANGERTSTEIN, 677 B
5. ADEL V. RHÖNFORST, 629 z
6. INGO V.D. METENA, 136 C

1956 No competition.

1957 DR. KLEEMAN and DIANA-AUSLESE PRUFUNG (both sexes) *(Bad Lippspringe) (erschienen 12, bestanden 7)*

1. ERRA V. WESERTOR, 1143 D. Diana-Siegerin.
2. K.S. CORALLE V. BRAUWINKEL, 498 E
3. FREYA V. KOHLWALD, 1150 D
4. BENN V.D. GOTTESSTIEGE, 579 E
5. MARGA V. BRIKENBAUM, 559 E
6. VASALL V.D. RADBACH, 1455 C
7. XELLA V.D. RADBACH, 1580 D

1958 (Seligenstadt bei Aschaffenburg) (erschienen 10, bestanden 5)

1. K.S. ZEUS V. BLITZDORF, 322 E. Kleeman-Sieger.
2. K.S. LÜMMEL V. BRAUMATAL, 301 F
3. K.S. BITTA V.D. GOTTESSTIEGE, 586 E
4. SEIGER'S SALTUS, 77 G
5. K.S. AESKULAPS GEMSE, 83 F

1959 (Wallerstein) (erschienen 10, bestanden 5)

1. K.S. LACKL V.D. FORST BRICKWEDDE, 729 F. Kleeman-Sieger.
2. K.S. ORLANDA V. GARTENSCHLAG, 1311 G
3. K.S. AXEL V. HEIDEBRINK, 241 F
4. K.S. ARCO V. NIESTETAL, 181 G
5. K.S. CORA V.D. BABILONIE, 1407 E

1960 No competition.

1961 (bei Kassel) (erschienen 8, bestanden 3)

1. K.S. ELCH V. BLITZDORF, 90 H. Kleeman-Sieger.
2. K.S. FALK V. ROTHENBERG, 531 I
3. K.S. DONNA V. GRUNEN Deich, 456 G

1962 (Stadhagen) (erschienen 19, bestanden 9)

1. K.S. CONNI V. MOORACHÜTZ, 888 I/59
2. K.S. BLITZ V. KLOSTERFIELD, 950 I/59
3. K.S. EDDA V. WILSEDER BERG, 921 H/58
4. K.S. SEIGER'S PARA, 161 J/60
5. K.S. ASSAN V. BÖHNENHOF, 212 J/60
6. JUCKER V.D. SELDE, 899 H/58
7. IMME V. HANSTEIN, 1275 G/57
8. ORION V. GARTENSCHLAG, 1310 G/57
9. K.S. EVA SAND, 308 H/58

1963 No Competition.

1964 (Speyer) (Bestanden 9. Entry figure not given)

1. K.S. SEIGER'S MUNGO, 173 L/62
2. FLECK V. GARTENSCHLAG, 975 K/61
3. K.S. ARNO VON SOLZ, 308 K/61
4. BURSCH V. BIRKENBACH, 1696 J/60
5. K.S. POLLUX V. BEDERKESA, 516 K/61
6. ARKO VOM NORDHOF, 1841 J/60
7. CAHN V. OSTERBERG, 451 L/62
8. BIRKE VOM GRÜNTAL, 1898 K/61
9. BIENE V.D. BUCHENHEIDE, 875 K/61

1965 No competition.

1966 (Bosau) (Bestanden 21—which appears to be a Kleeman record. Again no entry figure given)

1. K.S. MINGO V. HEIMERSHEIM, 2014 M/63
2. ONKO V. TODTENSEE, 921 M/63
3. K.S. JANUS DU RAPIDO, LOF 2522
4. ISSOS V.D. MÜRITZBUCHT, 1995 M/63
5. MOHR V. WASSERSCHLING, 364 N/64
6. K.S. MASCOTTE V. WASSERSCHLING, 368 N/64
7. SCHELL VON BEDERKESA, 533 N/64
8. ARTEMIS ERF, 1966 M/63
9. AXEL V. BLOMBERG, 156 L/62
10. BARON V. SIEBENBERGEN, 2061 M/63

11. EX v.d. Hünenburgwiese, 733 L/62
12. K.S. Seiger's Tenno, 1928 N/64
13. K.S. Ivos v. Wasserschling, 661 M/63
14. Pia v. Hanstein, 1224 L/62
15. Cilla v. Drostenhof, 854 M/63
16. K.S. Anje v.d. Porta, 608 M/63
17. Maja v. Klostermoor, 1803 J/60
18. Laia de la Motte, SHSB 115 951
19. K.S. Artemis Bolz, 1344 K/61
20. EX v. Osterberg, 1006 M/63
21. Duro a.d. Schottengasse, 483 L/62

1967 No Competition.

1968 (Kehl-am-Rhein) (Bestanden 10—24 erschienen)
1. K.S. Erra v. Sixenhof, 24 N/64
2. K.S. Amber Donaria, 205 N/64
3. K.S. Birke Aus Der Porta, 975 O/65
4. K.S. Cara v. Hohenfeld, 647 N/64
5. Alpha v. Goddbach, 510 P/66
6. K.S. Anke v. Ichenheim, 1306 N/64
7. K.S. Tasso v. Garziner Grund, 503 O/65
8. K.S. Pan de Lemania, LOF 8488
9. Mark v. Wasserschling, 361 N/64
10. Kox v.d. Müritzbucht, 161 P/66

1969 No Competition.

1970 (Bad Lipperspringe) (Bestanden 8–14 erschienen)
1. K.S. Quell Pöttmes, 735 Q/67
2. K.S. Axel v. Bügelhof, 69 Q/67
3. K.S. Graf v. Lindenkreuz, 739 P/66
4. K.S. Vock v. Wasserschling, 790 P/66
5. K.S. Fiesta Donaria, 625 Q/67
6. Bill v.d. Wildburg, 167 Q/67
7. Masscotte v. Moorschutz, 578 Q/67
8. Vina v. Wasserschling, 793 P/66

1971 No Competition.

K.S. Axel v.d. Cranger Heide, influential German stud.

K.S. Lümmel v. Braumatal, 301 F, wh. 1956, placed second to K.S. Zeus v. Blitz-dorf in 1958 Kleeman-suche, also has modern-day get in America.

4

The Early
American Scene

THE first German Shorthaired Pointer to be registered by the A.K.C. (1930) was imported Greif v.d. Fliegerhalde, wh. 1928. Actually, many specimens had reached the country before that time. FDSB already had many registrations on file, and old family-album snapshots survive to prove that quite a few hunting and pet dogs of earlier years that found their way here, unregistered, were German Shorthaired Pointers too.

There is no question, though, that the first true establishment of the breed was effected by Dr. Charles R. Thornton, then of Missoula, Montana. The time was 1925. Dr. Thornton, whose favored relaxation from medical cares was the harrying of upland game with his setters, had been accidentally attracted to the German breed by the chance reading of a magazine article featuring the Hohenbruck strain (*Zwinger Hohenbruck*) of Herr Edwardt Reindt, of Bruck-an-der-Leitha, Austria. These all-purpose dogs, thought the doctor, matched beautifully with his own father's teaching, remembered from his Ohio boyhood—a dog is worth keeping only for what it can DO. He passed the magazine article over to his wife with the observation that if these dogs could be bought for anything reasonably less than the earth, he was going to import himself a few.

Hohenbruck, for all the years since then, has been to students of the breed here no more than a name. The elderly Herr Reindt, with whom Dr. Thornton did business, is long dead. The strain has passed from existence. Yet, in its long-enduring day, it was of considerable prominence in Austria. Through the interest of Dr. Otto Fischer, of present-day Austrian Klub Kurzhaar (Vienna), there has recently been furnished to us an old broadsheet of Herr Reindt's kennel advertising. This establishes the strain foundation date as 1894. It is bordered on both sides with pictures of Hohenbruck dogs, and filled with references from satisfied buyers. Topping the list of these references—and the only one written in English, the rest of course being in German—is that dated 1928 and signed "Charles R. Thornton. " In it, he praises the cleverness and sense of his imported Senta v. Hohenbruck.

This historic bitch, wh. 1924 (Rih v. Hohenbruck ex Susi v. Hohenbruck) came to Missoula in whelp. A male that should have come with her was killed by a car the day of shipment. Her litter was the first German Shorthaired Pointer litter known to have been whelped in America. The timing was neat—July 4th, 1925, she produced it: *Siebenköpfigen* (seven-headed) as the German breeders count, by heads rather than noses. Six survived to be given the collective name of "Everyuse" by Dr. Thornton for his faith in their utility qualities in prospect. They were, otherwise, Frisky, Smarty, Pep, Queen, King and Bob—as well as all the colors there are: solid liver, ticked, clear white and liver.

It is unfortunate that breed students can get tangled up in respect to this historical bitch. Twenty years later, another Senta v. Hohenbruck, A-933184, wh. Oct. 1945, by Ch. Hans v. Waldwinkel ex Pointa v. Hohenbruck, was registered with the A.K.C. by a Wm. Connolly, of Iowa. The recurrence of the name has already confused some breeders who have found it in their pedigrees. Perhaps this will now make all clear. . . .

Dr. Thornton's interest in donating his records for the compilation of this new book enables a clear picture to be gained of his importations from 1925 on. The pedigrees, as preserved, also represent a mine of information concerning great German bloodlines of

Senta v. Hohenbruck, FDSB 125225, wh. 1924 (imp. Austria), arrived in U.S. 1925, whelped the first German Shorthaired Pointer litter in this country. Senta was imported by Dr. Charles R. Thornton of Montana.

This painting, treasured by Dr. Thornton, depicts his first two import studs, huge Treu v. Saxony and tidy John Neuforsthaus. Many oversize GSP can be traced to Treu. In Bitter Root Valley, Mont. *Photo: S. Bede Maxwell.*

the past. Even the merest scanning makes clear what quality came to Montana in those early years. It was the cream of German bloodlines, the produce of all-time historically acclaimed studs, mostly through bitches brought in whelp. Almost before he knew it, as the doctor now relates, he was involved out in Bitter Root Valley with a thousand-acre farm to grow the crops tilled by registered Belgian horses to feed the registered brown Swiss cows to make the milk to feed the pups to fill the pens and boost the strain that Charles built!

First, there was the trouble of getting a good stud. The first replacement for the one killed came here old and sterile. The next, Treu v. Saxony, was a beautiful-headed dog of eye-catching, light ticked color, a great-limbed one of distinction. But he weighed 90 pounds—in condition! Poster handsome as he was, with a dramatic style in the field, such a big dog could not please Dr. Thornton, who well understood the preference of American hunters for smaller dogs than this. He used Treu a few times only, waiting for another stud to come. Senta v. Hohenbruck produced a 1926 litter to Treu; two bitches from this crop up still, in western breedings especially: Belle of Montana and Senta's Vonnie. Senta v. Hohenbruck's imp.-in-dam daughter, Queen of Everyuse, an almost-white dog herself, also had two Treu litters (1926-27), registered as "v. Grassthal" —of which Marie, Girl, Bell, Trinket and Schoenheit were retained as broods. Those are also quite easy to locate in pioneer pedigrees. Following the wide distribution of stock from Dr. Thornton's kennels, it is quite possible that many big, pictorially handsome, light-ticked, good-headed German Shorthaired Pointers of today reach back to big Treu.

Dissatisfaction with the size of Treu set the doctor later to weighing and measuring his entire kennel stock. Fortunately, he recorded these statistics at the time on each separate registration certificate. These have interest nowadays as they pinpoint so exactly the size of the pioneer imports from the great German kennels of the time, correcting a somewhat general present-day impression that all dogs of that period were monsters. All quoted here are either direct imports or first-generation get from imports.

| ARTIST V.D. FORST BRICKWEDDE (imp.) | d. | 23¾ inches | 56 lbs. |
| GERO V. BUCHWALD (imp.) | d | 23½ " | 65 lbs. |

Fritz v. Bitterwurzel	d	23½	"	64 lbs.
Wanda v. Otterstein (imp.)	b	23½	"	54 lbs.
Peyda v. Weserstrand (imp.-in-dam)	b.	23¼	"	55 lbs.
Seiger's Lore (imp.)	b	22½	"	55 lbs.
Vogelein v. Bitterwurzel	b	22½	"	50 lbs.
Koenigin v. Weserstrand (imp.-in-dam)	b	22½	"	44 lbs.
Belle of Montana (by Treu)	b	22½	"	65 lbs.
Silva v. Weserstrand (imp.)	b.	22¼	"	57 lbs.
Kindchin v. Bitterwurzel	b	22	"	43 lbs.
Peggy v. Bitterwurzel	b	21¼	"	59 lbs.
Nancy v. Hohenbruck	b	21¼	"	59 lbs.
Diana v. Otterstein (imp.)	b	21	"	48 lbs.
Grille v. Weserstrand (imp.-in-dam)	b	20¾	"	44 lbs.

Such statistics match interestingly with the average size of present-day German imports, apparently making the point that the size over there has remained quite constant over the past 30 years or more.

The replacement for Treu v. Saxony was the 1926-wh. John Neuforsthaus, 322 b, (Taps Harrachstal v.d. Bürgerweise, 1474 U, ex Helga v. Neuforsthaus, 508 Y). His sire line stemmed v.d. Maylust, his dam was deep in debt to Edelmann Giftig, via Edelman and Horst Giftig as well, half-brothers these ex Asta Giftig (Waldo Bilin Schönerlinde, 441 F, ex Thyra Altenau, 67 H). As for size, though John does not figure in the surviving measurements of the kennel, in a beautiful on-point painting in Dr. Thornton's present-day home, he backs Treu v. Saxony's spectacular find and is, in size relation, to the big fellow as a cruiser to an aircraft carrier!

John and Senta, who worked so well, who bred the good stock, who helped school all the pups, figure most vividly in the memories that brighten the heart of the fire these days for Dr. Thornton. Senta—who could beat a duck at its own game in iced-over river slush. John—who could do everything, even herd cattle, so that on one occasion, by baiting a vicious bull, he saved a yardman's life! John's son was another in the same pattern—Fritz v. Bitterwurzel (by the way, Bitterwurzel was Dr. Thornton's German rendering of Bitter Root!). As "Little Fritz," the doctor recalls him: "Clever little Fritz," and the tales of his cleverness are endless. Look through your pedigrees; he can so easily be there.

Among the great-strain representatives that reached Montana between 1925-30, were Diana and Waldo v. Otterstein (Treff II v. Reulbach ex Cilly v. Zampital); Seiger's Lore (K.S. Tasso v. Winterhauch ex Seiger's Halli); Seiger's Holla II (Fuchsfelds Dolling ex Herta Winzler)—both these in whelp to Treff v. Waldhausen, the sire of R.S. & W.S. Heide v.d. Beeke. Sylva v. Weserstrand was another of this procession of in-whelp bitches (Hallo v. Weserstrand ex Kleinchen v. Hastedt), as was Senta v. Lob (Reck Konigsbrunn ex Tika v. Lob). Studs included Artist v.d. Forst Brickwedde (Treff Kalthoff ex Cora Ahlert); Arco v. Lillianberg (Prinz v. Schlosshof ex the Blitz Mülligen II daughter, Iris v. Dubro); Gero v. Buchswald (Blitz Mülligen II ex Carmen v. Buchswald); Donn v. Sulfmeister (K.S. Kobold Mauderode-Westerholt ex Hella v. Wilseder Berg); Cosak v.d. Radbach (K.S. Magnet v. Ockerbach ex the famed Siegerin, Hussa v.d. Radbach).

There are quite a few breed "experts" nowadays who affect the pose of shrugging away all mention of "Thornton breeding." It takes little probing to find such people seldom have the least notion of what "Thornton breeding" actually was. Such "experts" gloat happily over the exact same German great names where these chance to lurk behind any dogs *they* own.

In brief, "Thornton breeding" embraces half-brothers and sisters to Reichs-und-Welt Sieger Heide v.d. Beeke; a three-quarter brother to K.S. Bodo v.d. Radbach; the Prinz v. Schlosshof inheritance of cleverness and sharpness; the heavy leverage on the strains of Mars Altenau, Artus Sand, Edelmann Giftig. No one can shrug away breeding of that order, nor was it subsequently bettered by anything brought in elsewhere at later dates. What is, of course, as true as it is regrettable, is that in the then-prevailing state of the breed market, it was necessary to let the produce of these great German bloodlines go out to hunting men who so often had not the least idea what to do with it. Dr. Thornton preserved, and passed on to us here with unhappy comment, many photos that have reached him through the years—produce of dogs he has sold. Many are obvious crossbreds—half-Pointers, Setters, Springers, Retrievers, Coonhounds.

Where this imported blood was, however, valued at its worth and carefully bred from, grand results accrued. Most American strains of today owe their fair share to "Thornton breeding" if the gen-

Four pioneer stud dogs imported to Missoula, Montana by Dr. Charles Thornton.

Photo: *Dr. Charles Thornton*

erations are back-tracked far enough. And in our own day, one of the last of Dr. Thornton's direct breeding is that great matron, Ch. Yunga War Bride (5 chs. including 4 Duals) wh. 1951, from his own damline, long preserved. Dr. Clark Lemley, of Michigan, breeder and owner of the strongly-Thornton-influenced Dual and Nat'l Ch. Dandy Jim v. Feldstrom, says with truth: "We, now rightly to be called the Old Timers of the breed, know what we owe to Dr. Thornton's importing enterprise of those founding years."

Actually, it is hard for novices to recognize "Thornton breeding" in their extended pedigrees, for this kennel was never endowed with a distinctive name. Dogs carried all manner of endowment. However, where, in a far-taken pedigree, there occur American-whelped Hohenbruck, Waldhausen, Brickwedde, and Altenau especially, "Thornton breeding" is presumable. The operative words are "American-whelped." Famed German strain names are arbitrarily lifted all over in this country, and imports are seldom tagged as such.

An A.K.C. spokesman recently explained that when a dog is registered, the country from which it is imported is included on the face of the certificate. "If people don't choose to use this information later when showing their dogs or signing papers in connection with it, the matter is beyond our control," he added. Yet, and in all respect, it could be held that confusion of status as between import and homebred is as surely an error of particulars as a wrongly-stated date of whelping or a miscalculation of wins. That such errors as the latter are thoroughly subject to control is well understood by all who breed and/or exhibit dogs.

The pedigree services, in many ways very efficient, also tend to ignore the status of importation. Recently sighted was a pedigree, professionally-compiled, of a most prepotent, present-day stud. His fourth generation is 100 per cent German dogs. His third, with the exception of one son of imports, is all import. Yet, for all the serious-minded student could gain to the contrary from this handsome compilation, all his forebears could have been whelped in the lobby of the Empire State Building. This would matter less if, at the same time, there did not exist the local practice of appropriating famous German strain names. Herr Bleckman, of the famed v.d. Radbachs, is not the only German breeder who wonders what protection he could invoke against the wide, unauthorized filching here of his name property.

70

Importing and breeding from good dogs was not Dr. Thornton's only responsibility in those early years. He was also concerned with the necessary promotion and publicity. The matter of breed recognition, official sanction from the A.K.C., was another concern to occupy him quite seriously. That, of course, involved the matter of the name by which it was to be known. As the doctor recalls, the first intention of the A.K.C. was to recognize the breed as the "German Shorthair." He held out against this, taking the view that it should be known as "German Shorthaired *Pointer*," that the shorter name could mean just *any* shorthaired German dog.

One may look back now and wonder whether the adoption of the word "Pointer" was actually in the best interests of the breed— something that could not have been discerned in that earlier time. Historically, new breeds have not always benefited by being bracketed together with those longer-established in the like field. Shakespeare to the contrary, there is much in a name where dog breeds are concerned, chiefly because of the ready triggering of the association of ideas. Belgian Sheepdogs carelessly judged in many cases as German Shepherds is one instance. Brittany Spaniels, faulted by Springer or Cocker standards too often, is another.

The Germans, who commenced by knowing their breed as *"Deutsche Kurzhaarige Vorstehhund"* (literally, German Shorthaired Pointer), must have dropped the last word just as soon as they perceived the significance and dangers in association therewith. By 1938, Dr. Kleeman and Herr v. Otto had settled for the shortened version, entitling their famed breed monograph simply *"Deutsch Kurzhaar."* In their opening paragraph they analyze the names by which the breed is known throughout Europe—mostly in some form and translation of "German Braque." (French: *Braque Allemand.* Italian: *Bracco Tedesco.*) Officially, under the rules of the European Canine Governing Body, the F.C.I. (Federation Cynologique Internationale) it is also known as German Braque.

English "Dog World" explored the matter very thoroughly in 1958, (March 14 issue) when the newly-awakened interest in this breed began to be apparent in that country. The famed English sporting dog authority, Frank Warner Hill, started the ball rolling. He invoked the opinion of some Continental experts. The first quoted opinion came from Herr Waldemar Marr, a German sporting dog authority of note: "I see that the problem of what to call

71

in England the so-called German Shorthaired Pointer is still not solved. I advise the English K.C. to call the breed the German Shorthaired Gundog. *'Vorstehhund'* was the name of the breed about 35 years ago. Now, the title *'Vorstehhund'* (Pointer) has been abandoned in Germany and they call the breed *'Kurzhaar.'* I think the English could call the German breeds German Shorthaired Gundog, German Long-haired Gundog, and German Wirehaired Gundog." *(WALDEMAR MARR, Berlin.)*

The Italian sporting dog expert, Signor Zavaterro, also consulted on this occasion, made clear that he went along with the F.C.I. name-endowment of "German Braque," adding: "To call a breed a German Pointer when it is not a Pointer at all is indeed a grave error. The Shorthaired German Pointer (in Germany) is now called *Kurzhaar,* and the club the *Deutscher Kurzhaar Klub.* . . . As a practical shooting dog the Kurzhaar is an excellent worker . . . an excellent bird dog, very steady at point, a good backer, and with many other excellencies of a good gundog."

In "Dog World" of June 8, 1962, Frank Warner Hill again granted space for the airing of this discussion, adding as his opinion that "these great all-round gundogs are definitely not Pointers in the accepted sense of the term in this country. Their owners acknowledged this originally in applying to the Kennel Club for the name of 'Pointer-Retriever' for their breed. It was obvious that this trespass on a specialist breed could not be allowed to stand, and so as almost a last resource the name of German Shorthaired Pointer was adopted."

Referring to the careful re-classification the English Kennel Club has recently granted the breed, including its own special type of competition for Field Trials, Mr. Warner Hill makes plain the realistic approach of the English to the employment of the breed: "German Shorthaired Pointers by this or any other name (are) in the original strong, powerful dogs used for all types of hunting, and as this they can command a niche of their own in the Gundog world, but must be kept separate in appearance, work, and general characteristics." Adding that there might be a case made for finding a name along the same lines as those given the Viszla, the Weimeraner, Mr. Hill adds: "You cannot call a dog a Pointer when this is only a third of his work, the other two-thirds being hunting and retrieving both in and out of cover. The original description

72

of the breed, as an ideal, was one that would work in all conditions of weather and cover, would hunt, point, retrieve tenderly on land or in water, track wounded game, act as guard against poachers. To achieve these things, size and substance must be preserved—and don't try monkeying around with any English Pointer crosses. . . ."

Here, of course, one comes upon the bitter kernel of a hard nut for the cracking. In arbitrarily dubbing the breed a Pointer, there is issued to the unthinking, the ignorant, a strong incentive to "try monkeying around with English Pointer crosses." The English, with their long-time reputation as breeders of every kind of livestock from horses to canaries, know the pitfalls that can be dug. They have, themselves, formed in their time so many of the well-known dog breeds of the present age, as well as improved many others besides. They know very well that when a breed has been finally formed from radical basic crossing of diverse breeds, it is impossible, at a later stage, to re-introduce any of the "basics" without causing trouble. The "basic," as a matter of fact, has become wholly alien, and its reintroduction to the new breed is nothing short of cross-breeding again. The German Shorthaired Pointer, long since "fixed" as a separate breed, can no longer with safety re-absorb English Pointer crosses any more than it can absorb Schweisshund, or whatever form of scenting hound the 19th-century breeders borrowed from the German foresters.

This, then, is at least one of the dangers the English breeders of long experience discern in the name of the German breed as it is now recognized. For this reason, to take it outside the sphere of possible "monkeying," some of their wisest people are giving the matter great thought. They have even asked that the Americans also give consideration to helping them solve the problem. It will be interesting to see if, in the final analysis, anything comes of the intention to re-name the breed there, and whether, for goodness' sake, the English eventually range themselves with the Germans, and adopt the name the A.K.C. had here proposed in the first place, more than thirty years ago.

* * * * *

The second base for German Shorthaired Pointer breeding in America was also in the West, at Bennington, Nebraska. Here, in

73

1931, two hunting partners, Walter Mangold and Ernest Rojem, imported a dog and bitch. Both had had experience with the breed overseas. During World War I they had served on opposite sides, Rojem with the German army, Mangold with the American army. After the war, they met in Nebraska, the state running over with game—pheasant, prairie chicken, quail, grouse. Population pressure has now driven the game away, but just after the war the young men had great sport. Rojem's brother, Peter, living in Germany, was commissioned to find them a good pair of *Kurzhaar*. After long search he found in Schleswig-Holstein a six-months-old, Claus v. Schleswig-Konigsweg, wh. 1931, paying 80 marks for him. It took longer to find Jane v. grünen Adler, 341 l, and at two years old and trained she cost 180 marks. Claus was by Golo v. Gottorp, 754 c, ex Arna v. Altenberg, 606 h. Jane was by Horst Fürstermoor, 924 Y ex Toni v. grünen Adler, 661 U.

It took money, time, and some string-pulling to get them out of the country. Then, as now, the Germans tried to keep their best dogs in the country. Both were royally bred. Claus' sire, Golo v. Gottorp, was an Artus Sand son ex Karin Fürstermoor, 925 Y, she a Pack v.d. Bode daughter ex Ulme v.d. goldenen Mark, both stemming from Edelmann Giftig, the sire of Pack. Here, again, is an important basic pedigree subjected to compilation error. As Claus v. Schleswig-Konigsweg touches so many moderns, it is worth correcting. He was registered with FDSB, United K.C., A.K.C. Only the latter records his particulars correctly, and this compiler has sighted many pedigrees in which the error in the other two is carried along. His name (in these) is wrongly spelled, his sire's name is wrongly spelled, and he has been awarded an entirely different dam, recorded as Lena v. Schlenbarge. This must have been plucked from the air, as there is no bitch of that name in any part of his authentic German *Ahnentafel* (pedigree) here in our hands. The error is the more in need of correction in that Golo v. Gottorp, as an Artus Sand son, has merit. Misspelled, his name is a nothing. This strain name, by the way, still functions in Germany, registering dogs right into the late 1950's and beyond.

"Claus was a great dog for us," Walter Mangold writes. "It was tough getting the breed going, though—perhaps it was still a little close to war days in a small community. Dog judges showed prejudice, too. At one water trial, a judge looked at Claus standing

74

beside me, asked: 'Can HE swim?' After several dogs failed to re-trieve a dead duck in heavy waves, Claus swam out to a sandbar in the river, raised his head high for the scent, then swam directly to retrieve the duck. The crowd went wild with excitement when he was seen to catch the scent! He didn't waste time swimming circles, either, like some of the better-known water breeds did on the day. Funny—I didn't see anything of that judge later in the day, the one who asked me if Claus could swim. . . .

"He had the rugged constitution needed here, summers over a hundred, winters to thirty below, snow drifted to twelve feet and more quite often. We sent him through floating ice after duck. And he was a fireball on land, not even sand burrs stopped him. He was a gentle dog, too. As postmaster, I had him with me at the office. Children coming in for mail rode around on his back. But he was a good guard too, and no stray dogs ever bothered him twice. He got us lots of good dogs that were widely distributed, and lived to be very old. We buried him in what was native hay land east of here, but it's all built over now that we're the center of U.S.A."

In examination of pedigrees, and tracing beyond the convention-ally-given four generations, this compiler is forever coming up with Claus v. Schleswig-Konigsweg—in such as the wonderful producer, Little Gretchen's Brownie, dam and grand-dam of National Field Trial champions; as Dual Ch. Wag-Ae's Snowflake, with her fine produce of bench and field champions, and dozens upon dozens more beside. Lance McGilbrey, of Columbia River, who purchased his first German Shorthaired Pointer from Walter Mangold while living in Nebraska, owes to old "Claus-can-HE-swim," and maybe *you*, Mr. Breeder, owe to him too. Go look to see. . . .

＊　＊　＊　＊　＊

By 1932, the tide of importation flowed strongly into the mid-West. In St. Croix Falls, Wisconsin, a dedicated breeder sat nights over his homework, German field and show reports. This was Joseph Burkhart, one-time German gamekeeper. He made his choice on the basis of line-breeding to a fine-performed German bitch, Wandadora. Her son, by K.S. Benno v. Schlossgarten, her grand-daughter also by Benno, were partnered by a bitch by Benno's own sire, Bob v. Winterhauch, the Heidi Esterhof son. They were

Bob v. Schwarenberg, (K.S. Benno v. Schlossgarten ex Wandadora); Arta v. Hohreusch (K.S. Benno v. Schlossgarten ex Afra v. Schwarenberg); Feldjager's Grisette (Bob v. Winterhauch ex Edith v. Karlbach, a Junker v. Bomlitztal daughter ex Wanda v. Karlbach).

Impact of the three on American breeding is beyond hope of exact assessment. It is difficult to find strains from which they are totally absent. Maybe only the modern Danish imports exclude them to any degree, and this may not last indefinitely. There is just too much Minnesota breeding around for it to be kept forever out of a breeder's planning.

Joseph Burkhart not only chose well, he gained the confidence of people who bought from him, he taught them how to line-breed, saving what they had. A fully-extended pedigree of such as, say, Joseph Burkhart's own personal dog for so many years, Ch. Thalbach Waldwinkel Mark, is a model of practical application of line-breeding practice to prepotent basics. Mark's fourth generation could be the most "family" compilation outside that of the Fletcher Christians on Pitcairn Island! Joseph Burkhart's teaching was as direct as it was brief. Breed *only* the best *to* the best, not merely male to female. Nowadays, he says he has not changed his viewpoint, and feels the breed would benefit if such a practice were more generally followed.

Of the three imports, the palm must surely go to Arta v. Hohreusch. Feldjager's Grisette, much plainer looking, proved out her bloodlines, but not to the extent that Arta did. Bob v. Schwarenberg died of heat stroke less than two years after his importation. Fortunately, Arta, his half-sister, had whelped him two litters before then. Dr. Berg, a good friend of Joseph Burkhart's, took the pick bitch of the first litter, naming her Berg's Choice. Go on, look into your pedigree—see if you can't find her easily. She was good. From the second litter, the late Jack Shattuck picked a dog on the very day that Bob v. Schwarenberg died. Jack Shattuck named his pup Fritz v. Schwarenberg.

Too many of the litters, like those of Dr. Thornton, went to hunting men, many of whom didn't even bother to register their purchases. Feldjager's Grisette justified herself with Bessie v. Winterhauch (by Ch. Fritz v. Schwarenberg), but it is surely Arta that supports the entire strength of Minnesota breeding. After her litter that included Ch. Fritz v. Schwarenberg (the balance was all but wiped out by distemper, which in those days was not under control as it is now), she was sold to New York, where she had recently had imported for her a son of K.S. Frei Südwest, Hallo Mannheimia, from the breeding of Herr Carl Seidler, of Mannheim. It was a stipulation that Arta be bred to this dog, and that Joseph Burkhart have his choice of a pup. So he came to be possessed of Treu v. Waldwinkel. As the dam of Fritz and Treu, Arta's influence has to be conceded.

"And one old dog I have these days," Joseph Burkhart had written to then-novice breeder, Don Miner, of California, in 1947; "Eleven years old is this old dog now, and he has the record of being the sire of more champions than any living Shorthaired Pointer that we know of, though he himself was never entered in any show. . . ."

That was Treu v. Waldwinkel. . . .

"Treu v. Waldwinkel?" muses that other tower of breed knowledge, Hjalmer Olsen, of Georgia, the master of the Fieldborns. "How *very* much all we breeders owe to old Treu. . . ."

Before Treu though, remember, there had first to be Arta!

Treu v. Waldwinkel, whose record of prepotency has kept him with the top flight of studs in the U.S. (By Hallo Mannheimia, imp. Germany, ex Arta v. Hohreusch.)

The only surviving picture of Ernest Rojem (1) with Jane v. grunen Adler (imp. Germany), and Walter Mangold with Claus v. Schlesweg-Konigsweg (imp. to Nebraska from Germany in 1931).

Dual Ch. Rusty v. Schwarenberg with his owner, the late Jack Shattuck. Rusty was first of the breed to gain the Dual title.

Arta v. Hohreusch, one of the three original imports from Germany to Minnesota. Arta is the strongest bitch prepotent the breed received here.

5

Progress in

American Breeding

BY 1938, breed strength was gathered mainly in the Minnesota-Wisconsin areas with a lap-over into Michigan. This permitted making application to the A.K.C. for Parent Club status. First officers were Jack Shattuck, Jr., D. R. Lugar, J. MacGaheran, Beckwith Mayer, Joseph Burkhart, Henry Radle, H. J. Loring, H. B. Klein, G. Noltimier. Their first problem concerned a name for the club. The A.K.C. rejected the first proposal—The German Shorthaired Pointer and Retriever Club of America, Inc., exactly as the English K.C. was later to reject the same proposal from breeders in that country. Official view would seem to be that as pigs is pigs, so Pointers is Pointers. They cannot be Retrievers too. The plain fact, of course, is that they *are* Retrievers too.

Looking back, one wonders why the superb retrieving abilities of the breed have never gained official recognition here; why no opportunity exists for a German Shorthaired Pointer to prove himself competitively at retrieving skills and win points for it. At least, if the English K.C. denied the use of the double-barreled name, they have provided the means for exercising the ability. It may well be that the early-day insistence on recognition as a Pointer clouded the issue as to utility abilities. It may also be that at that time many people, newly-recruited to ownership of the German breed here, ill understood those potentialities that the ordinary hunting man had so quickly discovered. A contributing factor to misunderstanding of the breed aims may also have been the sad circumstance—still prevailing—that no one has ever provided German Shorthaired Pointer owners with training manuals fitted to the performance of their breed. The novice who wants to train his dog has to buy the books catering to Pointer/Setter performance and, inevitably, and unfortunately, as he reads, so he tailors his views as to what his dog should do. Lastly, many recruits to German Shorthaired Pointers came directly from Pointer/Setter activities. They brought with them their own measure of a Field Trial dog— a Bird Dog. They had known no other, and rather than change their viewpoint and training practices, they set out to change, to the best of their ability, the dog. People with such views were not likely to besiege the A.K.C. to provide a type of competition suited to the particular skills of the breed into which they had now insinuated themselves. Their ideal measure of performance remained as it had always been, and many of them worked hard to thrust it upon their associates in competitive activity.

The Parent Club application for a Charter, then, was eventually granted to The German Shorthaired Pointer Club of America, Inc. First responsibility was that imposed by Article IV (Sec. 5) of the Constitution and By-Laws of the A.K.C., ". . . that it was the duty and privilege of each Parent Member Specialty Club to define the true type of the breed of purebred dogs which it was organized to promote and improve." That meant a Standard to be compiled. Adapted from the German, with slight variation, it was officially approved in May, 1946. It has not since then suffered any revision, as have so many other Standards, especially over the past ten years. Yet the Parent Club, in its beginning, had recognized that such a revision could become necessary. The Amended Articles (1945) hold, as an added objective, "the need to improve the definition of the Standard for the true type of German Shorthaired Pointers from time to time, and to establish uniform methods of judging, either at Field Trials and/or Bench Shows."

As it is no secret that many Regional Club members would like to see the Standard gone over, it would seem that the Amended Articles of 1945 provide the basis for firm demand along such lines.

The Parent Club was first with Field Trial competition for the breed, promoting this first at Anoka, Minnesota, then at Ft. Snelling, also in Minnesota. So it presently became possible for German Shorthaired Pointers to work towards their Field Trial titles and the coveted Dual title, Field and Bench. As more and more Regional Clubs were formed across the nation, additional venues were provided.

The first A.K.C show championships (1936) were gained by Becky v. Hohenbruck (Trill v. Hohenbruck ex Lotte v. Hoellenthor) and Baron v.d. Brickwedde (Artist v.d. Brickwedde, imp., ex Dixie Queen Buchwald), Thornton-breds. First to make true gallery impact, though, was Ch. Fritz v. Schwarenberg (Bob v. Schwarenberg, imp., ex Arta v. Hohreusch, imp.). Championship honors never fell to old Treu v. Waldwinkel. His day was before that of Field Trials for his breed, and youthful curiosity in respect to the workings of a wolf trap disqualified him for show.

Ch. Fritz was widely campaigned, publicizing his breed in all ways his owner, Jack Shattuck, Jr., of Minneapolis, could contrive. Morris & Essex and Westminster are among his B.O.Bs, and he took four years in a row at Chicago International, including the first Breed Specialty held there. He is still a medium of breed publicity, by the way, posing for German Shorthaired Pointer conformation in the A.K.C. *Book of Standards* (Plate 2). His life was useful and long, Jack Shattuck reporting him still in great heart at age eleven, still a tireless hunter, with more than 3000 pheasants shot over him. He founded the long-enduring v. Schwarenberg strain here, and sired the first bitch of the breed to get her Dual (1949) in Dr. Zahalka's Schatz v. Schwarenberg (ex Helga v. Schwarenberg).

Contemporary with Ch. Fritz was another fine breed publicist in Ch. Sportsman's Dream, bred by Rudolph Hirschnitz, then of Wyoming, and owned by V. E. Lantow, of Denver, Colorado. Ch. Sportsman's Dream gained at least one honor that eluded Ch. Fritz—an all-breed B.I.S. It was the first for the breed, and taken at San Diego, California, in 1940. The judge, Col. E. E. Ferguson, recalled him as "a most exceptional dog of his time, so much so that if he were showing now he would compare well with our top winners in the breed. Coincidently, my B.I.S. at a 1960 show was later reported to me as a Sportsman's Dream grandson (Ch. Huntsman's Drumfire) proving that the dog of twenty years ago was not only good in himself but able to influence his breed."

Ch. Sportsman's Dream was sired by the Hirschnitz import, Astor v. Fischtal, 1736 k (Flott Teutoberg gen Ingo, 322 g ex Erna Teutoberg, 297 k), ex the American bred Sieglinde v. Meihsen, a granddaughter of Cosak v.d. Radbach, imp. Importing as early as the mid-1930's, Rudolph Hirschnitz also qualified as a breed pioneer. His experience was drawn upon during the earliest institution of field trials in California, in which he took interest to the end of his life. Sharing his German correspondence solved for me many problems of compilation, placing me deeply in debt for historical matter from his files and for advice as to where more might hopefully be sought.

Jack Shattuck's next star was to become a legend: the solid liver dog, Rusty v. Schwarenberg (Mars v. Ammertal, imp. ex Vicki v. Schwarenberg). As the first Field Trial Champion, the first Dual in his breed (1947), Rusty stemmed dam-side from the Burkhart imports, Arta v. Hohreusch and Feldjager's Grisette, his grand-dams. His sire, Mars v. Ammertal, also solid liver, was said to be a very good worker, an efficient cold-trailer, a little dour of temperament. As a phenomenal dog of any time, Rusty's record includes two Westminster B.O.Bs, three Breed Specialties, and an ability to switch from Field to Show and back again. The day after winning the 1944 Breed Specialty, he went out to win a First in an Open All Age Stake in the field. Competing often against Pointers and Setters, worked from a horse, his useful performances on such occasions did much to break down Pointer-men's prejudices against his breed; not that he was ever one to hug the horizon—merely that he gave useful performances practical men could evaluate.

Jack Shattuck, Jr., deserves to have his memory perpetuated by the breeders here. Not only did he campaign good dogs widely to advertise the breed, but he gave a great deal of time and energy to publicity work as well, though his health condition made exertion difficult for him. He was still young when serious disability overtook him. "A broken hip won't heal right," he wrote Don Miner, of California. "Now I can hardly walk . . ." In those final years of pain he had Dual Ch. Rusty with whom he could re-live old triumphs, the dog pre-deceasing him by only a few weeks in 1952.

It ought to be possible to give consideration to the possibility of perpetuating the memory of the outstanding breed pioneers in the same way as the Germans have done. They name their proudest competitions for those to whom the breeders are indebted, such as Prince zu Solms-Brauenfels and Dr. Kleeman. Obvious nominations in this country for such honorable recognition would certainly include Dr. Thornton, Joseph Burkhart and Jack Shattuck, Jr. It is not a right thing that the names of good men be allowed to slip away from knowledge of the breeders and owners of the future.

It is not possible to list by name all the Minnesota-Wisconsin breeders of the period. Many founded strong strains with good dogs. Among such count the late Dr. E. W. Berg, Henry Radle, Dr. and Mrs. H. Zahalka, Fr. Gerald Baskfield, the late W. A. Olsen, Hjalmer Olsen, and Joseph and Magdalina Deiss, all making the wisest use of the good breeding material Joseph Burkhart put into their hands. Their breeding activities formed an intricate mesh from the original imports and their descendants, harping heavily on the thread of Treu v. Waldwinkel.

Thus the Zahalkas followed up their Dual Ch. Schatz v. Schwarenberg with the handsome Ch. Searching Wind Bob (Treu v. Waldwinkel ex Maida v. Thalbach, his granddaughter). Bob, in turn, sired Searching Wind Topper (ex Fieldborn Katzie Karlbach) with whom his breeder-trainer, Hjalmer Olsen, completed the Dual in 1951. From Ch. Searching Wind Cita (Treu v. Waldwinkel ex Dual Ch. Schatz) came six champions, three sired by her half-brother, Ch. Searching Wind Bob, and three by Heinrich v. Karlswald (Treu v. Waldwinkel ex Senta v. Karlbach). All within the mesh pattern. . . .

With far fewer stud opportunities than fell to better-publicized dogs of his time, Treu v. Waldwinkel's record of champions sired, plus the produce of his prepotent daughters and granddaughters, must be viewed with respect. Of Treu's female descendants, Fr. Baskfield's Maida v. Thalbach (Ozzie v. Schwarenberg ex Bibi Winterhauch, she a Treu daughter ex Bessie v. Winterhauch) is also a standout. In addition to Ch. Searching Wind Bob, she produced Ch. Thalbach Waldwinkel Hans to Treu, this one becoming the base of the late W. A. Olsen's strain, the Waldwinkel taken proudly from old Treu. Ch. Thalbach Waldwinkel Heide (by Tell v. Thalbach) was a Maida one that did well for D. K. Johnson, and

Ch. Thalbach Waldwinkel Mark was Maida's son by Ch. Glanz v. Winterhauch (Treu v. Waldwinkel ex Bessie v. Winterhauch). Mark, who made a good winning record, lived on to an extreme old age with Joseph Burkhart, and it was a sad letter that reached us here, while this book was being compiled, telling that Mark, last direct link with the pioneer imports, was dying of leukemia in his thirteenth year.

Bessie v. Winterhauch, a singleton effort of Feldjager's Grisette to her mating with Ch. Fritz v. Schwarenberg, was owned by a close friend of Joseph Burkhart's, Henry Radle, who mated her to old Treu (who but!) to produce the future champion, Fritz v. Schlossgarten. With Fritz, Hjalmer Olsen got under way with this breed, winning the first Field Trial, he notes, promoted for German Shorthaired Pointers, held at Solon Springs, Wisconsin, April, 1940.

No one associated with German Shorthaired Pointers has won more lasting respect, from a wider cross-section of fanciers, than has Hjalmer Olsen, now of Cordele, Georgia, growing no younger, for sure, but still vitally interested in the progress of the breed—still able to rap the knuckles of the lunatic fringe when he deems their activities not in the best interests of German Shorthaired Pointers en masse. Frankly, and in print (*Dog World*, May, 1958), Hjalmer Olsen tells us that his true love is the English Pointer, doubtless the breed on which his first enthusiasms were built. However, he makes it abundantly clear that Pointers is Pointers and German Shorthaired Pointers are something else again, understanding the breed to which he has devoted so many practical-minded years as a breeder, importer, judge.

With the name of Hjalmer Olsen, too, is earliest associated that of a Thornton-bred he acquired as a pup, handled to within a few points of its title, and sold then to William Ehrler, of Michigan. This was Timm v. Altenau, who never actually finished, but who holds a place in breed history through having sired fifteen champions—for many years the record till Austrian import, Field Ch. Greif v. Hundsheimerkogel came to say move over, please! Timm was by the K.S. Kobold Mauderode-Westerholt son, Donn v. Sulfmeister, imp. His dam was also Thornton-bred, Dreizenheim v. Brickwedde (Artist v.d. Forst Brickwedde, imp. ex Seiger's Lore, imp.). Timm v. Altenau produced six of his champions from Distel v. Rheinberg (Tell v. Schoenwalde ex Wanda Gale Altmark); four from Distel's older sister, Dixie v. Rheinberg; three ex Tillie v. Rheinberg, his daughter ex Distel. There was another ex Distel's dam, Wanda Gale Altmark. The only champion outside the family pattern was Hjalmer Olsen's own Ch. Loal's Dot, ex Zest v. Horstig.

Wanda Gale Altmark, supporting the edifice on the female side of this fantastic production, was a granddaughter of the Thornton import, John Neuforsthaus, ex Marie v. Grasstal, already in these pages mentioned as a daughter of that big handsome Treu v. Saxony —remember? Wanda also has influence through her non-champion son by Timm v. Altenau—Duke v. Rheinberg. He sired future Dual Ch. Valbo v. Schlesburg, owned by Carl Schnell of Fraser, Michigan, long-time still active breeder there. Valbo's striking good looks may have owed something to big boy Treu, but here we consider him rather for winning the first A.K.C. Field Trial Championship in Michigan in 22 exciting days, at fifteen months of age. He was also the first Field Ch. handled by Russell Dixon! Dual Ch. Valbo v. Schlesburg's pedigree is an interesting one to reproduce here, presenting, as it does, most of the Montana and Nebraska imports we have discussed. This, of course, was still the time when so many owners strained after dogs that worked as well as they looked, that looked as well as they worked.

Those who have come with us so far through these pages will readily identify all the imports, while noting that none are indicated in any way as such. This could be usage, but one hesitates to describe it as good usage.

Carl Schnell had success also with his Ehrler-breds from Timm v. Altenau, finishing four: Bella and Hilda v. Rheinberg, Sweet Tillie Too, and Rita v. Altenau. Rita made 1948 a bonanza year, many B.O.B., Group placings, and the breed Specialty best under Jack Shattuck, Jr. Ch. Alsedda (Timm v. Altenau ex Tillie v. Rheinberg) gave Dr. Clark Lemley, of Detroit, his early successes.

Here, too, bowed in Del Glodowski, of Sturtevant, Wisconsin. His Baron v. Strauss, a Dual Ch. of 1953, also stems from the pioneer imports, his sire vintage Burkhart, his dam line chock-full of Thornton, being anchored on Sieglinde v. Meihsen, the dam of Ch. Sportsman's Dream. Sieglinde was by Monte v. Kissell, a son of the Thornton imp.-in-dam, Kamerad v. Waldhausen, by Treff v. Waldhausen (Germany) ex his half-sister, Weisse v. Brickwedde (Artist v.d. Forst Brickwedde ex Seiger's Lore, both imports). Sieg-

Name of Dog __Valbo v Schlesburg__ Sex __Male__ Stud-Book No. __S197,946__

Breed __German Shorthaired Pointer__ Vol. __65__ Color __liver, white and ticked__

Date Whelped __January 13, 1948__

Breeder __Thomas M. Adams__

Duke v Rheinberg
Sire A861718

Heida v Schlesburg
Dam S74106

Dean v Sulfmeister
Sire A151688

Dreisenhein v Brickwedde
Dam A28159

Kronos v Habichtshof
Sire 944182

Wanda Gele Won
Dam A146907

Flash Schleswig
Sire A332280

Minnie v Hohenbruck *
Dam

Monta v Kissel
Sire A153307

Judy v Burg
Dam A153308

Timm v Altenau
Sire A406109

Wanda Gele Altmark
Dam A803576

Baron Schleswig
Sire S11656

Beauty v Kisselburg
Dam A408186

Kobold Nauderode Westerholt
Sire

Heila v Klieger Berg
Dam

Artist v d Forst Brickwedde
Sire A8782

Seigers Lore
Dam 954365

Flako v Habichtshof
Sire

Hertha v Habichtshof
Dam

John Neuforsthaus
Sire

Marie v Graesthal
Dam

Claus Schleswig Konigsweg
Sire 999655

Braunne von Schmeling
Dam A77982

(Ch) Dilgrue Amour
Sire A799

Beck von Hohenbruck
Dam

Kamerad v Waldhausen
Sire

Weiss v Brickwedde
Dam A8160

Cosak V d Wedbach
Sire A1428

Nancy v Hohenbruck
Dam 873948

The foregoing is a true copy from the records of the American Kennel Club.

In witness whereof, the Official Seal is affixed hereto this 7th day of October, 1949.

linde's dam, Judy v. Burg, was by Cosak v.d. Radbach, imp., ex Nancy v. Hohenbruck (ex Senta v. Lob, imp.). That Sieglinde is a combination of the forces producing the great German dogs, K.S. Bodo v.d. Radbach and R.S. Heide v.d. Beeke, makes sense of the excellence of her descendants and something else again of the dictum of those who, on the basis of no knowledge at all, elect themselves to dispose contemptuously of "Thornton breeding."

This brief analysis should interest Colorado folk who owe to Ch. Sportsman's Dream and also currently to that dog's grandson, Dual Ch. Baron Turn and Taxis, owned by Mr. W. Barth. Also, it concerns all with descendants of Dual Ch. Baron v. Strauss, among which count his sons, Ch. Otto v. Strauss, Field Ch. Spiker and Mort v. Strauss. In the next generation is Dual Ch. Strauss' Working Boy (by Otto) and the National (A.K.C.) Field Ch. of 1960, Field Ch. Duke Strauss III (by Spiker), plus the bonus that Field Ch. Fritz v. Strauss also represents.

Burkhart basics built up the Oak-Crests of Joseph and Magdalina Deiss, of Minnesota. Joseph had worked with German Shorthaired Pointers in his native Germany, and was not long without one here, finding his first really good one in a litter sister to Dual Ch. Rusty v. Schwarenberg. This was Ch. Cora. Mated to Fr. Baskfield's Ch. Glanz v. Winterhauch, she rewarded them with Ch. Cora's Penny of Oak-Crest. Liking her, they presently sent Glanz another Arta v. Hohreusch granddaughter (as Cora had been) in Chimes Girl (Mars v. Ammertal, imp. ex Berg's Choice). This was sound linebreeding. It produced their Ch. Oak-Crest's Rick v. Winterhauch, who put to such good use his heritage, which is Arta-plus-Arta-plus Arta, that he is now honored with ten American champion get, including three Duals and that resplendent B.I.S.-winning bitch, Ch. Oak-Crest's Cora v. Winterhauch.

The pedigree of Ch. Oak-Crest's Rick is worth reproducing in full. By that old proverb holding that an ounce of seeing is worth a ton of hearing, it is an outstanding example of how the Minnesota breedings were carefully contrived, a lesson to the followers of the haphazard, and shows at a glance most of the dogs discussed in these pages.

Mrs. Deiss tells a grand yarn of their involvement with the breed. "We always had *two* German Shorthaired Pointers, even when we lived in the city," she reminisces. "To 'keep a few more,' as one says,

Field Ch. Kaposia's Chief of Oak Crest, pictured on his 13th birthday in 1965. This fine old personality dog was representative of the solid early-day type of solid livers within this breed, and faithfully passed along his inheritance. Breeders: J. and M. Deiss, Minnesota. Owners: Don and Betty Sandberg.

Ch. Oak-Crest Cora v. Winterhauch, the first bitch in the breed to take a BIS (1956). In addition to compiling a phenomenal show record, she is the dam of six champions.

```
                                                          ┌ Frei Sudwest -
                                          ┌ Hallo Mannheimia, 924,177
                                          │               └ Cita Mannheimia -
                      ┌ Treu v Waldwinkel, A-230,208
                      │ Sire of 10 Champions
                      │                   ┌ Benno v Schlossgarten -
                      │                   ┌ Arta v Hohreusch, 894,328
                      │                     Dam of 1 Champion
                      │                     └ Afra v Schwarenberg -
      ┌ Ch. Glanz v Winterhauch, A-494,473
      │ Sire of 3 Champions
      │                                   ┌ Bob v Schwarenberg, 885,741
      │                                     Sire of 1 Champion
      │               ┌ Ch. Fritz Schwarenberg, A-173,976
      │                 Sire of 7 Champions
      │                                   └ Arta v Hohreusch, 894,328
      │                                     Dam of 1 Champion
      │             ┌ Bessie v Winterhauch, A-279,248
      │               Dam of 2 Champions
      │                                   ┌ Bob v Winterhauch -
      │               └ Feldjagers Grisette, 894,329
      │                 Dam of 2 Champions
      │                                   └ Edith v Karlbach -

Ch. Oak-Crest's Rick v Winterhauch,
German Shorthaired Pointer (male)
Sire of 11 Champions       S-224,872
                                          ┌ Ajax Frankfurt (Main) -
                                  ┌ Heros v Ammertal -
                                          └ Hansa v Schertelspitz -
                      ┌ Mars v Ammertal, A-413,778
                      │ Sire of 6 Champions
                      │                   ┌ Hasso v d Schwarzwaldecke -
                      │           └ Asta v d Rohrhalde -
                      │                   └ Ella v Ammertal -
      ┌ Chimes Girl, A-676,166
        Dam of 1 Champion
                                          ┌ Benno v Schlossgarten -
                      ┌ Bob v Schwarenberg, 885,741
                      │ Sire of 1 Champion
                      │                   └ Wandadora -
        └ Berg's Choice, A-259,273
          Dam of 1 Champion
                                          ┌ Benno v Schlossgarten -
                      └ Arta v Hohreusch, 894,328
                        Dam of 1 Champion
                                          └ Afra v Schwarenberg -
```

we moved out onto seven acres. Before long we had *seventeen* German Shorthaired Pointers and had to make a choice which would quit eating, the dogs or the family. So, to ease the strain, we took a few boarders. Soon we had seventy dogs to take care of, plus our own breeding stock, plus the twenty-thirty puppies always in my care. By 1959 this was getting to be rather much. We sold the kennels and now we are where we started, we have *two* German Shorthaired Pointers." It is not by any means an unusual history of dog involvement.

The pride of Oak-Crest's earlier days was at one time Ch. Schatz v. Konigsheim, Ch. Cora's son by Ch. Fritz v. Schwarenberg. Sold as a pup, he was donated by his owners to the K9 Corps in World War II. His litter mate was killed on Saipan but Schatz came home, was de-trained for civilian life and restored to his owners. Maybe the de-training didn't take. There were incidents. He was returned to Mr. Deiss in hope something could be done with him. It took a year of patient training to make Schatz trustworthy again. Then, being six years old, he went to his first show, finishing smartly with three five-point majors. Thereafter, as Mr. Deiss' most dependable hunting and tracking dog, he lived out the useful life of a worker into his twelfth year.

This period also saw the first German import to gain an American championship in Alfred Sause's Ch. Dallo v.d. Forst Brickwedde, a Westminster and M.&E. Best of Breed. His sire, Artus v. Hasetal (Furst v. Fuchspass ex Cora v.d. Brickwedde, an Artus Sand granddaughter) was also the grandsire, through his daughter, Gerda v.d. Forst Brickwedde, of Berta Spiessinger v. Pfaffenhofen/Ilm, dam of the top American producing sire, Field Ch. Greif v. Hundsheimerkogel. Dallo's dam was a daughter of that fireball, K.D. Don v.d. Schwarzen Kuhle, who played such a big part in the foundation of the Seydels and Blitzdorfer strains in Germany.

Dallo was killed in a hunting accident, but his owner, Alfred Sause, has been connected with other good dogs, including Pheasant Lane champions Schnapps and Tomahawk. Dallo's direct breed influence is perhaps most usefully through his daughter, Ch. Katinka of Sycamore Brook, C.D. who, in the ownership of the Johns brothers, of Benton, Pennsylvania, produced two Dual Champions, Valkyrie and Junker v. Grabenbruch, the home-owned Valkyrie finishing in 1952 and Junker, owned by Mr. J. Lurba, in 1955. Both are by

90

Johns' Dual Ch. Blick v. Grabenbruch, who finished, in 1951, the first German Shorthaired Pointer Dual on the East Coast. His parents were the imports, K.S. Sepp v. Grabenbruch and Nanny v. Lückseck.

Sepp was the first German Sieger brought here, coming at the end of the war from the kennels of that breeding genius, Peter Kraft, of Hof Grabenbruch, Rhine-Hessen. It has always been hard to get good dogs out of Germany, and the Grabenbrucher's, like all kennels after the war, was down in numbers. It took Richard Johns a year of coaxing to get Sepp for America. Johns had noted that the vast flat fields, the partridge and pheasant country of Sepp's birth, were suited to the production of a wider-going, faster type of dog, and felt that Sepp, with speed, nose, and intensity on point, had something American strains could use. History would seem to support this very reasonable assumption.

It is one of the paradoxes of dog registration, from country to country, that Johns had trouble persuading the A.K.C. that this German Sieger from the famous kennel was registerable. As the matter stands, Sepp is FDSB, but not A.K.C., registered. However, his descendants, including his Dual champion grand-get, are all A.K.C. registered, achieving this through their sire, Dual Ch. Blick v. Grabenbruch, who was rendered acceptable on the basis of points won in competition. This brief explanation may help those whose research on Grabenbruch dogs here carries them back to the A.K.C. intimation that they have no record of K.S. Sepp.

Sepp's breeding, therefore, should be placed here on record for the sake of reference, apart from its worth. His sire, Reichs-Sieger Odin v. Weinbach, is a son of R.S. & W.S. Heide v.d. Beeke ex Mauki v. Schlossgarten, she a granddaughter of K.S. Bill v. Hirschfeld (solid liver) and Argus v.d. Weihermuhle, a well-known and well-performed son of Artus Sand. Sepp's dam, Leda v. Grabenbruch is ex a K.S. Benno v. Schlossgarten daughter, her sire a K.S. Frei Südwest son ex Asta v. Angetal (by Treu Südwest ex Jutta Mannheimia).

Sepp was small, and contemporary reports do not particularly praise his good looks, but he was full of terrific drive and burning desire to find game. He has been described as "a hunting demon." It was unfortunate that a virus carried him off so early, but his qualities were obviously preserved for the future in his son, Dual

Ch. Blick v. Grabenbruch, with his get including three Duals.

Blick lived the long life of the best German Shorthaired Pointers, long his owner's grouse and woodcock dog. His daughter, Dual Ch. Valkyrie v. Grabenbruch, a Dual at two-and-a-half, was also a good winner on the bench, including a M.&E. and the Eastern breed Specialty. In Gundog competition against Setters and Pointers at the famed Jockey Hollow Club, Valkyrie shone in 1954-5 and also topped similar competition in the first "shoot to kill" stake in Delaware.

Developed entirely on grouse, few dogs ever attained to better knowledge of this wily quarry, her owner, Dick Johns, reports. Mated to Ch. Tell v. Grabenbruch (by Int. Ch. Franco Beckum imp. ex Adda v. Assegrund, imp.) she produced Kenwick's Diana Beckum, dam of the 1957 Nat'l Field Trial Ch., Field Ch. Bobo Grabenbruch Beckum, owned by Dr. Wm. Schimmel of California. To bring the story a generation further, Bobo's get now includes the winner of the 1961 A.K.C. National, Field Ch. Von Saalfield's Kash, owned by Walter Seagraves, of California, and many other distinguished get, welcoming his first Dual champion in 1964, the elegant Bee's Gabby v. Beckum, owned by D. Briggs of California and handled by veteran trainer, J. Huizenga. Gabby's dam line brings in further strength in a strong background of the famous "Dixon" strain from Michigan.

Dual Ch. Bee's Gabby v. Beckum (ex F.C. Skid-Do's Bee).

Dual Ch. Valkyrie v. Grabenbruch (Dual Ch. Blick v. Grabenbruch ex Ch. Katinka of Sycamore Brook, CD). Breeder-owner: Richard S. Johns, Pennsylvania.

Field & Nat'l Ch. Bobo Grabenbruch Beckum, winner of 1957 AKC National and prepotent sire. Owner: Dr. William Schimmel, California.

6

German Shorthaired
Pointers on the
West Coast

CALIFORNIA'S first German Shorthaired Point-
ers were brought in during the later 1930's, introduced by practical
hunting men after they had seen these dogs working, either in
Montana or in the mid-West.

"What got us interested first was their trainability," recalled Geoff
Zander, of San Rafael, California, an early-day user of this breed,
along with his keen brother. "We soon found how well they suited
our kind of hunting, able to cope with the tough conditions of the
time. That was the days before all those Seabees came back from
the war, Army Engineers too, with all their modern earth-moving
equipment, and re-contoured the rice fields. That was the time
when a man could go hunting and find his dog up to its chest in
water most of the day. It was no trouble to our big, strong German
Shorthairs. They weren't what you'd call fast workers, but then
in that kind of going we didn't want fast dogs, seeing we had to

keep up with them. We couldn't use horizon-chasers at all, and it was our belief that we'd really found the ideal dog for our conditions. We used them on *everything*—upland game, though it was beginning to thin out a bit by those years, and pheasants didn't take too well, for some years at least, though when the rice fields were made over to their liking, that was a different story, of course. We used our dogs continually on duck, and experience was that the sitting in the blinds didn't worry them, as long as a man used common sense and didn't expect them to sit about forever, wet and cold.

"Their smooth coats sure shed the water. And there was another thing—no sitting around for hours to pick burrs, like out of our setters' coats. But the rice stubble could be hard on smooths too—dogs coming back with the hair rubbed from their faces, bitches with the tips chafed from their teats. A man who forgot to pitch-pine his dog's pads before sending it got it back in a mess. It was very tough hunting, but I want to say these were tough dogs. We never asked them anything they couldn't do—and we asked them *everything!* Conformation? We never thought about it, but they were nice to look at and our pups were in great demand."

Geoff Zander, who truly loved to work with dogs, is now no longer with us, but the breed he admired boomed in the West after original introduction. Practical hunting men have scattered it widely, especially towards the North, with greatest strength in Washington and California. While setter-loving New England and the Pointer-favoring South seldom saw a German dog in the show rings, the entries on the Coast were already very numerous. It took a good dog to win, and the proof of their quality is established by their position in the Production Tables, sires and dams.

Early-day western standouts were Mr. Bowley's brace, Johann v. Schwarenberg (Ch. Fritz v. Schwarenberg ex Gata v. Schwarenberg) and Brown Ace, solidly Thornton. Brown Ace is best to be remembered as the sire of Little Gretchen's Brownie, that great bitch of her time. Post-war years brought out good new ones, all used as a rule for practical hunting, and running in fun trials before the time of licensed competition, usually meeting again in the show rings. Dr. Ted Werner's Ch. Iron v. Schwarenberg was such a one, Nebraska-bred by Walter Mangold, a Dual Ch. Rusty v. Schwarenberg son ex Bess v. Schlesweg, who stemmed from the import, Claus

v. Schlesweg-Konigsweg. Schlesweg, by the way, is usually an indication of Nebraska breeding. However, it has also to be remembered that in America strain names, no matter how illustrious, can never be depended upon, for anyone at all times seems to feel free to take these at pleasure; they fall all over the pedigrees as generously as snow in a Grandma Moses painting.

Prominent, too, were Dr. E. F. Boyer's Ch. Max v. Stauffenberg, a Brown Ace grandson; E. & A. Radke's Ch. Wolfgang (Brook v. Schwarenberg ex Waterbury's Gretchen, the dam of Ch. Count v. Schlesweg (by Ch. Janecek v. Schlesweg). Johann v. Schwarenberg is also represented by four champions ex Henry Duus' Ch. Flora v. Schoenweide: Meigs, Freida, Uncie, Hansel. These originated a strain name still strong on the Coast, as in old Fritz v. Schoenweide, who shadows Mr. Ed. Francis, president of the GSP Club of Central California. Little Gretchen's Brownie produced a champion to Johann v. Schwarenberg, too: the California show winner, Ch. Helen's Lil Ladybug. From like West Coast breeding also stems a good East Coast prepotent, Ch. Alnor's Brown Mike, whose Thornton inheritance can be carried back, on both sides of his pedigree, to the very absolute pioneer introductions, so that it is plain that while diversion to competitive field activities, as in the case of Little Gretchen's Brownie and her get, could benefit from these bloodlines, the show ring could do the same, as made plain by the get of Ch. Alnor's Brown Mike, which includes such successful East Coast winners as Dual Ch. Robin Crest Chip, CDT.

To be counted in the West Coast picture, too, because so much of their winning was done there, were the Utah-breds of Carl and S. Nussbaum, of Salt Lake City. Their first star was Ch. Rex v. Windhausen, bought in 1944, from whom came the successful Ch. Flash v. Windhausen, to take the breed's second B.I.S. (1940 to 1950 was a long, barren period with regard to this honor!) in his home town. Ch. Flash was widely campaigned, even over to Westminster, where he won the breed and placed in the Group in 1950. This emphasizes how often the West Coast dogs have gone over to the East to meet what they may—and how often they have taken the honors for their enterprise. Ch. Flash was also a fine producer, with a tally not only of show, but of many Field Chs. as well, with a class one in his daughter, Field Ch. Princess Anna v. Windhausen.

Lasting impact was made by Ch. Davy's Jim Dandy, California-bred, last owned by Lance McGilbrey, of Washington, whose Columbia River strain bases on a Jim Dandy son, Ch. Pheasant Lane's Stormalong and Nebraska-bred Columbia River Tillie. Ch. Davy's Jim Dandy did much show winning under the handling of Porter Washington, and his prepotency must have been great. Unfortunately, we have no accurate record of his production, but his memory is secured in Dr. Clark Lemley's famed Dual Ch. Dandy Jim v. Feldstrom, in his own turn an excellent producer, drawing on his dam line as well, a neat meshing of Thornton and Burkhart breeding once again.

Jim Dandy's sire, Fritz, was a son of Donn v. Sulfmeister, imp. His dam, Weisse v. Brickwedde (Artist v.d. Forst Brickwedde ex Seiger's Lore, both imp.) had for her four grandparents Kamerad v. Waldhausen, Diana v. Otterstein, Thornton imports, and Tell v. Brickwedde, Vogelein v. Bitterwurzel, first generation Thornton imports. For many years, show judges have especially approved the good-looking, light-ticked Jim Dandy descendants. For that reason, it is interesting to note that the German word *weisse* means white.

By 1950 things were really humming with this breed in the West. At the same time that a mid-westerner was prophecying dourly that "there never have been any good dogs on the West Coast and, what's more, there never will be!" H. V. Garrard, of California, took his young Duchess High Hasit to the historic Trial grounds at Ft. Snelling, Minnesota, won the Limited All Age Stake with her at the Parent Club trial. At the same time, Little Gretchen's Brownie qualified for the Amateur Pheasant Ch. of America, and then prepared to whelp what proved to be the 1957 Nat'l A.K.C. Field Trial champion, Traude v.d. Wengenstadt (by imp. Aar v.d. Wengenstadt). In Washington, Columbia River Tillie was all set to produce that Ch. Pheasant Lane Stormalong litter of hers that, for several generations, would clamp a mortgage on the breed's B.I.S. competition, coast to coast. Also up in Washington, Col. W. A. Wolcott, of Seattle, had brought in a German import, Bella v. Hohen Tann (Bass v.d. Grossen Muhl ex Berta v. Schwarzenberg) that was to produce a whole raft of champions, including a Dual (Riga v. Hohen Tann) to Ch. Bill's Linzer Boy, a son of Ch. Pheasant Lane's Schnapps.

In California, many good dogs were being bred. Ch. Yankee Tim (Ch. Skyacre Timmad ex Roxy v. Waldwinkel) held trust for his great-grandsire, Cosak v.d. Radbach, and would soon prove his own prepotency. By the middle of the 1950's more names were appearing: the Weidenbachs of Mrs. M. Combs; the Erdenreichs of Miss Irene Pauly, already credited with a B.I.S. winner in Mrs. G. Greer's Ch. Erdenreich's Beau v. Gardsburg (Ch. Buck v. Gardsburg ex Can/Am Ch. Erdenreich die Zweite).

It was the Salinas area of California, the area served by the German Shorthaired Pointer Club of Central California, that added, however, the most spectacular chapter to West Coast breed history. That was when a new name was introduced as the 1950-whelped Field Ch. Yunga v. Hundsheimerkogel began to rack up his wins. Solid liver, ex Bettina v. Schwarenberg, a Rusty daughter, he was bred, owned, handled, by Sgt. Bob Holcomb, then of Ft. Ord, California. With his half-sister (ex Ch. Freida v. Schoenweide), Field Ch. Karen v. Greif, owned by the late George Richardson, Yunga carried the new name with pride. A mouthful, isn't it? It came from their obscure sire, an Austrian import—also then owned by a Ft. Ord soldier who had brought him to this country—named Greif v. Hundsheimerkogel (by Alf Gindl, DK 1490 A ex Berta Spiessinger v. Pfaffenhofen/Ilm, the Markus Freising bitch already mentioned in these pages).

The years of Yunga and Karen's appearance were also the best ones for Little Gretchen's Brownie. Her owner, Tom Hanna, was saying he'd rather not breed her again; he didn't want to spoil her shape, or lose his pleasure in working her. She had never lost him a bird, or run unplaced in competition. Perhaps there was sense in his reluctance to trade the substance of a good competing bitch for the elusive bird-in-the-hand that would be her likely get. Great bitches—and Little Gretchen's Brownie *was* a great one—do not necessarily always throw as good as themselves, let alone better. Davis Tuck, in *The Complete English Setter*, has explained why, quoting the operation of a force he calls "the drag of the breed" that is always towards the norm, the middle way, up or down. That is why, so often, very good dogs can come from rather moderate parents, and why a mating of the two most spectacular champions in circulation sometimes disappoints by yielding specimens not as good as either.

Fortunately, demand for Brownie's produce induced Tom Hanna to change his mind. That season, then, she whelped a litter that

The famous Austrian breeder, Herr Viktor Rohringer, of Vienna, breeder of America's top prepotent, Field Ch. Greif v. Hundsheimerkogel, is shown with Greif's dam, Berta Spiessinger Pfaffenhofen Ilm.

Photo: Dr. Otto Fischer, Austrian Kurzhaar Klub, Vienna.

included a future field champion, Brownie's Pat McCarthy. In the ownership of Larry McCarthy, of Burbank, California, Pat produced Field and Nat'l Ch. Brownie's Greif McCarthy (1960). And just to tie things together, this precocious one, who took the Futurity and the National in the same year, happened to be the seventeenth champion sired by that obscure Austrian import, got in the eleventh year of Greif's age.

By then the import had a new owner, the late D. Hopkins, of Watsonville. Dave Hopkins enjoyed practical hunting, was uninterested in any form of competition for dogs. He had schooled one German Shorthaired Pointer to suit his own hunting ways, and when he went afield, that was the dog he took. The "spare tire" that was the Austrian import stayed at home, exercising a considerable charm, since recognized as a strain characteristic, on Mrs. Hopkins, and eventually getting into mischief, chasing chickens yet!

That led to a visit to the kennels of trainer J. Stanley Head. Stan confesses German Shorthaired Pointers had interested him little—till he met this Greif. After that, two years went by, with Dave Hopkins still uninterested in running his import at all seriously in competition. An outing or two—it was nothing. Time went by . . .

Then, the reliable old hunting dog fell ill. Dave Hopkins took Greif instead. Stan Head tells of being wakened one morning—3 A.M., a phone call from hundreds of miles away. Dave Hopkins was saying, with some awe: "Stan—I got me a DOG!"

After that, Greif went to Stan for field trial training. He was eight years old. Competition in the West was mighty tough by then, with Greif's own get really hard to beat. By May of 1955, in for a five-point major at Washington, Greif was handicapped when Stan Head took ill. Handled by an amateur, a stranger to him, Ivan Brower, Greif got the win he needed, stern test of his temperament. Recovered, Stan took the great old dog over to that year's A.K.C. National Field Trial in the mid-West. The entry included, among others, 22 Field Chs., two Dual & Nat'l Chs., and a German Sieger with an American title. It is history that there were some who laughed when they looked at Stan Head's charge, that old white-face with the jaw-breaker name. But Greif made it through to the Final Series, when most of the above listed long-experienced champions had gone down the drain. He ran the last brace with Dual Ch. Wendenheim's Fritz, the winner of the previous year's National, a spankingly good youngster of three. Well, Greif didn't win that National, but he was right into the death, pitchin' hard (that was Field Ch. Gunmaster's Jenta's year). It was his swansong, too, no use to keep him campaigning; he had his title, he was old, and his owner was not very enthusiastic. He'd rather take a dog out hunting, anyway.

Time and geography have denied me sight of many of America's great in German Shorthaired Pointers. At least, I saw Greif. The experience was unforgettable. New to California, taken visiting to see Stan Head's kennels, then at Paicenes, I asked him to show us his best dog. It was with amazement we saw him come down the track with an old, old white-face, still hard and tough and eager as a colt. Now, who could then have foreseen the possibility that I would ever be compiling this breed book—yet what a break, to have seen Greif when so few, so *very* few, even in California, ever actually did. When he had been running that brief twilight burst in competition a few years earlier, no one cared—he had been just another dog. And when Stan Head showed him to us, rising twelve, he had not been seen in public for years.

Stan sent him down into the birdfield and that was a display to remember, too. Afterwards, he posed for what may be the only color slides of him in existence, the eagerness, the drive he possessed, easily to be discerned in his stance. These slides are treasures now. So much did Greif impress me that within a few days, under my byline, articles went out to canine journals in many parts of the world. The famous sporting-dog specialist, Frank Warner Hill, of *English Dog World*, probably thought the California sun had been too much for me when I sent him the claim to have that day seen the greatest sporting dog in any breed shown me since my arrival in the U.S.A. The year was 1958.

Greif did not live long after that, but the since-compiled record of his prepotency more than supports the impression of greatness gained that day—and great dogs, the world over, had been for many years under my eyes, lodged in my memory. His production record that includes 17 champions, Field, Bench, as well as four Duals, to count up to an all-time breed record, were secured not from one or two line-bred bitches, as in the case of many top-producing studs, but from a few widely-assorted locals brought in from here and there, haphazardly; for be sure, no track ever was beaten down to

101

the yard in Watsonville where this great dog lived in obscurity for so many of his later years.

Inquiry in Austria concerning his background brought response from Dr. Otto Fischer, of Austrian Klub Kurzhaar, Vienna (1961). The Zwinger (strain) of Hundsheimerkogl (no "e"), bred by Herr Viktor Rohringer, of Vienna, "comes up continually here still with success in our best breedings, in our trials and in practical hunting," advised the club official.

It was long thought Greif was the only one of the strain to come here, but research pinpointed a half-sister, Flora v. Hundsheimerkogel, with B.O.B's in Asheville, North Carolina, and Charlotte, South Carolina (A.K.C. Gazette, June, 1947). She was a year older than he ("F" litter to his "G"), wh. 1946. Ex Berta, she was sired by Adon v. Cilony, also a Czech dog, as Greif's had been. Flora was bought in Vienna from her breeder by Colonel L. K. Ladue, of Asheville. Colonel Ladue lost his life in Korea, but Mrs. Ladue remembers Flora as the best hunting dog she has seen in a lifetime spent among fine hunting dogs and horses. "Even as a pup, when we took her in the Vienna Woods, she *hunted*. My husband enjoyed good sport with her in America too, and her strain must have been superb." Sadly, after Colonel Ladue's death, Flora was never bred.

From 1958, when he was dead, commenced the sequence of Greif's Duals, these including the three sisters establishing a record in single ownership—the E. E. Harden's of Salinas. The fourth of the Duals, a dog owned by their breeder, J. Huizenga, also of Salinas, is Oxton's Bride's Brunz v. Greif. The sisters are Dual Ch. Oxton's Leiselotte v. Greif, winner at age seven of the breed Specialty under Max Riddle in 1962; the Duals Madchen Braut and Schoene Braut, both v. Greif. Carrying Greif's name another generation down, three sons of Dual Ch. Oxton's Bride's Brunz v. Greif became prominent in West Coast competition, Dual Champions Brunnenhugel Balder and Jarl, and Oxton's Minado v. Brunz.

The West Coast's first Dual Ch. was Riga v. Hohen Tann (Ch. Bill's Linzer Boy ex Bella v. Hohen Tann, imp.), whose owner, Robert Fletcher, of Seattle, is seemingly too modest to boast (or even tell) of what is a truly lovely bitch. California's first Dual was Gretchen v. Suthers, owned in Novato by Paul and Fran Putnam. On this Coast, too, owned also in Seattle, is Gretchen v. Greif

Dual Ch. Oxton's Bride's Brunz v. Greif. Owner: J. Huizenga, California.

Dual Ch. Oxton's Leiselotte v. Greif, specialty winner, 1962. Owner: E. E. Harden, California.

Dual Ch. Madchen Braut v. Greif. Owner: E. E. Harden, California.

Ch. Yunga War Bride, wh. 1951. One of the last dogs bred by Dr. Thornton, "Bridie" holds the record of four Dual Chs. and a show championship. All were sired (two litters) by Field Ch. Greif v. Hundsheimerkogel (imp. Austria). Owner: J. Huizenga, California.

Dual Ch. Schone Braut v. Greif. Owner: E. E. Harden

Ch. Lisa v. Greif, BOS Westminster, 1959. Owner: Miss B. Eschen, California.

(Yunga v. Hundsheimerkogel ex Field Ch. Karen v. Greif—half-brother-sister mating). Gretchen's unique honor was in being separately a Dual Ch. in America and in Canada. There seems no area in which she did not excel—dam of champions, she made the A.K.C. National every year. Whelped in June of 1953, she again made the second Series at the 1962 National in Colorado. Her bench championship was gained against odds. She was a solid liver, her measurement just on the minimum. Count two strokes against her in many a showring, but count credit also to those judges who recognized her worth. Her achievements would seem to suggest that the application of blanket prejudice by showring judges in respect to size and color is at least to be questioned. At age nine also (1962), "Sandy," as she is called, came in second at the Chukar Trial at Prosser, Washington, to the tune of better than $300 in prize money (and $20-plus her owner's wife won in a Calcutta pool, betting on her!). The trial was run in hour heats, over very steep, rough terrain, in multiple course, on wild Chukars, in competition with 12 English Pointers, two English Setters, 11 German Shorthaired Pointers, three Brittanies and one Weimaraner. That added up to an impressive placing, apart from the fact that she was the only "short-tailed" dog to place in this Stake during the three years it had been run.

Along the way, she still made her wins and placements in All-breed trials and German Shorthaired Pointer Trials. Try and match the pride the owners, Ralph and Frances Park, take in this little bit of solid-liver dynamite. In status of double descent from Greif, she surely adds luster to his name.

In life, scarcely any dog could have been more obscure than Field Ch. Greif v. Hundsheimerkogel, living out his last years with Stan Head at Paicenes. And then, suddenly, with all these dogs finishing, Greif was news as well as dead! *Popular Dogs* gave a whole page to him and his get in an Annual Sporting Dog issue. Someone started counting up Yunga's get as well. . . .

It was like that old Cockney Music Hall thing of long ago:

> "Mrs 'Odkins wuz nothin', 'ad nothin', noo nuthin'. . . .
> But she wuz the bloomin' Queen o' Sheba. . . .
> WHEN SHE DIED. . . . ."

Greif's Duals cannot be discussed without bringing in their dam,

104

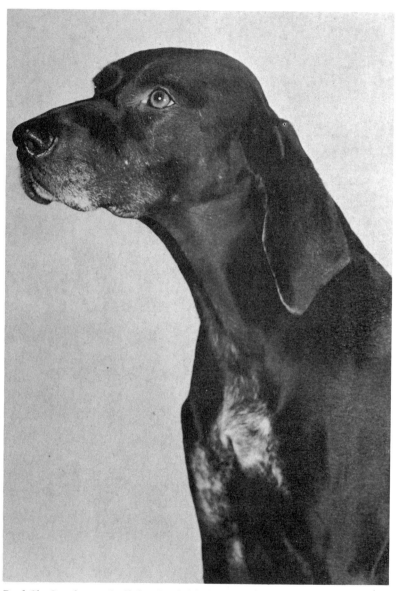

Dual Ch. Gretchen v. Greif; her Dual title individually in both U.S. and Canada, a unique record. At the age of nine she could still make her presence felt in the nation's top competition. Owner: Ralph Parks, Sen., Washington.

Jake Huizenga's Ch. Yunga War Bride—which brings us full circle again to Dr. Thornton. He bred the Bride in 1951. Her sire, Major V. S., his hunting dog, was v. Schwarenberg on his male side, original Thornton back to Kamerad v. Waldhausen and Lady Brickwedde on the female. Bride's dam, Lassie Man o' War, owes to Hjalmer Olsen's breeding through Ch. Pagina's Young Lover and the Timm v. Altenau daughter, Sue v. Dusseldorf. In the far-down corner lurks Minnesota in Dual Ch. Rusty v. Schwarenberg and two Waldwinkels. Bride was bought as a pup by Bob Holcomb, a destined bride for Yunga—Yunga's War Bride, but the apostrophe was lost in registration. Jake and Sally Huizenga took a fancy to the puppy, bought her away from Bob, made her their personal dog about their house. Those privileged to know what they were seeing (which is not at all times the case with gallerysiders!) will long remember "Old Bride" in Brood Class at the Breed Specialty at the Del Monte K.C., Carmel, California—standing at the head of her four Dual Champions, her Westminster winner. It could be long enough before the like is seen again.

Greif's influence neither began nor yet ends with Duals. The influence exerted by his sons and daughters bridges the decades, especially in National Field Trial competition year by year. As from Field Ch. Brownie's Greif McCarthy's Am. Field National (1960) by way of multiple win and place successes of his grandget by Field Ch. Von Thalberg's Fritz II ex Field Chs. Mitzi and Patsy Grabenbruch Beckum; by Nat'l Field Chs. Thalberg Seagraves Chayne (1968), Blick v. Shinback (1969), and Patricia v. Frulord (1971), the direct line is to trace on down.

Nor can it be overlooked that the owners of these good dogs did right by them. *Potential* must be bred for, but it is wasted without *development*. Greif's own Cinderella story points the moral; his potential always existed, but so easily he could have lived out his days obscurely as a hunting man's "spare tire" dog. As in the *Sound of Music*, "A bell is no bell till you ring it!" The wisest dog folk have always known this. Lack of sustained owner effort keeps many good dogs of all breeds out of the limelight. The fine dog man Down Under, Len de Groen, briefed this writer in her novice days: "Your good dog will be worth exactly what YOU put into it. Good dogs are *made*, every bit as much as they are born." It's very hard to get the usual novice to believe that.

106

A parallel truth, of course, is that not even the most conscientious embroidery will make a silk purse out of that sow's ear!

* * * * *

Another West Coast strain national in impact is Columbia River that early-on encouraged judges to look at Shorthairs in the BIS ring. Lightning, Cochise, Jeepers, Ranger, Vagabond, Thunder-cloud, preceded Ch. Gretchenhof Moonshine (all C. Riverbred) with her 15 BIS and 50 Gl and Top Sporting of her year. Columbia River bloodline is still a force to respect.

This strain rests on a Mangold-bred bitch, Columbia River Tillie, mated to Ch. Pheasant Lane's Stormalong. Tillie's multiple-win-ning B.I.S. son, Ch. Columbia River Cochise, owned in Richland, Washington, by B. K. and Mrs. Maxson, proved himself extremely durable as did also his brothers Lightning (four BIS) and Chief, in the home yard at Kennewick. At home, too, in 1961, old but more durable than any, was Columbia River Tillie, then aged six-teen! Tillie had much to show the camera. Age could not hide her superb forehand, correctly-sloped shoulders, long upper-arm, putting her forelegs where they belonged, solidly underneath her. Her shoulder-slope gave her a strong, short back, such shoulders as the Germans took care to breed into their developing breed for all-purpose retrieving chores, and which the speed-only fans here would kiss goodbye without a qualm. Yet, precisely such shoulders, when lost, can represent the first lack in an eventual down-grading of breed type, even of soundness. Show the knowledgeable a sport-ing-dog strain with newly-straightened shoulders, and they will recognize a sporting-dog strain in danger of being on the way down—and out!

Tillie's hindquarters were in balance with that forehand, good stifle-bend, straight hocks, but no straight-stick legs. (Too few folk, including judges, keep in mind that proverbial wisdom so long quoted: "Crooked as a dog's hind leg!") Her size was medium, her color soft liver roan, her head extremely well-balanced, no coarse-ness, though rather spoiled by long houndy ears, her worst fault. Her

107

Ch. Columbia River Lightning, multiple BIS winner and strongly prepotent sire. Owner: L. V. McGilbrey, Washington.

Ch. Columbia River Cochise, litter brother to above (Ch. Pheasant Lane's Stormalong ex Columbia River Tillie), also a multiple BIS winner and prepotent sire. Owners: B. K. and Mrs. Maxson, Washington.

Ch. Columbia River Jeepers, son of Lightning, has six BIS's. Owner: L. Barnett, Texas.

feet were still a miracle—at age sixteen! Neat, with strong pasterns, thick pads, arched toes. They, of course, doubtless owed to all her years as Lance McGilbrey's pheasant dog.

We may only now regard Columbia River Tillie as a living fossil, a link with the pioneer past, when the highest regard here was still set most widely on the breed's utility qualities. It had been a miracle to come and find her still alive, to set her up for the color slides for which she posed maybe a little shakily. These have gone into the file to show what the early breeders had, against which pictorial evidence there can be no dispute. Just such shoulders as Tillie's could have well served her forbear, Claus v. Schleswig-Konigsweg, the Artus Sand grandson, the day the river ran so high and wide and the judge asked could HE swim!

There is thought-provoking matter, too, in the realization that for years and years, judges, including America's greatest, most knowledgeable all-rounders, have shown such a liking for Tillie's children, grandchildren and great-grandchildren, so many of whom have taken from her the mechanics of her construction, though inclined to exceed her in terms of size. There appears to be some interesting sex linkage here. Tillie's male descendants are usually hefty, her female descendants often elegant. Line breeding the produce of her sons, Lightning and Chief, eventually produced Ch. Gretchenhof Moonshine with her 15 B.I.S.'s.

It is good to be reminded by an old-time one like Tillie that there was such a sound construction valued in pioneer breeding, that weediness was not liked, that the discernible trend in some quarters today is not necessarily progress—as Hjalmer Olsen has taken the trouble to warn. In working towards a dog of an entirely different frame shape, in which Tillie's kind of forehand is traded back for the exact kind the Germans originally sweat blood to breed out of their developing strains—the short upper arm that puts a terrier front undesirably into a sporting dog—some breeders may be invoking a force that has been already operative in other breeds of sporting dogs, that had to be paid for by later generations. It can be a wedge to help split type, split the breed. In dog breeds, as in geometry, it is not hard to prove, either historically or empirically, that the part is never greater than the whole.

Tillie's mate, Ch. Pheasant Lane's Stormalong, also stems notably. This Pheasant Lane's strain, in the ownership of W. H. and Mrs.

Warren, of South Dakota, is inextricably twined with all manner of breed achievement. It rests on Ch. Four Winds Gretchen, a bitch blessed with many multiples of Arta v. Hohreusch, distributed on both sides of her inheritance. By Herr Pete ex Frau Gretchen, she is most strongly followed by her daughter, Ch. Pheasant Lane's Deborah (by Ch. Kraut v. Schwarenberg). Deborah's produce includes a B.I.S. in Mrs. J. W. Gordon's Ch. Pheasant Lane's Storm Cloud (1951); Chs. Tomahawk, Lightning, Liesel, are also hers, all of Pheasant Lane. Deborah's background is somewhat awe-inspiring as, to her dam, Gretchen's strongly "Arta" inheritance, is allied that of her sire, Ch. Kraut v. Schwarenberg, with one half of his breeding solid accumulation of K.S. Benno v. Schlossgarten, through Arta and Bob v. Schwarenberg, of course, and the rest dominated by Claus v. Schleswig-Konigsweg.

It is also necessary to consider Ch. Pheasant Lane's Schnapps, sire and grandsire of two present-day Duals in Peter Bruner and Riga v. Hohen Tann, and through his son, Ch. Bill's Linzer Boy, grandsire of seven champions; a Dual, two Field Chs. and four bench champions, plus three in the next generation sired by a non-champion son from the same breeding. Pheasant Lane Apache (Ch. Rex v. Krawford ex Ch. Pheasant Lane's Deborah) is the sire of a notable Midwest-owned one in Field Ch. Sandra v. Hohen Tann.

It is not possible to list all good West Coast strains, let alone dogs, individually. Yet many names can scarcely be overlooked. Perhaps most interesting is the undertaking of Miss Irene Pauly, at Sonoma, who, following her retirement from a distinguished career in education, took up German Shorthaired Pointer breeding by way of relaxation!

To wind up what's to see in the West: during a visit to Washington for the 1961 A.K.C. National Field Trial, this compiler's great privilege was to stop by and visit with Dr. Charles R. Thornton. Growing physically no younger for sure, bravely in his mid-eighties, Dr. Thornton assures us he still has his eye for a good-looking horse, a good-looking dog—and a good-looking woman! It is unspoken commentary on the inexorable press of the years, though—those decades since he introduced those great basics in a then-new sporting breed to Missoula in the 1920's—that the dog-about-the-house in his present home, at College Place, Washington, is a Chihuahua!

Timm v. Altenau (Donn v. Sulfmeister, imp. Ger. ex Dreizenheim v. Brick-wedde). Twenty years atfer his death, this Thornton-bred still exercises influence. Breeder: Dr. C. Thornton. Owner: Wm. Ehrler, Mich. *Photo: Hjalmer Olsen (lent by Mrs. C. Carlson, Ohio)*.

Ch. Columbia River Jill (Ch. Columbia River Chief ex Helga v. Krawford), a main conveyance of prepotent factors behind Gretchenhof. Interesting to compare picture with that of her granddam, Columbia River Tillie, p. 291. Breeder: L. V. McGilbrey. Owners: Gretchenhof Kennels, Calif.

7

From the 1960s
into the 1970s

As Dual Champions are not only the breed pride, but also the life insurance premiums invested for the breed future, it is heartening to count up how many of these have finished since old Dual Ch. Rusty v. Schwarenberg first showed the way to the honor twenty years ago. Nor is it necessary to beat one's brains to bits to discover whence come these good dogs. It is perfectly obvious that the good ones come from exactly where one should expect— from other good ones.

Many fine Duals have already been discussed, referred to sometimes in comments on their sires and dams. Now we have to look at some more, as, say, Dual Ch. Fritz of Sleepy Hollow, owned in pride by Fred Z. Palmer, of Canaan, N.Y. Fritz's sire, Ch. Donar v. Schlangenberg, is by Dual Ch. Blick v. Grabenbruch. His dam, Susabelle v. Catskill, is a granddaughter of Ch. Pheasant Lane Schnapps, a Dual Ch. Rusty v. Schwarenberg son. A good producer in his turn, Dual Ch. Fritz is a long-lasting popular dog wherever he appears, and has amply justified the long-term opinion expressed by veteran Hjalmer Olsen who judged him as a Derby. Young Fritz, on that day, did everything wrong, but he did it with joy and verve, most spectacularly, and this was what the judge assessed.

Dual Ch. Captain v. Winterhauch, bred and owned in Minnesota by Millard W. Axelrod, a past president of the Parent Club, is also a B.I.S. winner, a rare combination of honors. Here is another Dual whose background requires little explanation. His dam, Duchess v. Hotwagner produced five champions, including two Duals and two with B.I.S. wins. She, too, stems from the great Minnesotan basics combined with the best Thornton breeding through Cosak v.d. Radbach and Kamerad v. Waldhausen, imp. both. Captain's sire, Ch. Rick v. Winterhauch is high among the great producers. Captain's litter brother, Dual Ch. Able v. Eltz, owned by Mrs. K. Metcalf Allen, now of California, topped a successful show career by starting out after Field Trial honors at the age of seven. That he was not long finishing might usefully be noted by the owners of other good show dogs, seeking fresh fields for conquering. It may be difficult to say just when a good German Shorthaired Pointer could be too old to start his Field career; Mrs. Allen's Able is by no means the oldest to start. Greif v. Hundsheimerkogel was rising eight, as was, in 1961, the matron, Ch. Wag Ae's Snowflake, C.D. An outstanding show career behind her, three champions to her production credit (two bench, one field), Snowflake also started for her Dual in her eighth year, achieving it within a few months to finish in May, 1962. Others have done the like. Dual Ch. Lucky Lady v. Winterhauch commenced and finished her Dual honors *years* after her Dual Ch. daughter, Kaposia's Firebird, was already dead. Dual Ch. Alfi v.d. Kronnenmuhle, also the dam of a Dual (Miss B'Haven v. Winterhauch) was nine when she got up there.

In view of such achievements—and there have been many others besides—there could possibly be something of a surprise in store for those who, in connection with field trial activities, consistently shrug away the idea of "show dogs" in German Shorthaired Pointers. Experience with this breed seems to suggest that where owners undertake to launch their good show dogs into field trial work, they tend to find themselves, in good time, the owners of Duals. That more "show dogs" do not qualify in the field is not of necessity because the instinctive ability to do a good job of work is bred out of them; rather it is for reasons their owners hold valid. Some owners are just not interested. Others consider the expense of field trial training and participation too high. Unable to afford the services of a professional trainer, and lacking the know-how to do the job themselves, even many who take their "show dogs" hunting have to

113

Dual Ch. Able v. Eltz (litter brother to Dual Ch. Captain v. Winterhauch and Ch. Oak-Crest Cora v. Winterhauch), photographed with the author, Mrs. C. Bede Maxwell, at Pebble Beach, California.

let the extra honor go unsought. There are others who view with anxiety the chance that too much "putting on a bit of pressure" (as it is euphemistically styled) might hurt a valued dog's temperament. It has happened. . . .

Pursuing the theme—that the good ones come from other good ones —it is discoverable that they also come as door prizes as did Lucky Lady v. Winterhauch into the grateful hands of Parent Club official Al. Frush, of Minnesota. They come as Christmas presents—"to Papa with Love"—as did Ch. Pheasant Lane Schnapps to E. E. Andrews, of Akron, Ohio. Schnapps got in return for the Andrews their Dual Ch. Peter Bruner ex Hunter's Lady Heflin, she by Ch. Sporting Butch, Nebraska-bred by Walter Mangold (Ch. Fritz v. Schwarenberg ex Braunne v. Schmeling, who hails by grace of old friend *Claus-can-HE-swim!*).

Dual Ch. Peter Bruner finished in the field at age two, and in the showring soon after with a five-point major at Morris & Essex. Mated to (now) Dual Ch. Wag Ae's Snowflake, C.D. he is responsible for Group-winning Ch. Wag Ae's Sheba Bruner and her litter sister, Ch. Quaker Cliff Gretchen.

Dual Ch. Wag Ae's Snowflake, C.D. a Dual at eight years of age, cannot be overlooked. She has also produced, to German import, Ulk v.d. Radbach, a show champion in Wag Ae's Zit v. Radbach, and a Field Ch. in Wag Ae's Helga v. Radbach, proving that she can not only perform in the Dual sense competitively, but also productively. So, now, where does *she* hail from, having ability to throw her quality into either scale? Bred in Akron, New York, by J. A. Wolak, her sire was Spike of Clover Club, her dam Princess Rosie— which conveys nothing till we probe. Then we find that Princess Rosie is a Skriver's Sofus daughter ex Helga v. Waidmannsruh (Ch. Fritz v. Schlossgarten ex Duchess of Johnson). This treads a familiar path, for Ch. Fritz is by Treu v. Waldwinkel ex Bessie v. Winterhauch. Duchess of Johnson runs to Bob v. Schwarenberg and Arta v. Hohreusch along her sire line, and her dam line goes to Claus v. Schleswig-Konigsweg. Spike of Clover Club is a grandson of that same Ch. Sporting Butch that got Dual Ch. Peter Bruner's dam and the same Duchess of Johnson (above). So—back to the old proved lines when seeking where the Duals come from!

The amazing factor, too, in the production record of some of the most versatile matrons, able to whelp field and show champions

Am. & Can. Dual Ch. Timberlane's Ace, another of the Northwestern Shorthairs to hold the two-country title. Owner, Mrs. Wayne Davis, Seattle.

Dual & National Ch. Wendenheim's Fritz (1954) posed with owner, Frank Nuzzo of Illinois, and judge Richard S. Johns.

both, is that so many of them share so much of a common inheritance. This, then, could be as good a time as any to introduce another outstanding producer in Can/Am. Ch. Susanna Mein Liebchen, C.D., owned by Mrs. Maxine Collins, of Michigan. Susanna's multiple get includes three Dual champions in Fritz of Hickory Lane Farm; Gustav Mein Liebchen; and Marmaduke Mein Liebchen, the most recent to attain the honor, a dog whose show wins include B.O.B. at Westminster (1960) and three times best of breed at the Chicago International, and already credited with five champion get of his own. So, whence comes this Susanna? Her sire, Pat of Sonja Lee Lodge, has imported Donn v. Sulfmeister twice through Timm v. Altenau. And, perhaps just as interesting, the very same Sue v. Dusseldorf is found figuring behind Susanna as behind the prepotent sire, Ch. Sobol's Pointing Jay Mer, and Ch. Yunga War Bride of the four Duals. And Sue v. Dusseldorf is by Timm v. Altenau ex Zest v. Horstig, which takes us straight back in large doses to Donn v. Sulfmeister. As the distinguished matrons, Susanna and Bridie, share from Hjalmer Olsen's Ch. Pagina's Young Lover, we are also inevitably back again to Ch. Fritz v. Schwarenberg and Arta v. Hohreusch. Columbia River Tillie, with *her* record of production, also marches in close line here. Though mostly owing to Claus v. Schleswig-Konigsweg, her dam line matches the Sun Valley Bob/Nietschke bitches of Susanna's background.

That the outstanding prepotents across the country find so much common linkage cannot be ignored. Two more to bracket are Helga v. Krawford, from Lance McGilbrey's strain in Washington, with her long tally of champions, and Dual Ch. Big Island Spook, owned by George Reudiger, Minnesota. These two bitches, so far as the back line of their breeding goes, could almost swap pedigrees. The main divergence is in Helga's indebtedness to Claus v. Schleswig-Konigsweg through Trudy v. Schlesweg, and a single contribution from imported Ch. Dallo v.d. Forst Brickwedde. Helga and Spook, through their sire, Ch. Rex v. Krawford, owe and *OWE* to Arta v. Hohreusch. Spook's dam, Graffs Lady Lou, is all Minnesota basics (plus Mars v. Ammertal), sire-wise, and her dam, Silkie v. Schlossgarten, is by Art v. Berkemeyer (Hallo Mannheimia/Arta v. Hohreusch) ex Queen v. Baskfield (St. Croix Fritz/Berg's Choice), which is doubly back to Arta again.

That such distinguished present-day producers have genetically

117

Am. & Can. Ch. Ricki Radbach v. Greif, fifth in this same ownership to gain the two-country title—a record that may go long
unbroken. Owners: Ralph and Frances Park, Washington. *Photo:
D. W. Owens.*

Can. & Am. Ch. Susanna Mein Liebchen, C.D., dam of Marmaduke.
Her produce includes four Duals and two show champions. Owner:
Mrs. Maxine Collins, Michigan.

so much in common is something for breeders to mull over in quiet hours now and then.

It is worth mentioning also that Ch. Fieldborn Tempo II, to whom Susanna produced prepotent Dual and Can. Ch. Marmaduke Mein Liebchen, was sired by Ch. Fieldborn Hiawatha II, owing mainly to Arta, whilst his dam, Alfa, could have been whelped in Dr. Thornton's yard: Donn v. Sulfmeister, Pedya v. Weserstrand, Bitter Root Duke. Even Montana Belle's there—she the produce of the first-ever imports, Senta v. Hohenbruck and Treu v. Saxony.

With all this braiding between present great prepotents and performers and the basics of the pioneers, will all who still want to shrug aside the basics please stand up and be counted? (The basics, by the way, that established the breed in its great public favor here in the first place.)

It is *most* important that newcomers to the German Shorthaired Pointer breed understand the operation of these proved forces. The dogs behind these Dual Champions, including those continually finishing in our own time to the greater glory of the breed—these superb modern insurances against the pitiful breed-split that overtook Pointers and Setters and Springers—are, for the overwhelmingly greater part, also the exact same dogs on which the present-day popularity of this breed was originally built. These basics, plus their produce, are the ones that aroused the public interest, even coaxing to themselves many dedicated Pointer/Setter men for what must have been good and valid reasons. The registration figures soared sky-high over the years. These were the dogs that came here, were bred, their produce first sold to hunting men and then to those who enjoyed a good-looking, nice-natured companion. They soon found their way to the showrings, did well there, as Best in Show and Group records clearly prove. They proved themselves in practical Field Trial competition in the sphere for which, as a utility breed, they were designed. Their popularity continues to rocket as that of Pointers and Setters, by comparison, has declined. This is not opinion; this is from *official figures*.

Demonstrably, the public is *not* to be brain-washed in respect to what does or does not constitute a good dog. Over the past thirty years, the public went for the competent, handsome German Shorthaired Pointer. These dogs caught and held the public's attention, won its regard, and are the exact same dogs that appear now in the background, generation after generation, of today's best specimens, as the title of Dual Champion defines these. So, Mr. and Mrs. Newcomer to German Shorthaired Pointers, next time some "expert" undertakes to brain-wash you about the original imports being no good, and tries to point out some spindly little mere running machine as "an improvement in the breed," don't let yourself be too impressed. That type could be headed, with its future produce, into much the same trash basket into which that same type of Pointer and Setter was heartlessly, relentlessly dumped by the general dog-buying public after the split was imposed on these glorious breeds. Just look that "expert" in the eye and comment that the weather's nice, the sun shining, or the rain falling. . . .

The brother Duals, Captain v. Winterhauch and Able v. Eltz are matched by fine sisters; half-sister Dual Ch. Lucky Lady v. Winterhauch (ex Hephizbah Holzman) has a daughter Dual, and Ch. Oakcrest Cora v. Winterhauch, their full sister, has six champions and more pointed.

Still tracing family: Dual Ch. Captain v. Winterhauch's seven champions already include two Duals. The sweet ghost of Arta v. Hohreusch, so strong behind his family, could review its production with pride. Four of Cora's champions are by Ch. Gunmaster's Ricki, a B.I.S. dog owned by Richavling Kennels, Akron, Ohio. That Ricki has a sister who is a National Field Ch.—Gunmaster's Jenta—fits into the pattern, too, with their sire a Dual: Doktorgaarden's Caro, owned by their breeder, Dr. Wm. Hartnell, of Utah.

Cora, first GSHP bitch to take an all-breed B.I.S., also did well in Group. Lower placings apart, A.K.C. Gazettes of 1956 record for her 21 times G1 in 52 showings. Her record suggests that good bitches can gain the judge's eye in the rings, yet it was a long dry stretch till the next one showed—1962, that *anno mirabalis* in GSHP history. Of seven B.I.S. awards to the breed that year (there were none the year before), three fell to the crowd-pleasing Ch. Gretchenhof Moonshine, owned by Gretchenhof Kennels, California. These, with her many Group wins, put her on top of the breed for 1962. In January 1963, Moonshine won the prestigious West Coast show, Golden Gate K.C., her fourth B.I.S. The breed and G2 followed at Westminster. During 1963 she continued her run, including B.I.S., Santa Barbara, three B.I.S. in three days, Oregon circuit, and Top Sporting in the nation.

Ch. Moonshine's record is the more remarkable in view of her sex. American judges in the main show preference for males in making BOB awards, thus cancelling the opportunity for good bitches to go further. Many good bitches, too, are sidelined because owners *cannot wait* to hurl them into maternity, enterprise only too often yielding stock nowhere near the quality of the dam. This is about the oldest and often the saddest owner-discovery to make in dog-breeding. British breeders, for the most part, show better judgment in the management of flyer bitches. They keep them in competition as shop window advertisement, and can trust most British judges not to hold their sex against their quality. They breed sisters—mothers—brothers and sell on repute of the flyer.

Ch. Moonshine taught American judges to look at Shorthairs in BIS line-ups and perhaps as a member of a short-haired breed, her sex was less to her a hindrance.

In the compilation of production statistics, the contribution of good bitches has too often been played down in favor of the studs that benefited from alliance with them. It is however worth noting that it is oftenest the strains that establish a strength in fine producing bitches that endure to produce good stock generation after generation. There are several such strains in the United States and these provide, in terms of perpetuity, sharp contrast to strains built shakily as they needs must be on the performance of some single stud. With the cessation of such a stud's activity, the strains for the most part vanish. No space here to trace these additionally to the presentation in the Production tabulations, but certainly two that come readily to mind are the Kaposias and the Albrechts. The Kaposias were founded on a brace of Dual Ch. matrons in Lucky Lady v. Winterhauch and her daughter, Kaposia's Firebird. The Albrechts rest imposingly on the produce of Ch. Katrina v. Albrecht and her magnificently prepotent daughter, Field Ch. Albrecht's Countess Tena. These are not the only strains with such an endowment, but serve as excellent examples of the truth proposed already four hundred years ago by the Elizabethan sportsman, George Turberville (1576): "If you would have a faire Hound you must first have a faire Bitch, which is of a good kind, strong and well-proportioned in all parts, having her ribs and flanks great and large." Such matrons support ANY breed, and it is to less than the honor of too many judges that they do not always secure merited honor in show ring placings.

Ch. Buck v. Gardsburg, repeatedly the nation's top show-winning German Short-haired Pointer till his retirement in 1961. Buck and his handler, the late Roland Muller, always made an eye-catching team. A prolific stud, with versatile get. Owner: D. D. Williams, California.

In a magnificent water leap, Dual Ch. Sager v. Gardsburg demonstrates excellence of construction and balance of fore and after parts. He proved out the lasting ability of a properly built dog, winning in top company into old age. Owners: R. & L. Sylvester, Georgia.

Dual Ch. Kaposia's Firebird, foundation of this successful Minnesota establishment of "Kaposia." Owners: D. and B. Sandberg, Minnesota.

Dual Ch. Richlu's Terror, a daughter of Dual Ch. Sager v. Gardsburg (facing page). She combines pioneer American/modern German/best Danish inheritances. Breeders: R. and L. Sylvester. Owners: C. and S. Carlson.

8

The Danish Strains

THE earliest recorded importations of Danish strains appear to have been the brace brought to Ohio by Lee W. Rodgers, of West Richfield for personal shooting pleasure. Gelsted's Bob and Gelsted's Sita were by Gelsted's Rap ex the brown-white Nybjerg's Freja, also behind imports Dual Ch. Doktorgaarden's Caro and Field Ch. Moesgaard's Ib.

Dr. W. Hartnell, then also of Ohio, followed with the subsequent importation of the 1945-whelped Skriver's Jens. Jens, short-lived, is honored by his best-known son, Ch. Sobol's Pointing Jay Mer (ex Cocoa Queen, she strong pioneer American breeding through granddam, Sue v. Dusseldorf). Jens was tick-patch color (*braunschimmel,* as the Germans say, and *brunspœttet* as in Danish). Jens' well-performed parents, Danish Chs. Bobby af Bjerringbro and Kraglands Ulla, stem from good German basics.

Over the years there appears to have been engendered a widely-held belief that Danish breeding is to be bracketed only with the brown-white, pointer-patterned jacketing which so many dogs within this national division of Shorthair interest carry. However, it is not true that the predominant color patterning in Denmark runs to such. Some years ago, when putting together a first edition of this Shorthair breed book, through the kindness of Dr. Lewis L.

Kline, then president of the German SHP Club of America, it was possible to study the several issues of the very informative magazines issued by the Danish breed club (*Korthaarede Hønsehund Saerklubben*). These publications carried a wealth of information, much of which served also to clarify the maze of German strain repetitive names (the Dianas, Hektors, Treffs, in their multiplicity), providing reg. numbers and whelping dates, along with photographs and the clarifying of color by indicative markings. Thus a solid liver dog was identified by a small blacked-in circle. A brown/white was identified by a circle half-white, half black. A tick-patch Shorthair was indicated when no qualifying color symbol was present.

With such exact aid, it was possible to discover that by no means —NO means!—were the majority of Danish Shorthairs brown-white pointer-patterned. Solid livers and tick-patches were there in the majority just as elsewhere in the world.

Many great dogs within the Danish breed were solid livers, tracing oftenest to that famous German basic, K.S. Michel v.d. Goldenen Mark, in most instances through a white-footed son, Danish-bred Rolf Toften. Golo Holzweiler, another famous German breed basic was also behind many Danish greats, he with his own *published* pedigree tracing to the brown v. Mansfields through Nimrod Otzenrath.

Behind many of the best-known imports from Denmark to the U.S. is to be found the strongest of solid liver influence, as through such as Brugschampion Bob Køge and his son, Casper Køge, including also the much-publicized Moesgaards strain that virtually dominated field trial competition for a few years mid-1950s-1960s. These showed no evidence of carrying a factor for the color so strong in their Danish forbears. The strain name became synonymous with brown-white pointer-patterned stock, with a tick-patch but rare. There was also startling divergence from accepted Shorthair breed appearance in many specimens. Successive generations, often overclosely inbred, showed still further divergence from accepted breed type not only in conformation but also in work pattern.

Predictably, the drift from world-recognized Shorthair breed type gave rise to speculation that from time to time lapsed into frank querying of possible breed impurity. Whether cross-breeding was the source of this strongly fixed and alien strain type has not been possible to establish in any acceptable legal sense. It is however also entirely possible that the undesirable divergence has actually resulted from what can only be described as a fantastic degree of inbreeding. Not since the complete degenerative ruin of the Llewellin setter in the early years of this century, consequent on like unprofitable breeding practice have sporting dogs in the U.S. seen such a doubling up, generation-by-generation on one dog as was effected in putting Field Ch. Moesgaards Ib to his daughters repeatedly, to his grand-daughters, his great-granddaughters in unbroken succession—and then to compound, by further mating the sibling produce in the third and fourth generations. And, inevitably, as the Llewellins were run out as is water into sand, so, too, may one expect to find eventually dispersed the strain that came out from Friday Island in Washington State, except as individual weldings are made with outcrosses to other supporting, dominant lines.

The breeding theory behind the process was never explained. Requests for information and/or photographs to use in the first and second editions of this Shorthair book went unanswered, and the accidental death of Mr. Ivan Brower some time ago cancels out hope of any clarification provided for this third. One is left, then, looking at those pedigrees. One doubts the equivalent exists even in the most inbred Llewellin compilations. Late 1960s saw the finishing of several field champions resultant on the mating of Field Chs. Moesgaards Coco and Moesgaards Angel. Their four grandparents are Field Champion Moesgaards Ruffy and Moesgaards Sis (paternal) and Moesgaard's Joe and Moesgaards Dee Dee (maternal). All four result from repeat matings of Field Ch. Moesgaard's Ib to his daughters. Ruffy and Joe are ex M. Arta, Sis and Dee Dee are ex imported Field Ch. Doktorgaarden's Lucky. Carry back another generation and one has M. Arta the produce of M. Ib and D. Lucky and Lucky, in her turn, the produce of M. Ib and Doktorgaarden's Bunny.

It can scarcely be argued that the produce of this compression down into the fifth generation provides dogs that possess rather less than happy commitment to world accepted Shorthair type, but undoubtedly there is as much reason to ascribe this to the effects of the continued inbreeding to one dog as to the commonly-discussed theory held among Shorthair people of the likelihood of an outcross to another breed having been made.

Water under the bridge, in any case. Inbred or crossbred, Short-

126

Field Ch. Skriver's Jesper. Owner: Chuck Petersen, Iowa.

Field Ch. Moesgaard's Lucky II. Owner: Dr. L. L. Kline, Florida.

Can. & Am. Ch. Skovmarken's Sep (imp. Denmark). Owner: James A. Karns, Ohio.

Scandinavian Ch. Adam (imp. Sweden). Winner Int. Ch. at Brussels, Belgium, 1959 and also in Sweden, Finland, Denmark. Owners: John H. & Mrs. Wilkins, Virginia.

Ch. Holevgaard's Wotan II, distinguished Danish taproot sire, and his sister, Ch. Holevgaard's Nora. Breeder-owner: T. Jensen.

Dual & Nat'l F.T. Ch. Moesgaard's Dandy. Owner: Dr. L. L. Kline, Florida.

hairs (of whatever strain) that do not conform to accepted world conception of breed type and breed working utility qualities may have a short space of fashionable approval in respect of qualities not even proper to the breed, but over the long haul, as precedent teaches, time nudges them out of the continuing breed history.

It needs to be emphasized that color *alone* is not a suspect characteristic. There have always cropped up in this breed the occasional throwback to the original mixture that formed the breed. One does not see brown-whites in European competition, though a small percentage—officially reported at a fraction of 1%—is reported among whelpings. Most are likely done away with in the nest—as are whites in Boxers here, and in German Shepherds, reds in Gordon Setters. The world disapproval of the Pointer-patterned brown-white Shorthair is not necessarily *because* of color per se, but because this serves too handily to cloak possible unethical practices. The argument raised in defense is usually in terms of a recessive factor, providing screen against challenge.

It becomes necessary to differentiate as between such inbreds as the Moesgaards and the far wider sweep of the better-managed Danish imports brought here over the years, mostly through the promotion of Hjalmer Olsen, drawing from his native land. Several Danish imports have given this country a splendidly valuable legacy of true-type, exceptionally well-performed dogs, able to endow their progeny in due course with like virtues and excellences. In the majority of these cases it will be found that the imports were mated away from their own national background, combined oftenest with strong and valuable early American pioneer import German lines. Such breedings have produced far fewer brown-white Pointer-patterned, but a strength of tick-patch, often presented in the poster handsomeness of a very light-tick-patch much valued by breeders of Shorthairs in every country of the world, Germany included.

In Europe, the good Czechoslovakian lines have currently a rich endowment of tich-patch to this pattern, useful currently for Germany breeders swamped with their solid livers by the Axel v. Wasserchling flood. In the United States the eruption of solid liver in a pedigree strong in Danish bloodline will oftenest reveal a hitch back to v. Schwarenberg, the strong liver Dual Ch. Rusty v. Schwarenberg, down from his solid liver sire, Mars v. Ammertal, draws to itself the solid liver Danish inheritances down from Bob Køge. Back of many clear brown-white Danish is Dan. Ch. Holevgaard's Wotan II, through his get from Ally of Fangel-brother-sister brace, Fangels Rolf and Rossy. These are behind good dogs from Dual Ch. Doktorgaarden's Caro (by Rolf) and Dan/Am Ch. Skovmarken's Sep, whose grand-dam was Rossy. Rolf and Rossy were tick-patched. Their dam, Ally of Fangel stems tick-patch over five generations with but two exceptions. Rolf Toften, solid liver with white front feet, is in her fifth generation, and a grand-dam was white-brown from tick-patch parents.

Doktorgaarden's Bunny, dam of imp. Field Ch. Doktorgaarden's Lucky, is also by Rolf, ex Holevgaard's Cora, dam of D. Caro, above. Cora is ex Nybjerg's Freja (Ch. Holevgaard's Wotan II—Ch. Moesgaard's Leddy). Leddy was tick-patch, her dam Ketty was light-tick. Her sire was Bob Køge the solid liver, taking the solid color back five generations, and passing it to a famous son in Casper Køge. Bob's dam Pax, was liver, as was Casper's dam, Fanny, and Casper in his turn sired Nybjerg's Rit—dam of Field Ch. Moesgaard's Ib. All very interesting to the dedicated student of color inheritance—a science which, it has always seemed to me, works optimistically in the face of considerable difficulty, in that way-backs have to be clarified from surviving particulars, and the matings of dogs, in terms of surviving records, is but a speculative thing at best. If it is a wise child that knows its own father, it is a wiser pup that can count the name of his own sire. Even *one* misrepresentation on a surviving record can throw the best of color inheritance theories down the drain!

The American scene does owe more than a little to Danish influence of the well-managed persuasion. Such as Skriver's Jens represent a plus, and Field Ch. Skriver's Jesper (imp. 1955) is another, he by Skriver's Seks ex Skriver's Jette. Jesper combined well with pioneer American lines, and his best son was a good producer, Ch. Skriver's Streak. Skriver's Sofus (also ex S. Jette) is remembered through his grandson, the famous Ch. Buck v. Gardsburg.

9

The German Shorthaired
Pointer in Britain

IN the practical sense, the German Shorthaired
Pointer was introduced into Britain immediately after World War
II. In the later 1940's, home-returned officers, especially, thought the
frustration and expense of the long quarantine period worthwhile
to be able to keep the good dogs they had hunted with in Germany.
Some dogs came with papers, some without, as modern-day pedigrees
attest, but when that matter was evened out, as is possible under
English K.C. Rules, some extremely useful sporting dogs began to
attract notice, especially where practical hunting men—roughshoot-
ers, as the English call them—were concerned.

In a historical sense, though, the introduction of the breed was
actually made in England in 1887. That was newly proved in 1961,
when, in response to an inquiry initiated by this compiler, the
English K.C. delved into its Archives and, through the courtesy of
the Assistant-Secretary, Mr. C. A. Binney, made available some most
interesting material. The clue had been originally provided by
an award made "in London" on the record of a German brood,
Holla Hoppenrade, owned by Herr Julius Mehlich, of Berlin.

"1887 records do show that for some reason classes for German Shorthaired Pointers were scheduled at the K.C. event at Barn Elms, London, June 28/29/30 and July 1st. when Herr v. Schmiederberg judged the class. There were at that time no quarantine regulations, and to the best of our knowledge, dogs passed freely between this and other countries. A strong contingent of these dogs was brought over for the show and, I assume, re-exported soon after. A number were registered in June 1887, and as we cannot trace any registrations in previous or subsequent months, they may have been all exhibits at the show. Nor are any subsequent registrations to be traced, nor any records available to show that classes for this breed were scheduled again in this country till after World War II."

Mr. Binney, along with the above explanation, also forwarded the particulars of the 22 exhibits, plus the critique of the judge. As it seems likely that the exhibit comprised a sort of "Show-the-Flag" gesture on the part of the German breeders in that very new stage of the breed's development, the critique is especially interesting. Surely, one may guess that the dogs sent over were the best specimens currently available. Shortly after this English historical matter came to hand, the Danish magazines lent by Dr. Kline also became available, and, in the well-compiled histories of the Hoppenraden and v. Lemgo dogs, provided supporting proof that dovetailed exactly with the records as they were preserved in England— miraculously, one would say, through the years, the wars, the blitz!

The exhibitors included some of the most active of early-day German experimental breeders. Not only Herr Mehlich, of the famed Hoppenraden, was represented, but also Hofjaeger F. Isermann, later known as the breeder of Frigga v. Berry, the dam of the breed pillar, Nidung. With Herr Z. U. O. Borchert, the Hofjaeger provided 14 of the 22 entries. Seven of the entries were sired by the breed basic, Treff 1010. Caro (Mr. W. Schutze's) by Treff ex Diana, is of the same breeding as Hektor 64, sire of the famed Waldin. Edda (Mr. Borchert's) was by Harras Hoppenrade, 312. Feldmann (wh. 1885, so not the caricature-cross Feldman of a decade earlier) was Isermann-owned, ex his Juno 192, and she traceable through the Danish publications as basic to some great German strains. Holla (Hoppenrade) 395, was by (another) Caro ex Cora, 180, a Hektor 65 daughter. Treff II was also ex Juno 192 (by Treff 1010), and Juno's breeding is established as by another unidentified

132

Feldman, and an unidentified Diana. As her surviving photograph shows, Juno 192, wh. 1882, was just such another near-Spanish pointer type as Hektor I, the original studbook entry. One well may marvel at the breeding skill of the Germans in refining all such cloddy material (as Dr. Kleeman later described it scathingly) into the beautiful dogs of the 1890's and onward to our time.

Uncas II and Uncas Bravo were both by Uncas I, whose registration number of 94 places him very close to the starting line. Such may have been also the case with Adda (ex Aunsel), wh. 1886, whose owner, Herr Seydel, stirs interest for us. Unfortunately no one, not even Frau Maria Seydel herself, can now link him with her family exactly—though she thinks he must have been a relative of her deceased husband.

Gaining the B.O.S. placing to Holla Hoppenrade's B.O.B. was Waldo II, 211, also known as Bosco, the property of Herr Mehlich, here listed as from the full brother and sister, Waldo I and Hertha, litter mates of Waldin, 175—particulars at variance with the Danish-published version. Historically valuable as the earliest catalog of the breed in competition that has yet been located, the list is worth re-publishing for the record. (*Courtesy, The English K.C.*)

The Cataloged Entry of German Shorthaired Pointers,
Barn Elms, London, 1887

ADDA	Mr. Seydel's	(Uncas-Aunsel)	Wh. 4/15/1886
CARO	Mr. W. Schutze's	(Treff-Diana)	1/13/1885
CAROLA OF GOTTENBACH	Mr. C. Georg's	(Unknown)	1886
COSAK OF GOTTENBACH	Mr. C. Georg's	"	1886
DIANA	Hofjaeger Isermann's	(Treff-Sally)	8/20/1886
EDDA I	Mr. Z. U. O. Borchert's	(Harras-Colla)	1885
EDDA II	Mr. Z. U. O. Borchert's	(Uncas I-Edda I)	Feb. 1887
FELDMANN	Hofjaeger Isermann's	(Treff-Juno)	4/9/1885
FUTTA	Mr. W. Schutze's	(Uncas II-Wanda)	3/6/1886
HEKTOR III		(Treff-Sally)	8/20/1886
HOLLA (Hoppenrade)	Mr. J. Mehlich's	(Caro-Cora)	4/16/1885
HYDRA	Hofjaeger Isermann's	(Treff-Sally)	8/20/1886
MENTOR	Mr. Saatweber's	(Unknown)	Jan. 1880
NIMROD	Hofjaeger Isermann's	(Treff-Sally)	8/20/1886
TREFF	Mr. W. Schutze's	(Uncas II-Wanda)	3/6/1886
TREFF II	Hofjaeger Isermann's	(Treff-Juno)	5/8/1886
TREFF III	Mr. G. Englestadt's	(Mentor-Zampa)	2/10/1884
TREUMANN	Mr. Z. U. O. Borchert's	(Uncas II-Wanda)	Nov. 1884
UNCAS II	Mr. Z. U. O. Borchert's	(Uncas I-Juno I)	May 1883
UNCAS BRAVO	Mr. Z. U. O. Borchert's	(Uncas I-Edda I)	Oct. 1886
WALDO II	Mr. J. Mehlich's	(Waldo I-Hertha)	5/18/1886
WODAN	Hofjaeger Isermann's	(Treff-Sally)	8/20/1886

We are also indebted to the courtesy of the English Kennel Club for the critique of the judge, Herr v. Schmiederberg, who was at that time a top official of the newly-formed breed club in Germany. This matter is also unique, possibly the only detailed critique of pioneer dogs that still exists in the world:

"*Waldo II* is a strong, powerful dog, just what many German sportsmen want; his color, head, and especially ears are excellent, but his hindquarters not fully developed, and will probably show better next year; the forefeet turn out slightly. *Hektor III* is light in build, his ears set too low, must lay on more muzzle. Of the same description is Wodan. He too has the forefeet outturned, as has Nimrod. They deserved the v. highly commended award however, considering their young age, and that German pointers develop slower than English. *Feldmann* was the best in the class, but he too might have the ears set higher. *Treff II* is very light and shows all the ailings of his brothers. *Treumann* would strike the eye of most German amateurs, he has that stumpy body that is much liked, but lacks quality and his ears are too pointed. A puppy—name not given—won third. I think he will grow into a likely dog, his color and head are promising. *Holla* (Hoppenrade) is an excellent bitch all over. She was without doubt the best of the entry, not too heavy for work. *Diana* resembled her brothers, but showed her shortcomings less and might have been in better condition. *Hydra,* a sister, resembles her. *Edda* is a strongly built bitch, but lacks quality. Her skull is far too broad, but on account of a litter I thought she deserved a commended mark. Her age was stated wrong in the catalog, she is much older. The other dogs of the class were inferior in type and need not be mentioned, though the pluck of their owner, a young breeder, is to be praised."

Many of the faults noted by the German judge are still in the breed today: too broad skulls, outturned feet, lack of muzzle, even sometimes pointed ears. One would like to have had more detail concerning Holla. That she was excellent is proved by her progeny after her return to Germany (Morell and Maitrank Hoppenrade). No picture of this bitch has as yet been located. Maybe some English breed enthusiast, with the above dates to guide him (or her) may now undertake a search through the British Museum newspapers and periodicals of the time. The "Illustrated London News" is a likely source.

Seventy years later, and against some opposition from conservative hunting dog interests, the German Shorthaired Pointer returned officially to England, post-war, in 1945. However, Frank Warner Hill points out that isolated specimens actually were in England before that date. Specifically, he refers to meeting with a Mrs. Locker Lampson in 1935, when that early-day German Shorthaired Pointer owner was concerned about finding a mate for the bitch she then owned in England (*Dog World*, June 8, 1962).

After the war, the breed had a better chance to take hold in England than it could have had earlier. The new tax structure had whittled away at the guarded hunting privileges of the Squire and His Relations, and the organized shooting drives. Gone were the days when the great Arkwright of the Pointers could fill a *train* with his dogs and kennel help, en route for the shooting in Scotland. The fashion had begun to return to individual hunting, fur and feather, and for this the all-purpose German dog was able to show his worth.

Michael Brander's *Roughshooter's Dog* and *Roughshooter's Sport* (published by MacGibbon & Kee, London) describe how the wheel of hunting sport in England turned full circle over a century and a half. Now, again, it was for the man who went individually and afoot, and his need was for an all-purpose dog. Once again a dog was being asked not only to point game, but to retrieve it when it was down. New? Not really—it was the chore of early-day Pointers too, as the accompanying George Morland picture from the British Museum collection establishes; the period was the later part of the 18th century, as the artist was dead by 1804.

British difficulties with the German dog were first, as Michael Brander describes them, to discover how the breed wished to work, what it could do. He solved his own problem by letting his dog teach *him*. His "Max" actually wrote his *Roughshooter's Dog* for him, he says! Since then, the breed has been taken up by the gamekeepers who neither show them nor run them in trials—they *work* them!

Here, then, is another parallel—the initial fostering by professional gamekeepers, as in Germany. The breed can scarcely fail to benefit by its firm establishment in Britain, for these are a people with a genius for producing good dogs, who value conformation but insist that their sporting dogs shall retain their working qual-

135

The Pointer in England was originally a retrieving dog, too. This picture, by the famed 18th century sporting dog artist, George Morland, is reproduced by permission of the British Museum, London. Note the sitting bitch, still of the heavy "old Spanish" type. In the colored version of this painting she is of recognizable German Shorthaired Pointer color.

ities, and completely refuse them the honor of a full championship unless they do.

Breed popularity is being further boosted on a high level of Church and State. Anna, the dog-about-the-Palace (Lambeth) where the Archbishop of Canterbury lives, is a German Shorthaired Pointer. H.R.H. Prince Phillip, the Duke of Edinburgh, has accepted a brace from the Rt. Hon. the Lord Ferrier, and indeed, has been using this breed already for some years, working over some of Michael Brander's dogs when in residence at Balmoral. In this conservative country, such an acceptance means much, as those who have seen the results that accrued to the Welsh Corgi, after Royal acceptance years ago, will understand.

Founded in 1951, as the German Shorthaired Pointer Club, the Parent Club has been busily occupied ever since. As in Minnesota in 1938, there was the first responsibility to prepare the Standard for official adoption. The K.C. had to be approached for the provision of challenge certificates for show competition in due course, and for the formation of the rule under which the breed would run in field trial competition too. There was considerable time given to the problem of just where this breed fitted into the field trial scheme of things, and the eventual result was that the Kennel Club has been pleased to provide separate rules and aims in competition for "Any Variety of German Pointers, Weimeraners, Viszlas, and other Pointing/Setting breeds carrying out the Pointing/Retrieving schedule." Under these rules, dogs are required to quarter in the open, in cover, find game, point, flush, drop to shot, mark and retrieve to hand to order. Each dog also has to do a water retrieve. Within the official view, this constitutes "a test of practical working abilities that mere quartering at speed against pointers and setters never could provide. It adds up to a real test of working ability, and no purely 'trial' dog ought to win," is the interesting comment made there.

That the British rule not only permits but actually requires a dog to indulge the sporting breeds' deepest, centuries-old instinct of dropping to shot will permit cooperation with German breeders, avoiding the complications that can result in America when trained adult German dogs are imported and pressured to forget what has been bred and drilled into them—often with disastrous result.

Under the new Kennel Club rule, an aspiring British champion

137

must "win two prizes at two different Field Trials in Open and All Aged Stakes. One of the above wins must be in a Stake open to all breeds which hunt, point, and retrieve."

As a practical British German Shorthaired Pointer owner-breeder points out, this means that the Kennel Club has now fully recognized a new category of Gundog, a Pointer-Retriever. This, in the past, it has always refused to do. In other words, as this knowledgeable commentator emphasizes, the wheel in his country has come full circle again. Weimeraners, Draathaars, Viszlas, are of course the "other breeds" to which the new rule would appear to apply, but there is no such qualification as has elsewhere applied with the use of the description of "German" breeds. As read, the rule seems to put no obstacles in the way of Pointer/Setter folk who may also wish their dogs to retrieve.

English Kennel Club rule now places Pointers and Setters in a separate category from "breeds that hunt, point, and retrieve," so rendering the older breeds ineligible for utility type trials. For a time there was fear that as Pointers-Setters are no longer shot over in Britain (other than in Scotland on grouse) the division would collapse interest in P/S trials. In fact, these are now better supported than ever. The removal officially of all incentive or temptation to work the Germanic breeds in terms of the specialized and traditional P/S pattern has not only encouraged utility work interest but discouraged cross-breeding by making it unprofitable. From lack of such protection in the United States stem all the troubles that beset this breed in its working sphere here.

The new category of Gundog now recognized in Britain, where changes are never lightly made, is the first officially recognized since the Spaniel (in 1900), in which category there had also been a struggle to gain maid-of-all-work classification.

In the immediate past, individual German Shorthaired Pointers have competed in British and Irish Pointer/Setter trials, often with considerable success, if not always with the blessing of the devotees of the longer-established breeds. Indeed, the 1959 International Field Trial, held in Ireland, surprised with a German Shorthaired Pointer, Senta of Fellowes, in first place.

By 1960, the new but active British Club had gained sufficient support to justify the formation of local training classes in various parts of England. Some of these presently provided the impetus for the formation of Regional Branch Clubs, of which the first were

138

formed in South-Eastern England, and in the Midlands. Held during the summer, these classes are for schooling owners to get their dogs into training and themselves into the way of handling. They are followed by Spring Trials for pups up to sixteen months old and for young novice dogs to be tested in bird-finding and in retrieving dummies from land and water. Later in the year, Field Trials are conducted under full shooting conditions.

The 1961 Year Book Committee was kind enough to grant permission to quote here from some of the copyrighted matter which, obviously, makes considerable sense. "Our Club Trials are never to be regarded as frightening occasions in which dogs are expected to put up some vague and meaningless performance called 'Field Trial Standard.' They have rather two very real and constructive purposes—to show what a German Shorthaired Pointer is capable of doing in the Shooting Field, and to assist Breeders to select the strains most likely to improve the standards of work in the breed."

While "dedicated to protecting the German Shorthaired Pointer against the possible depredations of the purely show folk," the Club yet recognizes and advocates showring competition for publicity purposes, for allowing owners to see and compare quality. (This same view is held by some of the best breeders in America, too. Quoting the Sandbergs, of Kaposia: "Every dog we sell is sold as a hunting dog, but we like to have our dogs in the showring as a means of getting them before the public.") The British Club is also much concerned that the breed judges be Field Trial judges as well. "In the field and the showring the breed must be one breed. So far, here it is. (The majority) of champions till now have competed in Field Trials and been regularly shot over. But the Field Trial owners have a responsibility to bring their dogs into the showring, too," points out the Club President, Mr. G. C. Sterne.

Just as the American field competition has its two main Trials (Nationals) of the year, the British have two main trials, run annually by the Club. These are held in the autumn, the dogs shot over in realistic shooting conditions. The trials are held under Kennel Club rules, with two judges. The number of dogs in each stake is usually limited to twelve. "Our judges have a long day's walking to give each dog a fair run," points out Mrs. Mary Godby, of the Public Relations Committee, "but quite obviously do not have so many dogs to deal with as in American trials."

Nothing amazes British (and Irish) sporting dog owners more than to hear of American judges *riding* the braces. "I quite see your chaps are likely to need them on the big meetings in open rolling country," comments another well-known Britisher. "I'm willing to bet they wouldn't be refused by quite a number of our judges on the moors either, but the riding is tricky as there are plenty of holes and most of the judges can't ride anyway. . . ."

A most comprehensive description of why Field Trial judges walk in Ireland was provided by Mrs. Eustace Duckett, Hon. Sec. of the South of Ireland Gundog Club: "The natural game for Pointers/Setters in this country (or England) is grouse, and they are found on the mountains or moors, neither of which it would be possible to ride on as they are heather and bog. When trials are run on partridge or pheasant, the terrain is restricted by fences and the dog is penalized if he crosses the fence. Our entries are never so large that we cannot get thro' a novice and an open stake in two days, starting at 9:30." By quartering the ground systematically it is not possible for a dog to get beyond sight of his handler, but in America's 'wide open spaces' the dogs are simply required to range straight out for as far as they can till they find birds. Small wonder the judges have to ride. . . . All in all, what it amounts to is the completely different type of terrain over which the trials are run in America and here . . ."

"We are constantly trying to improve our stock in this country and, of course, are battling incessantly against too much inbreeding," notes Mary Godby. "We try to steer a middle course between the good-looking, badly handled, and consequently scatty performers, as some of our early dogs undoubtedly were, and the useful working type where (not enough) regard has been paid to conformation, gait, stance. My own particular axe continues to grind noisily on correct conformation for a capable working dog."

British breed judges, never easily pleased, were at first critical of the conformation of German Shorthaired Pointers that came before them in the rings, but are now reporting type improvement, this to be considered tribute to British breeding skill. Original German imports were few, and as to complementary qualities, sire and dam, quite unplanned. The quarantine fence is six months of cold, imposing discouragement and expense, as well as wreaking sometimes sad havoc on a dog that must endure it. Yet the bloodlines stand in need of reinforcement, and further importations therefore have had to be planned for, though the quarantine hurdle cannot be avoided.

Quarantine laws, especially within the British Commonwealth countries, are very severe. To wish to avoid introduction of rabies is, of course, quite a laudable aim, but the same penalty of detention is placed on dogs from countries admittedly rabies-free. And difficult as the British hurdle is, it does not compare with what applies Down Under. Importation of a "foreign" dog—which means any dog from any country other than Britain or Northern Ireland—to Australia or New Zealand involves first a six-month quarantine in England, then a freighter voyage, as air introduction is not allowed, then another two months at the port of entry. No wonder these countries took time to become acquainted with Shorthairs. The occasional specimen appeared first in New Zealand, but it was some time before interest was spearheaded in Australia by Mr. Jack Thomson, of Melbourne. As earlier in England, the Old Hands were "agin" and prejudice was for combating. Thomson had a hard time to gain acceptance for an all-purpose bracketing for his imports.

Major award in Field Trial competition is the President's Cup, annually awarded. To date this has been won by:

1955	CH. NEVERN JASPER	Owned Sqn/Ldr. D. W. Atkinson
1956	OCTAVA	" Mr. W. B. Mottram
1957	OCTAVA	
	SPRINGFARM SANDPIPER	" Mrs. E. S. Johnson
1958/9/60	LITTLESTAT SEIDLITZ	" Mr. S. Zanussi
1961	DUKE OF FRIULI	" Mr. S. Zanussi
1962	LITTLESTAT BARKER	" Mr. Mettram
1963	F.T. CH. LITTLESTAT SUSIE	" Mrs. Jeffries
1964	LITTLESTAT CURRY	" Mr. Mettram
1965	MAX OF BEROLINA	" Mr. I. Healey
1966	INCHMARLO HEIDI	" Mr. I. E. T. Sladden
1967	No trials—Foot/Mouth Disease outbreak in cattle.	
1968	INCHMARLO GRAFF GREIF OF PRAHA (sub. Dual Ch.)	" Mr. I. E. T. Sladden
1969	F.T. CH. HIE-ON-DINA	" Capt. T. H. Grace
1970	CH. INCHMARLO CORA	" Mr. I. E. T. Sladden

* Duke of Friuli is a son of Littlestat Seidlitz.

141

The Meredith-Hardy Club Cup for BOB at Crufts, London, has been won by:

1955	Ch. Nevern Jasper	Owned Sqn/Ldr. D. W. Atkinson
1956	Nevern Bruce	" Mr. M. Meredith-Hardy
1957	Ch. Blitz of Longsutton	" Mr. J. Gassman
1958	Springfarm Sandpiper	" Mrs. E. S. Johnson
1959	Ch. Zita Sand	" Mr. J. Gassman
1960	Ch. Mordax Morning Mist	" Miss J. Farrand
1961	Sh. Ch. Springfarm Duskie	" Mr. A. Lindquist
1962–63	Ch. Mordax Morning Mist	" Miss J. Farrand
1964	Ch. Larberry Link	" Miss J. Farrand
1965	Sh. Ch. Tojory Wildkrieger	" Mrs. P. Jenkins
1966	Sh. Ch. Patrick of Malahide	" Miss M. Ward
1967	Ch. Littlestat Condiment	" Mrs. L. Petrie-Hay
1968	Sh. Ch. Patrick of Malahide (and Group 1)	" Miss W. Ward
1969–70	Sh. Ch. Anna Liebe	" Mrs. W. Hancock
1971	Ch. Midlander Eider	" Mrs. M. Layton
1972	Sh. Ch. Postwood Luther	" Mrs. R. J. Schooling

British Shorthairs stem from best German strains, but as from the casual nature of acquisition in postwar years, there was wide divergence of type of dogs originally brought in. An early-day stud of distinction was the 1947-whelped Isgo v. Blitzdorf, a gift from Herr Böllhoff to Major-Gen. de Haviland. His dam, Grete v. Blitzdorf, was robbed of competitive opportunity during the duration of the war, but she stems notably, her four grandparents being Weltsieger Heide v.d. Beeke, Juno Goldbach, K.S. Dax v. Veronikaberg and Adria v. Blitzdorf. Isgo's sire, Opal v.d. Radbach was a Claus v. Veronikaberg son ex Klio v.d. Radbach, she by K.S. Seiger's Zett.

Also owing to Heide v.d. Beeke was Ch. Nevern Jasper, wh. 1953, through maternal grandparents K.S. Quandus and Vilvora v.d. Forst Brickwedde. Jasper sired the first Shorthair to make impact in British show rings, Ch. Mordax Morning Mist (ex an Isgo v. Blitzdorf daughter, Weedonbrook Wunder). Isgo also sired the winner of the 1956/7 President's Cup, Octava, her dam, Johanna of Walna one of several Shorthairs registered as of "breeding unknown owing to war conditions."

The breed club sponsorship supports versatile working interest with annual trophies, show and field, plus a trophy (the Lois Sterne) for the *breeder* of the stud whose progeny has qualified

First British Dual Ch. Inchmarlo Graff Greif of Praha. His pace, penalized in the breed outside USA, makes necessary running him miles behind a car prior to a trial to slow him down! Tell that around the Chuck Wagon in the USA! Owner: I. E. T. Sladden, MRCVS, Eng.

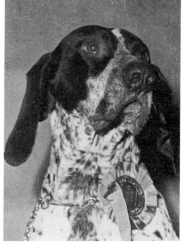

Ireland's first German Shorthaired Pointer champion, Ch. Halstead Ranger, brother to Sh. Ch. Deanslane Dawn. Owner: Mrs. Maybury.

Show Ch. Appeline Chough, BOB at the first Specialty held by the GSP Club, England. Owners: Mr. & Mrs. D. Appleton, Norfolk.

English Sh. Ch. Midlander Eider, distinguished show champion, field competitor, matron. Out of retirement, BOB 1971 Crufts from F.T. class. Owner: M. Layton.—*Photo, Cooke.*

by winning most awards at Field Trials under K.C. rules and at Open Class show competition. Many Shorthairs hold the "Qualifier" to make a show champion over to a "full" champion as required by English K.C. rules for sporting breeds. This does not require a finished field trial performance, but the demonstration to qualified Field Trial judges that the dog has the basic sporting breed instincts of desire, nose, etc.

Few trials are held in Britain, compared with USA, making slimmer the chances to finish a Dual—a matter of numbers, people and dogs. 1971 welcomed the first British Dual Ch. Shorthair in Inchmarlo Graff Greif of Praha (Fritz of Praha ex Deanslane Daystar of Praha) owned by Mr. I. E. T. Sladden. Also carrying "full" title under the same strain name are Graff-Greif's get, Inchmarlo Cora, reportedly near her Dual, and Inchmarlo Dunkeld, whose C.C. under me at the 1968 Specialty at age 7 months made breed history, (substantiated by his subsequent career), most recently (to time of writing) BOB at the 1972 breed Specialty, aged five.

The British first Field Trial champion was bred by the late Brian Mettram, Littlestat Barker, later in ownership of the Club president, Mr. G. E. Sterne. The Midlander strain of David and Mrs. Layton has also qualified "full" champions and many other British Shorthairs are similarly endowed.

The British show scene presents a wealth of good bitches, pattern set first by "full" Ch. Mordax Morning Mist, heading a Royal Procession of Great Ladies. Ch. Brownridge Marga was next, followed by her daughter, Ch. Midlander Eider (by Morning Mist's brother, Ch. Larberry Link). Eider retired after heading off the young C.C. winner, Dunkeld, at the 1968 Specialty under me, but by request of newer owners wishful to see her, entered Field Trial class at 1971 Crufts. She took the breed again, being 8½ yrs old. Last count of her record was 17 CCs, 3 Irish Green Stars, 6 FT awards, first winner of GSP Stake (1968) and twice (once with 100% mark) the Open All-Breeds Working Gundog Tests. Between times she whelped four litters, several representatives of which have reached their titles.

When Eider yielded First Ladyship and breed eminence, it was again a bitch that dominated competition—Sh. Ch. Anna Liebe, with 1969/70 Crufts BOBs among her many wins. Male challenge for breed supremacy has not yielded many stayers in Britain, but history was certainly made by Sh. Ch. Patrick of Malahide, whose second BOB at Crufts was followed (1968) by the Group, the first ever such for his breed.

As in other countries, the solid livers took time to become acceptable to the judges, mainly for the numerical superiority of tick-patched. This has been much changed through the influence of a solid liver stud that served a few bitches during quarantine detention in England, en route to Australia. The stock from this Irus v.d. Saaner Mark has made tremendous impact, and Britain's next Great Lady in this breed may well be the Irus daughter, Sh. Ch. Wittekind Erica.

The German Shorthaired Pointer in Ireland

The breed club in Ireland was formed in 1961, headquartered in Dublin. Pending increase of numerical strength, Shorthairs competed with Pointers/Setters.

Mrs. W. L. G. Dean, first President of the new club, acknowledged an amazing growth in interest and numbers since she established her own kennel with Tullyweary Spot. From Spot stem some interesting dogs in Ireland's first champion in the breed, Ch. Halstead Ranger, owned by Mrs. Maybury, and his sister, Sh. Ch. Deanslane Dawn, who has also been doing her share to help the breed along, being in the continued ownership of Mrs. Dean. Tullyweary Spot, their dam, stems v.d. Brickwedde, and the sire of Spot's successful produce, Spreccles of Hollybrook, brings in the familiar names of K.S. Frei Südwest, R.S. Odin v. Weinbach, Jäger's Naso.

Mary Godby, who confesses a great admiration for Sh. Ch. Deanslane Dawn, a beautiful, almost white, ticked bitch of good substance and conformation, describes her as a distinct personality as well, conceding, too, that Mrs. Dean has an eye for a good-looking dog. In the practical sense, Mrs. Dean describes how she and Dawn hunt all kinds of terrain, peat bog, marsh, fields, woods, mostly for pheasant, snipe, duck, and the few rabbits left since myxomatosis disease struck.

"We used to be over-run with rabbits, my game book shows I shot an average of five hundred a year, to my own gun alone, not counting those shot by friends. Now the dog has to hunt hard even for an occasional one, and the bag totals less than thirty for the past year. All game has to be hunted hard for in this country now, and

145

poaching has increased so greatly even the keepered estates have trouble to "keep the poachers out."

Interest in Shorthairs has grown to support classes at all top shows, plus an annual, well-supported Specialty. Since 1968 it has become possible to promote for the first time in Ireland Field Trials for Shorthairs exclusively, over shot pheasants. This was distinct innovation for Ireland where Pointers and Setters had never been shot over in Trials. Annual winners have been:

1968	PRINCE OF THE GAP	Owner Mr. T. McEvoy	
1969	CH. PREUSSE OF FALLOWS	"	Mr. E. J. Cunningham
1970	YELLOW GAP GREIF	"	Mr. P. W. Mooney
1971	HEIDI OF WOODFIELD	"	Mr. E. J. Daly

Mrs. Dean, bowing to time, no longer works Shorthairs in Ireland, but her teaching that a dog must look as well as it works is honored. An Irish requirement. This compiler is reminded of a wonderful day spent on Tullygrawley Bog, in County Antrim, where the heather-rich terrain was, as Mrs. Duckett refers to it, unrideable, all deep peat ditching and heather-screened holes big enough to swallow dog, man or horse; where (careful) foot progress is the only way, but game abounds. Dominie Russell took me shooting—he with gun, I with camera. Working two beautiful English Setters, Pegamoid and Mab of Fairy Thorn, he said: "Shooting sport is my recreation, has been all my life. To keep me happy I must have Ireland's best working dogs. But the Irish eye of me has to see beauty too, it can't be satisfied with a dog not made as a good sporting dog must be made, a delight to watch . . ."

Now Irish eyes all over are on the German Shorthaired Pointer, and only good can result from such assessment.

10

The Field Trial Dog

KONRAD ANDREAS *(Germany)* 1956.   *"Hunde mit denem man jagen kann, so weit der Himmel Blau!"*

MCDOWELL LYON *(U.S.A.)*   1956.   *"It is the great field dogs, the real ones, with noses and heart, style and intensity, that actually carry the whole breed."*

As good a reason as any for the modern-day popularity of Field Trials could be that when a man has a really good dog he welcomes the opportunity to show his friends what it can do. The prosperity of the times also contributes to this popularity—more money, more leisure. As the family station wagon takes everyone along to share the fun, Field Trials have become glorious picnic occasions. They are further held to be a substitute for Grandpa's blessed privilege to hunt where and as he pleased—though one does not gain the impression that Grandpa ever favored taking the women along. However, other times, other manners. Many of the gals now are as keen, or keener, than their husbands. Besides, when all is said and done, who takes care of the dogs? So, who goes for the old stuff about all work and no play?

Along with Grandpa's other hunting privileges went the freedom of the land. Now it is a nation of fenced and posted areas, shortened hunting seasons, shrinking bag limits. Grandpa's grandsons turn to the Field Trials, where the season is year-around, areas not posted, and no trigger-happy, lethally careless "hunters" roam to snick the ash of a distant cigarette along with the smoker's head.

For more than 30 years, first unofficially for fun, and eventually for points, German Shorthaired Pointer owners have been engaging their dogs in competition. The earliest imports were tested proudly thus: fur and feather, retrieving from land and water, cold-trailing, and at times a little coon-hounding or cat-harrying, just to see if those Germans told the truth about what the dogs could do. From such free-and-easy occasions was eventually reached, by the mid-1940's, Field Trials under license, at which the dogs could work towards points.

First with promotion was the German Shorthaired Pointer Club of America, Inc., Michigan Club next in line, and eventually the Regional Clubs, as these became formed, coast to coast. That was how it became possible presently for old Rusty v. Schwarenberg to gain his new title of Dual—an honor rarer than rubies so far as any Pointing/Setting breeds were till then concerned.

It is necessary to recognize that Field Trial performance and practical hunting performance are not necessarily one and the same thing. Most hunters would not want their dogs working as fast or wide as Field Trial performance requires. Many good hunting Shorthairs might not show to advantage in the Trials. Yet, as the best type of organized competition of today still aims to find inherited skills, it is also true that many big-winning Trial dogs in this breed are actually very useful to their owners in the practical sense as well. Many fine Dual Champions have lived out a long life later as personal hunting dogs. Doubtless, discussions of type distinction, as between the Trial and the Hunting dog, are akin to the Field/Bench argument, wherein all parties hold strongly that there should be but a single type of German Shorthaired Pointer—and everyone has a differing and not-so-private opinion of what that type should be.

In the earliest days of competition the breed's unique place within

148

Harro v. Klostermoor (later exp. USA) kills his fox in Germany to earn his "Sharpness" certificate, the award of M.S.

Weedonbrook Werra, owned and trained by Mr. Michael Brander of Scotland, author of "The Roughshooter's Dog." *Photo: Michael Brander.*

Thornton imports and their get worked as a pack in Montana, could tree 'em with the best.

Photo: *Dr. Charles R. Thornton.*

the Sporting Group seems to have been thoroughly understood. In 1943, the late Jack Shattuck, Jr., was describing old Rusty as "a first-class practical gundog, retrieving on duck and capably handling upland game. This is what the breed is meant to do. It is not meant to be a wind-splitter, but is as close to the ideal as a man can get with a pointing dog to follow on foot. It is not entered in the Big Trials for Pointing dogs, because it is not bred for that. It is a top shooting dog. That is why its trials are run with birds to be pointed, killed and retrieved." (*Letter to Don Miner, of California.*)

On such recognition of breed character has been based the present-day type of Field Trial competition for German Shorthaired Pointers and German Pointing Breeds generally. It has been found impractical to include all the tests to which German dogs are subject —the sharpness, work on deer and furred game generally, and the tracking of wounded animals. Sharpness tests (the German award of M.S.), in which a dog is sent into an enclosure to kill a fox or a cat, would not be tolerated here. Even in Germany it has been outlawed as a public spectacle since the mid-1930's. Nor do American game laws favor working deer with dogs. Many states legislate against this. Even where such a law does not exist, there is a great difference between the German privilege of hunting preserve-raised, virtually tame deer and the American hunting of free-running antlered game.

A belief is also expressed here by some German Shorthaired Pointer Field Trial adherents that the breed is no good for tracking, is outclassed by the nearest Beagle or Foxhound. Actually, as experience in other countries shows, it is difficult to be too definite about which dog breeds can or cannot track. The magnificent tracking of police-trained German Shepherds, for example. . . .* In their Kurzhaar, the Germans *bred* for this ability, fixed it strongly. Where breed purity has been honestly maintained, tracking ability—putting down the nose—can be found when required.

None of these skills, however, are competitively required now, here or in England. In England, the sharpness tests would come close to promoting riot and revolution! However, practical men know that when law and/or opportunity permits, their good Ger-

---

* *THE COLD NOSE OF THE LAW.* C. Bede Maxwell (Angus & Robertson, Australia).

This sled team includes three champions. Leader: Furie v. Lohengrin; Point: Ch. Kristi v. Lohengrin and Ch. Waldmann's Valdis; Wheel: Ch. Val-Valle's Heyoka v. Waldmann and Waldmann's Streif. Owner-driver: C. Lowe, Michigan. Heyoka is owned by F. Mainville.

A good German Shorthaired Pointer wastes no time in a water retrieve. Prince v. Blitzen goes for his bird. *Photo: T. Hanna, California.*

man Shorthaired Pointers can make useful showings at them all.

While the deletion of these German skills makes good sense here, less good sense seems to be made by omitting from competition the breed's superb waterworking skills, especially as these same water skills are those that help sell pups to hunting men. And while it is reasonable to hold that a smooth-haired dog should not be asked too much in terms of exposure to extreme icy conditions, as may a Labrador or a Chesapeake, it is also true that not all American duck-hunting (and/or Field Trials) is necessarily carried out under such climatic rigor.

Experience seems to be that a German Shorthaired Pointer blessed with the water-repellent coat the Germans took pains to breed for can hold his own in waterwork with specialist retrieving breeds. In Germany the view is held that one comes closer to nature's wisdom in adapting a smooth coat for water work. It is pointed out that wild aquatic animals develop protection through close, insulated jacketing, not from length of hair. Where, then, the German Shorthaired Pointer has the correct coat texture—"short, thick, tough and hard," as the Standard asks, and as the Germans bred for (show judges please note!)—it endures all but extreme discomfort in waterwork very well. But where it carries—as some do—the fine silken jacketing of Pointer texture on thin Pointer skin, it quickly becomes, under chill and wet, the same picture of shivering misery as would its water-hating, cold-avoiding English cousin. Nothing hates water more than the true-bred, aristocratic, fast-going English Pointer—as the Germans recognized nearly a hundred years ago, in all their infighting within Klub Kurzhaar, to keep further Pointer blood out of their developing utility dog. One is reminded of the fairy-tale Princess whose Royal blood was proved by her sensitive reaction to the single pea placed under the mattress of her bed. So, too, a test of the possible infusion of extra, unreported English Pointer blood into a German Shorthaired Pointer might likely be contrived anywhere in the world through a mere sprinkling with a hose!

It is now more generally understood that there is poor percentage in screening out inbred skills of the truebred utility sporting breeds. The revised rules (Jan. 1971) for AKC-licensed field trials now require a Water Test as additional to prevailing demands for finishing a Field Trial champion, divergence from narrowed aims of

Pointer/Setter run. There has been grumbling, of course, loudest often from those with least understanding or true interest in the breed. Most vocal is complaint that the rule imposes hardship on owners living distant from water. However, a whole ocean is NOT mandatory. In Europe, Shorthairs work duck competitively and in training in quite small streams and sloughs.

Sharpness and trailing, then, remain permanently out of the Field Trial picture. As to land-retrieving, there are dedicated bird-dog buffs who would gladly be rid of that too, if they could—pitch out the baby AND the bathwater. Opinion is strongly argued as to the breed ideal in Field Trial performance. Not officially, of course— the Rule Book still governs the A.K.C.-licensed Field Trial. The conflict would seem to be between those who would prefer to retain the character of the all-purpose gundog that first won the breed its following here, and those who long to turn it into what could at best be only a rather pale carbon copy of the Big-Running Pointer of the Classic Trials.

Those who appear ready to barter all that the German Short-haired Pointer inherits in hope to squeeze a bit more speed from it may be the most vocal, but their ranks do not necessarily include the wisest of the breed's adherents. For example, the demand for horsing German Shorthaired Pointer Trials ("Horses vs. Walking," by J. S. Brown, M.D., *German Shorthaired Pointer News,* September, 1961) is balanced by the wise observations of Hjalmer Olsen in the January, 1962, issue of the same publication. Mr. Olsen points out that it is doubtful if the aim to have the German Shorthaired Pointer outrun Pointers and Setters is necessarily something to describe as progress. "It is sad," he writes, "to see Shorthairs nowadays, running like streaks through the fields and not quartering them properly, and not taking in every likely spot where game may be hiding. I don't like a slow pottering dog, but a dog can be fast, covering his field in a schooled and well-organized fashion—something we seldom see nowadays."

And from Joe Stetson (*Field and Stream*) comes the query: "If the aim is to use the German Shorthaired Pointer as an ordinary bird dog, pushing it out further and further, faster and faster, why not have a Pointer or Setter, a wide-ranging, high-stepping, stylish specialist?" Indeed, why not?

There is a good case to be made for not yielding too many more concessions to the extremists. Those sighing for Pointer pace might reflect that it was the average Field Trial supporter's *retreat from* Pointer pace that popularized the German Shorthaired Pointer in the first place. Concentration on any one character in any breed of dog is always made at bitter cost—as history well establishes. Over-concentration on Pointer pace brought that breed to a frightening low, and thrust it out of public popularity, as registrations here accurately show.

It is never with the extremists—either end of the scale, show or Field—that the hope of a breed will rest. Rather is it with the far-seeing who preserve a normal balance between working merit and physical quality, such as the Dual Champion worthily represents. In this connection, useful notice could be taken by those exposed to much brain-washing on the subject of Speed for Speed's Sweet Sake that, in the December, 1961, issue of the A.K.C. *Gazette,* responding to a question, the breed columnist for Pointers writes sadly that Pointer folk must "hang their heads in shame" when it comes to the matter of Dual Champions. Not a single one has been finished in this breed within known memory!

The plea for the dog of well-balanced abilities does not mean that it has to be a clumsy bumbler falling over its own slow feet. Nor do available records suggest that the best early imports were as slow as the "racehorse" enthusiasts of today would like one to believe. Merely, in those blessed years when game was so plentiful, a dog could take his time because it wasn't necessary for him to search over so much ground. Now, dwindling stocks make it necessary for the dog to go faster, and selective breeding and improved training methods have been able to take care of this need within the framework of the breed's approved type and working style.

"With birds so few and far between, it becomes impractical to have a dog which hunts game too close to the gunner," a widely experienced mid-Westerner points out. "Smart pheasants merely run away, and the dog and hunter just don't find them . . . So, now you have to have a dog with range—one that will get out and find birds which are likely running before the hunter. A smart pheasant dog will go way out, find and pin the pheasant, holding it till the gunner can come up. This is what the Field Trials should try to illustrate—the ability of the German Shorthaired Pointer to adapt himself to the cover he hunts wherever he happens to be set down, the variety of the game, and the type of the hunting available to us today. . . ."

In this, then, is a word-picture that cannot be improved upon in depicting the working qualities of a good modern German Short-haired Pointer Field Trial dog that is, at the same time, not so grotesquely out of touch with hunting realities as the type some judges, so many of whom have always been recruited from the ranks of Pointer/Setter work, delight in seeing. Half a county away is quite a distance for that gunner to come up, as some dogs are pushed out at present.

Range and speed within the Pointing/Setting category must always be regarded comparatively. If the German breed were pushed to the utmost limits of any foreseeable capacity, it still could not match the range and speed of the top strata of big-running classics. There is no gainsaying that the classics are thrilling to follow (on horse!), but comparison of registration figures soon shows where John Q. Public, who buys the pups and often cannot afford a horse, finds himself the more comfortable as owner and competitor—which is on his own two feet!

As Nature's laws remain eternally Nature's laws, with no new thing under the sun, it could be interesting to review the pass to which concentration on speed alone brought the English Pointer in its native land at the exact time when the Germans were forming their new breed. It helps explain still further why those Germans fought to keep more Pointer out of their developing Kurzhaar. Let us look through the eyes of that fine dog writer, "Idstone," a Pointer/Setter man himself in England at that time (1872).

"Following the period when the 'improved' Pointer first became fashionable here, fetching enormous sums, some ghastly objects came to bear the name," he writes. "There was deficiency of nose, probably from some rash adventurer crossing with the greyhound (for speed); there was no lashing of stern, no high-ranging, no dash and discipline combined, no quick turn and quarter, no vigor, pluck, or constitution . . . Shyness has become one of the breed failings, temperament so irritable and excitable as to render whole litters occasionally, and for no assignable reason, afraid of the gun, or any sudden noise . . . Most certainly, such weakness is hereditary. The timid produce a nervous offspring, and this is a sign that inbreeding, though perhaps unsuspected, is doing its work. I have a suspicion that we shall have to go to a distinct cross, probably that of the Foxhound, 'diluted,' if I may use the word, to the 5th or 6th generation, to obtain again that courage and verve which are so essential in an animal bred for field sports, nor can I see any other remedy. In a prize-winner, the chances are that it propagates its faults, is the head of a race of nameless, shivering idiots." (*THE DOG, Idstone, pp. 114 et seq.*)

See, then? There *is* nothing new under the sun, it has all happened before! "Nameless, shivering idiots" have been produced before in the world, in the guise of "improvement" by wrongly-slanted breeding practice, by outcrosses hidden in falsified registration particulars, by over-close inbreeding, generation after generation. Trends some American breeders of wide experience now discern here in some emerging German Shorthaired Pointer strains of the present time may carry the seeds of wreckage similar to that which all but ruined the Pointer in England in that earlier period. The proud table of the German Shorthaired Pointer Dual Champions is, however, the best hope that sanity will prevail in this country to fend off the machinations of the would-be "improvers" of what is fine as they already have it.

The English wreckage was eventually salvaged after much work and a new building of the breed, in which the famous William Arkwright had so much part, thereby making his name a legend—preserving the working character, the physical stamina, even preserving the characteristic dish-face that in time has become known as an "Arkwright head," though he did not form, only salvaged it, from the "improvers." It is also true that many other English Pointer strains lost the dish-face, this becoming replaced by a straight or bumpy profile as is to be seen, too, on many German Shorthaired Pointers of the present, and earlier, times. What put that profile into the English Pointer all those years ago may have been just some such hound introduction as "Idstone" forecast as providing the likeliest hope of breed salvage.

Interestingly, we note that after 30 years of breeding German Shorthaired Pointers, Hjalmer Olsen confesses (*Dog World,* May, 1958) that his heart still belongs to the English Pointer—"the kind Mr. Arkwright used to raise," he is careful to qualify. That kind (Arkwright's) is a far cry from what Mr. Olsen would have found available to him here from run-of-the-mill field breeding—which

157

may explain why he turned, as did many other Pointer/Setter folk, along with that old friend of ours, John Q. Public, to the German dog.

Hjalmer Olsen is but one of the many clearsighted breeders who set their faces against ill-advised ambition to make the German Shorthaired Pointer over into something it was never meant to be; who deplore the results of possible irregularities the lunatic fringe might risk in order to bring this about. The safe and solid, which is the firmly-convinced majority of German Shorthaired Pointer breed opinion, is well aware of the disastrous split in other sporting breeds, brought about in past decades, of the impossibility of mending what was destroyed in the cleavage, the useful uniformity of good-looking dogs that could work as well. Such few present-day German Shorthaired Pointer breeders as have been led astray by alien aims, who now begin to suffer such disappointments as having some well-sold dog returned by a disappointed purchaser for inability to do a hunting dog's work (and it happens!), might usefully check some specimens of previously-split sporting breeds. Look not only to the top-heavy, over-coated "show" dogs; look also to the hapless "running machines," often but one remove from mongrel status in their overall appearance. Look at some of the less-admirable among the "field Pointers," with snipy muzzles and tails yelling "greyhound" to the knowledgeable. The thick-butted, short, bee-sting-tip tail of the true-bred Pointer is recognized the world over as the certificate of the purity of its blood. It is also one of the first visible sacrifices to "experimentation" in breeding and can be recognized even a dozen generations later, ringing the bell, telling the tale. No doubt, the original "experiment" was contrived also, all those years ago, in the interests of "improvement"!

So are wedges driven to split breeds, section from section. It can happen to the German dog too, if the guards are lowered, even if as yet no truly discernible split exists. No other sporting breed, excepting the Brittany, matches the Duals produced in German Shorthaired Pointers, not only in past years, but as a still-continuing process. Where the split could be held to threaten, wise breeding, wise training aims and the careful briefing of novices can still hold it at bay.

The following list of the Duals in all their pride is proof positive that all is well with Shorthairs here.

158

Dual Champion German Shorthair One Hundred!

Dog world historians must needs recognize such a statistic in terms of what has gone before—the woeful shying away over more than a century by tunnel-visioned breeders and owners of competitive sporting breeds from the obligation to produce and foster dogs uniting the essential qualities of proper conformation with proper working spirit. Thus in the two breeds that dominated the world of field competition for more than a century—Pointers and English Setters—there remains yet to be finished a *first* Dual Champion! Such a lack can scarcely constitute a pride to those who stubbornly maintained a division between the conformation and the working sides of dog development.

Some other breeds within the Sporting Group—notably Irish Setters, Labradors, Golden Retrievers, Springers and Cocker Spaniels—have over a long term of years also carried representatives to the Dual honor, but in a count to Dual Champion One Hundred, only the Brittany Spaniel in the United States marches sturdily with the Shorthair and justifies such a best management by dedicated owners.

For those watching with interest where the proud statistical figure would fall within the Shorthairs, there can scarcely fail to be satisfaction that it should have rested upon a representative of a strain carefully fostered in terms of Dual Champion interest over several generations. Dual & Amtr. Field Ch. Albrecht's Tena Hy has for dam a magnificent producing bitch in Field Ch. Albrecht's Countess Tena, already blessed by two other Duals, as well as field and show titled champions, plus a Dual grand-daughter, as the production tabulations in another section of this work establishes.

In reviewing the ever-lengthening tabulation of Shorthair Duals it should not be overlooked that the Duals attaining *first* their show title outnumber those that gained first their field title by near enough two-to-one. Which brings to memory that Pointer breeder in another country who said: "A working dog you can *make*. A show dog you have first to *breed!*"

The wisdom is incredibly ancient—think of Master Falconer Vicentino, five centuries ago, instructing dog owners in the responsibility to "breed them first and *then* to make them good!" European governing bodies in matters canine still wholly repudiate in the working sphere any dog that cannot pass preliminary conformation assessment. Dog owners in these United States have now the full benefit of a century's repudiation of this wisdom to ponder in the case of breeds that were once top of the popularity poll—and which modernly are in state of somewhat sad declension. So, for Shorthairs, let's draw on the skirl of a proud march-by of the bagpipes and transpose to "A Hundred Duals and all and all . . . A Hundred Duals and all. . . ."

Rusty v. Schwarenberg
Owner: Jack Shattuck, Jr., Minnesota
(Mars v. Ammertal, imp.
ex Vicky v. Schwarenberg)

Schatz v. Schwarenberg
Owners: Dr. H. and Mrs. Zahalka, Minnesota
(Ch. Fritz v. Schwarenberg
ex Helga v. Schwarenberg)

Valbo v. Schlesberg
Owner: Carl Schnell, Michigan
(Duke v. Rheinberg
ex Heide v. Schlesberg)

Searching Wind Topper
Owner: Hjalmer Olsen, Wisconsin
(Ch. Searching Wind Bob
ex Fieldborn Katzie Karlwald)

Blick v. Grabenbruch
Owner: Richard S. Johns, Pennsylvania
(K. S. Sepp v. Grabenbruch, imp.
ex Nanny v. Luckseck gen Senta, imp.)

Valkyrie v. Grabenbruch
Owner: Richard S. Johns, Pennsylvania
(Dual Ch. Blick v. Grabenbruch
ex Ch. Katinka of Sycamore Brook, C.D.)

Baron v. Strauss
Owner: Del J. Glodowski, Wisconsin
(Toby B
ex Patsy v. Strauss)

National Ch. Dandy Jim v. Feldstrom
Owner: Dr. Clark Lemley, Michigan
(Ch. Davy's Jim Dandy
ex Ch. Joan v. Feldstrom)

National Ch. Wendenheim's Fritz
Owner: Frank Nuzzo, Illinois
(Fritz v. Pepper
ex Wendy v. Windhausen)

Doktorgaarden's Caro, imp. Denmark
Owner: Dr. Wm. F. Hartnell, Utah
(Fangel's Rolf
ex Holevgaards Kora)

Trailborn Mike, C.D.
Owner: Carl L. Johnson
(Erick v. Reffup
ex Trailborn Scholar)

Junker v. Grabenbruch
Owner: J. Lurba, Pennsylvania
(Dual Ch. Blick v. Grabenbruch
ex Ch. Katinka of Sycamore Brook, C.D.)

Fritz of Sleepy Hollow
Owner: F. Z. Palmer, New York
(Ch. Donar v. Schlangenberg
ex Susabelle v. Catskill)

Big Island Spook
Owner: G. Reudiger, Minnesota
(Ch. Rex v. Krawford
ex Graff's Lady Lou)

Captain v. Winterhauch (also BIS)
Owner: Millard W. Axelrod, Minnesota
(Ch. Oak Crest Rick v. Winterhauch
ex Duchess v. Hotwagner)

Kaposia's Firebird
Owners: Don and Betty Sandberg, Minnesota
(Count Snooper v. Dusseldorf
ex Dual Ch. Lucky Lady v. Winterhauch)

Jones Hill Friedrich
Owner: Dr. Eugene R. McNinch
(Ch. Pardner, C.D.
ex Ch. Wilhelmia v. Kirsche, C.D.)

Peter Bruner
Owner: E. D. Andrews, Ohio
(Field Ch. Pheasant Lane Schnapps
ex Hunter's Lady Heflin)

160

HEIDIE V. MARVON (also Can. Ch.)
Owner: Charles Puffer, Michigan
(Necker's Arno
ex Wilhelmina v. Marvon)

RIGA V. HOHEN TANN
Owner: Robert Fletcher, Washington
(Field Ch. Bill's Linzer Boy
ex Ch. Bella v. Hohen Tann, imp.)

GRETCHEN V. SUTHERS
Owner: Paul Putnam, California
(Field Ch. Frederick Wolfgang
ex Paul's Vinkel)

GRETCHEN V. GREIF (also a Dual in Canada)
Owner: Ralph A. Park, Sr., Washington
(Field Ch. Yunga v. Hundsheimerkogel
ex Field Ch. Karen v. Greif)

OXTON'S LEISELOTTE V. GREIF
Owner: E. E. Harden, California
(Field Ch. Greif v. Hundsheimerkogel
ex Ch. Yunga War Bride)

AL-RU'S ERIC
Owner: R. J. Burnand
(Tell v. Grabenbruch
ex Gretchen Barikstettle)

STRAUSS'S WORKING BOY
Owner: Hermann Foss, Wisconsin
(Ch. Otto v. Strauss
ex Rita's Cocoa)

LUCKY LADY V. WINTERHAUCH, C.D.
Owner: A. Frush, Minnesota
(Ch. Oak Crest Rick v. Winterhauch
ex Hephzibah Holzman)

OXTON'S BRIDE'S BRUNZ V. GREIF
Owner: J. Huizenga, California
(Field Ch. Greif v. Hundsheimerkogel
ex Ch. Yunga War Bride)

BARON TURN & TAXIS
Owner: Wm. A. Barth, Colorado
(Heide's Dream
ex Astarte v. Svealand)

ABLE V. ELTZ
Owner: Mrs. K. Metcalf Allen, California
(Ch. Oak Crest Rick v. Winterhauch
ex Duchess v. Hotwagner)

MADCHEN BRAUT V. GREIF
Owner: E. E. Harden, California
(Field Ch. Greif v. Hundsheimerkogel
ex Ch. Yunga War Bride)

TIMBERLANE'S ACE
Owner: Mrs. W. G. Davis, Wash.
also a Dual in Canada
(Fritz v. Sulfmeister
ex Katherine v. Eugen)

FLICK V. HEIDEBRINK
Owner: Not Reported
(Wehrwolf v. Braumatal
ex Dina v. Heidebrink)

SAGER V. GARDSBURG
Owners: R. and L. Sylvester, Georgia
(Ch. Buck v. Gardsburg
ex Ch. Valory v. Gardsburg)

HANS V. ELDRIDGE, C.D. (also BIS)
Owner: R. Eldridge, Wisconsin
(Baron Strauss II
ex Strauss's Pamela)

ALFI V.D. KRONNENMUHLE, imp.
Owner: R. C. Bauspies, Illinois
(K.S. Gernot v.d. Heidehöhe
ex Heide v.d. Emmstadt)

BIG ISLAND RECS
Owner: Duane Petit, Minnesota
(Big Island Skinner
ex Big Island Queen)

ROMMEL V. RUMPELSTILZCHEN
Owner: K. T. Jensen
(Elbing v.d. Forst Brickwedde
ex Karen v. Hesselbach)

GROUSEWALD'S BLITZ
Owners: N. and J. Goodspeed
(Dual Ch. Blick v. Grabenbuch
ex Debby v. Hollabird)

DALLO V. HESSELBACH, C.D.
Owners: C. W. and Mrs. Flinn, Illinois
(Ch. Ace v. Barikstettle, C.D.
ex Calyx v.d. Forst Brickwedde)

WOODY V. RONBERG
Owner: J. Christensen, Wisconsin
(Field Ch. Kim v. Waldheim
ex Strauss' Glamor Girl)

MISS B'HAVEN V. WINTERHAUCH
Owner: R. C. Bauspies, Illinois
(Dual Ch. Captain v. Winterhauch
ex Dual Ch. Alfi v.d. Kronnenmuhle, imp.)

161

SKID-DO'S BONNIE KAREN
Owners: Mr. and Mrs. J. C. Pope,
California

(Field Ch. Dixon's Skid-Do
ex Field Ch. Dixon's Bonnie)

WAG-AE'S SNOWFLAKE, C.D.
Owner: E. D. Andrews, Akron, Ohio

(Spike of Clover Club
ex Princess Rosie)

FRITZ OF HICKORY LANE FARM

Owner: William Gill, Michigan

(Dual & Nat'l Ch. Dandy Jim v.
Feldstrom
ex Can/Am. Ch. Susanna Mein
Liebchen, C.D.)

GUSTAV MEIN LIEBCHEN

Owner: Otto Harris, Michigan

(Dual & Nat'l Ch. Dandy Jim v.
Feldstrom
ex Can/Am. Ch. Susanna Mein
Liebchen, C.D.)

MARMADUKE MEIN LIEBCHEN
Owner: Maxine Collins, Michigan

(Ch. Fieldborn Tempo II
ex Can/Am. Ch. Susanna Mein
Liebchen, C.D.)

BRUNNENHUGEL BALDER
Owner: Norman Revel, Calif.

(Dual Ch. Oxton's Bride's Brunz v. Greif
ex Ch. Weidenbach Suzette)

SCHOENE BRAUT V. GREIF
Owner: E. E. Harden, California

(Field Ch. Greif v. Hundsheimerkogel
ex Ch. Yunga War Bride)

BRUNNENHUGEL JARL
Owner: N. Revel, California

(Dual Ch. Oxton's Bride's Brunz v.
Greof ex Ch. Weidenbach Suzette)

BIFF BANGABIRD
Owner: Dr. C. P. Gandal, New York

(Chadwick of Hollabird ex
Grousewalds Berta)

ESSO V. ENZSTRAND (imp.)
Owner: D. Glodowski, Wisconsin

(Cato v. Grabenbruch ex
Dina v. Enzstrand)

NAT'L. F.T. CH. MOESGAARD'S DANDY
Owner: Dr. L. L. Kline, Florida

(Field Ch. Moesgaard's Ib ex Field
Ch. Doktorgaarden's Lucky)

ERDENREICH'S EARTHA
Owner: Miss I. Pauly, California

(Erdenreich's Able v. Yankee ex Am.-
Can. Ch. Erdenreich die Zweite, C.D.)

NAT'L. F.T. CH. KAY V.D. WILDBURG
(imp.)
Owners: R. Johns and J. Eusepi, Penna.

(K.S. Pol v. Blitzdorf ex
Cora v. Wesertor)

BEE'S GABBY V. BECKUM
Owner: Donald Briggs, California

(Nat'l F.T. Ch. Bobo Grabenbruch
Beckum ex Field Ch. Skid-Do's Bee)

ALBRECHT'S BARON CID
Owners: M. and L. Albrecht, Kansas

(Ch. Big Island Spotter ex Field Ch.
Albrecht's Countess Tena)

ALBRECHT'S BARONESS CORA
Owners: M. and L. Albrecht, Kansas

(Ch. Big Island Spotter ex Field Ch.
Albrecht's Countess Tena)

DINO V. ALBRECHT
Owners: Happy Hollow Kennels, Md.

(Ch. Big Island Spotter ex Ch.
Albrecht's Apache Breeze)

STREAK'S HERBST VERSPRECHEN
Owners: J. Lee and S. Meredith, Ohio

(Field Ch. Skriver's Streak ex Ch.
Lady Patricia Valbo)

ROBIN CREST CHIP, C.D.T. (and
Canadian champion)

(Ch. Alnor's Brown Mike ex Ch.
Montreal Belle)

NAT'L F.T. Ch. BARON FRITZ V. HOHEN
TANN
Owner: Ray C. Bauspies, Illinois

(Baron v. Heidebrink ex Field Ch.
Sandra v. Hohen Tann)

FIELDACRES KATIA
Owner: James R. Jares, Ohio
(Ch. Boy Howdy ex Fieldacres Geisha)

HEWLETT GIRL PEBBLES
Owner: Herman Levee, New York
(Dual Ch. Biff Bangabird ex Field Ch. Hewlett Girl Greta)

ZIPPER DER ORRIAN
Owner: O. L. Borland, Oregon
Field Ch. Von Thalberg's Fritz II ex Zetta v. Fuehrerheim)

KAMIAK DESERT SAND
Owners: L. & G. Dorius, California
(Field Ch. Lutz v.d. Radbach—imp. Ger.—ex Field Ch. Kamiak Bold Bark)

SATAN V. SCHNELLBERG
Owner: Wilson H. Lufkin, Massachusetts
(Eros v. Scheperhof—imp. Ger.—ex Field Ch. Freda v. Schnellberg)

NAT'L F.T. CH. LUCKY BALL
Owner: Dr. L. L. Kline, Florida
(Dual & Nat'l F.T. Ch. Moesgaard's Dandy ex Pearl of Wetzler)

RADBACK'S ARKO (Also Can. Ch.)
Owner: Alvin Schwager, Washington
(Field Ch. Gert v.d. Radbach—imp. Ger.—ex Katja v.d. Radbach—imp. in utero, Ger.)

JANIE GREIF V. HEISTERHOLZ
Owner: Elaine Stout, Colorado
(Am/Can. Dual Ch. Arrak v. Heisterholz—imp. Ger.—ex Am/Can. Dual Ch. Gretchen v. Greif)

RITZIE
Owner: George de Gidio, Minnesota
Field Ch. Chocolate Chip II ex Big Island Sheba)

ERDENREICH'S JETTA BECKUM
Owner: C. D. Lawrence, Washington
(Field Ch. Stutz Beckum ex Am/Can. Ch. Erdenreich Die Zweite, C.D.)

GRUENWEG'S DANDY DANDY
Owner: Ralph Z. Neff, Ohio
(Dual & Nat'l F.T. Ch. Moesgaard's Dandy ex Ch. Tessa v. Abendstern)

ARRAK V. HEISTERHOLZ (imp. Ger.)
Owner: Ralph A. Park, Sr., Washington
(Lummel v. Braumatal ex Astrid v. Grossenvorde)

RICHLU'S TERROR
Owners: C. & S. Carlson, Ohio
Dual Ch. Sager v. Gardsburg ex Ch. Richlu's Jan Oranian-Nassau)

RICHLU'S DAN ORANIAN
Owners: C. & S. Carlson, Ohio
(Ch. Dax v. Heidebrink ex Ch. Richlu's Jill Oranian—Dau. of above)

RAMBLING ROCK
Owner: Hal G. Ward, Virginia
(Dual Ch. Albrecht's Baron Cid ex Albrecht's Countess Abey)

BLITZ V. JAGERSLIEBE
Owner: R. M. Bancroft, Wisconsin
(Ch. Kurt v. Osthoff ex Frau v. Jagersliebe)

HOCHLANDER'S TITELHALTER
Owner: A. J. Hok, Illinois
(Field Ch. Mars v.d. Radbach ex Gretchenhof Tradewind)

CEDE MEIN DOLLY DER ORRIAN
Owner: Dean Tidrick, Iowa
(Dual Ch. Zipper Der Orrian ex Dual Ch. Erdenreich's Jetta Beckum)

BIG ISLAND SILVER DEUCE
Owner: Robert Smith, Minnesota
(Big Island Junker ex Big Island Lori)

HURCKES STEEL VICTOR
Owners: R. & L. Hurckes, Illinois
(Ch. Whitey v. Brunnthal ex Hurckes Gretel v. Becker)

BO DIDDLEY V. HOHEN TANN
Owner: T. Schwertfeger, Illinois
(Nat'l F.T. Ch. Shockley's Pride ex Field Ch. Susan v. Hohen Tann)

GERT'S DENA V. GREIF (Also Dual Ch. in Canada)
Owners: Ralph & Frances Park, Washington
(Field Ch. Gert. v.d. Radbach—imp. Ger.—ex Am/Can. Dual Ch. Gretchen v. Greif)

KAJOBAR V. STONY BROOK
Owners: H. & T. Strauss, New York
(Dual Ch. Robin Crest Chip, C.D.T. ex Jodie v. Hohenneuffen)

RADBACH'S DUSTCLOUD (Also a Dual Ch. in Canada)
(Dual & Can. Ch. Radbach's Arko ex Anka v. Niedersachsen—imp. Ger.)

German Shorthair Dual Champion One Hundred! Dual & Amtr. Field Ch. Albrecht's Tena Hy (Field Ch. Albrecht's Count Gustav ex Field Ch. Albrecht's Countess Tena). Owned by Myron W. and Lorraine E. Albrecht, Kansas.

Dual Ch. Streak's Herbst Versprechen, through his paternal grandsire, Field Ch. Skriver's Streak (imp. Denmark) and his maternal double-grandsire, the early-day, American-bred Dual, Valbo v. Schlesburg, inherits great bench, field, and water-retrieving talents. Owners: J. & S. Meredith, Ohio.

FEE V.D. WILDBURG
Owner: Richard S. Johns, Pennsylvania

GERT'S DURO V. GREIF (Also Dual Ch. in Canada)
Owners: Ralph & Frances Park, Washington

BRIARWOOD'S PEPPERMINT PATTY
Owner: Tom Cross, New Jersey

OXTON'S MINADO V. BRUNZ
Owners: K. & I. Clody, California

TIMBERLAND'S FRITZ
Owner: Mes. W. Davis, Washington

TIP TOP TIMBER
Owner: H. Brunke, Illinois

FREI V. KLARBRUK, U.D.T.
Owners: Joseph & Julia France, Maryland

TELSTAR DIRECT
Owner: Ralph Laramie, Michigan

RIDGELAND'S FRAULEIN
Owners: J. & B. Cuthbertson, Illinois

DEE TEE'S BARON V. GREIF
Owner: Dr. Stanley W. Haag, Iowa

DINO'S BARONESS MARTA
Owner: George Gates, Colorado

ROGER'S HANS
Owners: Roger & S. Claybaugh

T. K. EASTWINDS DANDY
Owner: Susan McHugh, New York

BIG ISLAND SASS-A-FRASS
Owner: Mary G. Finley

ALBRECHT'S TENA HY (also Amtr. F.T. Ch.)
Owners: M. & L. Albrecht, Kansas

(Dual/Nat'l F.T. Ch. Kay v.d. Wildburg—imp. Ger.—ex Field Ch. My Ritzie Fer Gitunburdz)

(Field Ch. Gert. v. Radbach—imp. Ger.—ex Am/Can. Dual Ch. Gretchen v. Greif)

(Field Ch. Fritz v. Smidt ex Sallie v. Hollabird)

(Dual Ch. Oxton's Bride's Brunz v. Greif ex Am/Can. Ch. Sorgeville's Happy Holiday)

(Am/Can. Ch. Lutz v.d. Radbach—imp. Ger.—ex Timberlane's Honey)

(Field Ch. Tip Top Timmy ex Ute Trail Wild Rose)

(Dual & Nat'l F.T. Ch. Kay v.d. Wildburg,—Ger. imp.—ex Ch. Gretchenhof Cinnabar CDX)

(Field Ch. Zerone Direct ex Trish v. Tess)

(Kettle's Fritz ex Chevron Dinah)

(Dual Ch. Oxton's Minado v. Brunz ex Dual Ch. Cede Mein Dolly Der Orrian)

(Dual Ch. Dino v. Albrecht ex Field Ch. Albrecht's Baroness Freya)

(Clarie Junker ex Nestle Bayrer's Alpha)

(Dual & Nat'l F.T. Ch. Kay v.d. Wildburg, ex Field Ch. Tina of Sleepy Hollow)

(Big Island Notchaway ex Big Island Chaska)

(Field Ch. Albrecht's Count Gustav ex Field Ch. Albrecht's Countess Tena)

(NOTE: The German Shorthair folk honor in this spot their Dual Champion One Hundred. *Albrecht's Tena Hy* was honored by this recognition by the Parent Club.)

DEE TEE'S BASHEN V. GREIF
Owner: Gary Short, Iowa

RICKI RADBACH V. GREIF
Owners: Ralph & Frances Park, Washington

WALDWINKEL'S PAINTED LADY
Owner: Helen B. Case, Arizona

FRITZ V. ZIGUENER (Also Can. Ch.) C.D.
Owner: John Marks, Ohio

(Dual Ch. Oxton's Minado v. Brunz ex Dual Ch. Cede Mein Dolly Der Orrian)

(Am/Can/ F.T. Ch. Lutz v.d. Radbach —Ger. imp—ex Lulubelle v. Greif

(Big Island Junker ex Waldwinkel's Gertrude's Joy)

(Ch. Fliegen Meister's Gunner ex Gretchen v.d. Ziguener)

EASTWINDS T. K. REBEL
Owner: Franz X. Benz, New York

FRITZ V. TREKKA RADBACH
Owner: Milton Donner, Wash.

(Dual & Nat'l F.T. Ch. Kay v.d. Wildburg ex Field Ch. Tina of Sleepy
Hollow)
(Am/Can. Ch. Lutz v.d. Radbach—Ger.
imp—ex Trekka La Mer)

DUAL CHAMPIONS FINISHING FIRST
AS FIELD CHAMPIONS

	Field	Show
VALBO V. SCHLESBERG	1949	1950
DANDY JIM V. FELDSTROM	1957 (Sept.)	1957 (Dec.)
RIGA V. HOHEN TANN	1954	1955
WENDENHEIM'S FRITZ	1954	1955
KAPOSIA'S FIREBIRD	1957 (April 7)	1957 (April 13)
GRETCHEN V. GREIF	1955	1958
OXTON'S BRIDE'S BRUNZ V. GREIF	1959 (March)	1959 (May)
LUCKY LADY V. WINTERHHAUCH	1958	1959
BARON TURN & TAXIS	1958	1960
GROUSEWALD'S BLITZ	1960	1961
SKID-DO'S BONNIE KARIN	1961	1962
BIFF BANGABIRD	1961	1963
BRUNNENHUGEL JARL	1962	1963
ALBRECHT'S BARON CID	1961	1963
ALBRECHT'S BARONESS CORA	1963 (Sept.)	1963 (Nov.)
MOESGAARD'S DANDY	1961	1964
KAY V.D. WILDBURG	1959	1964
BEE'S GABBY V. BECKUM	1963	1964
SATAN V. SCHNELLBERG	1964	1965
LUCY BALL	1965	1966
RADBACH'S ARKO	1964	1966
ERDENREICH'S JETTA BECKUM	1966 (March)	1966 (June)
ARRAK V. HEISTERHOLZ	1963	1966
RICHLU'S DAN ORANIEN	1965	1967
RAMBLING ROCK	1964	1967
BIG ISLAND SILVER DEUCE	1967	1968
BO DIDDLEY V. HOHEN TANN	1967	1968
OXTON'S MINADO V. BRUNZ	1967	1969
GERT'S DURO V. GREIF	1966	1969
RADBACH'S DUSTCLOUD	1968	1969
TIMBERLANE'S FRITZ	1969	1970
TIP TOP TIMBER	1969	1970
RIDGELAND'S FRAULINE	1969	1970
ROGER'S HANS	1970	1972
DEE TEE'S BARON V. GREIF	1971	1972
T. K. EASTWIND'S DANDY	1969	1972
RICKI RADBACH V. GREIF	1969	1972
BIG ISLAND SASS-A-FRASS	1971	1972
FRITZ V. TREKKA RADBACH	1969	1973

166

DUAL CHAMPIONS FINISHING FIRST
AS SHOW CHAMPIONS

	Show	Field
RUSTY V. SCHWARENBERG	1942	1947
SCHATZ V. SCHWARENBERG	1948	1949
BLICK V. GRABENBRUCH	1950	1951
SEARCHING WIND TOPPER	1950	1951
VALKYRIE V. GRABENBRUCH	1951	1952
BARON V. STRAUSS	1947	1953
BIG ISLAND SPOOK	1953 (May)	1953 (Oct.)
DOKTORGAARDEN'S CARO	1954 (June)	1954 (Oct.)
TRAILBORN MIKE, CDX	1955 (Aug.)	1955 (Sept.)
JUNKER V. GRABENBRUCH	1955 (May)	1955 (Oct.)
FRITZ OF SLEEPY HOLLOW	1955 (Sept.)	1955 (Dec.)
JONES HILL FREDERICK	1955	1957
PETER BRUNER	1957 (May)	1957 (Oct.)
CAPTAIN V. WINTERHAUCH	1953	1957
GRETCHEN V. SUTHERS	1957 (Feb.)	1957 (Nov.)
STRAUSS WORKING BOY	1957	1958
OXTON'S LEISELOTTE V. GREIF	1957	1958
AL-RU'S ERIC	1956	1958
HEIDIE V. MARVON	1955	1958
TIMBERLANE'S ACE	1957	1960
SAGER V. GARDSBURG	1957	1960
FLICK V. HEIDEBRINK	1960 (Jan.)	1960 (April)
ABLE V. ELTZ	1960 (June)	1960 (Sept.)
MADCHEN BRAUT V. GREIF	1960 (Sept.)	1960 (Dec.)
ROMMEL V. RUMPELSTILSCHEN	1960	1961
HANS V. ELDRIDGE, C.D.	1958	1961
BIG ISLAND RECS	1958	1961
ALFI V.D. KRONNENMUHLE	1956	1961
WOODY V. RONBERG	1961 (June)	1961 (Sept.)
MISS B'HAVEN V. WINTERHAUCH	1957	1961
DALLO V. HESSELBACH	1961 (Feb.)	1961 (Oct.)
SCHOENE BRAUT V. GREIF	1959	1961
FRITZ OF HICKORY FARM LANE	1960	1962
WAG AE'S SNOWFLAKE	1956	1962
GUSTAV MEIN LIEBCHEN	1959	1962
ESSO V. ENZSTRAND	1958	1962
MARMADUKE MEIN LIEBCHEN	1958	1962
BRUNNENHUGEL BALDER	1962	1963
ERDENREICH'S EARTHA	1963	1964
DINO V. ALBRECHT	1963	1964
STREAK'S HERBST VERSPRECHEN	1961	1964
ROBIN CREST CHIP, C.D.T.	1958	1965
BARON FRITZ V. HOHEN TANN	1962	1965
FIELDACRES KATIA	1960	1965
HEWLETT GIRL PEBBLES	1965 (Aug.)	1965 (Sept.)
ZIPPER DER ORRIAN	1964	1965
KAMIAK DESERT SAND	1964	1965
JANIE GREIF V. HEISTERHOLZ	1965	1966

167

	Show	*Field*
RITZIE	1965	1966
GRUENWEG'S DANDY DANDY	1964	1966
RICHLU'S TERROR	1964	1966
BLITZ V. JAGERSLIEBE	1963	1967
HOCHLANDER'S TITELHALTER	1967 (Aug. 4)	1967 (Aug. 16)
CEDE MEIN DOLLY DER ORRIAN	1965	1967
HURCKES STEEL VICTOR	1965	1968
GERT'S DENA V. GREIF	1967	1968
BRIARWOOD'S PEPPERMINT PATTY	1966	1969
KAJOBAR V. STONY BROOK		1969
FEE V.D. WILDBURG	1969 (July)	1969 (Aug.)
TELSTAR DIRECT	1965	1970
FREI V. KLARBRUK, U.D.T.	1966	1971
ALBRECHT'S BARONESS MARTA	1966	1971
ALBRECHT'S TENA HY (also Amtr. F.T. Ch.)	1966	1972
DEE TEE'S BASHEN V. GREIF	1971	1972
WALDWINKEL'S PAINTED LADY	1966	1972
FRITZ V.D. ZIGUENER, C.D.	1967	1972
EASTWINDS T. K. REBEL	1973 (July)	1973 (Oct.)

Dual Ch. Frei of Klarbruk, U.D.T. (Dual & Natl. Ch. Kay v.d. Wildburg ex Ch. Gretchenhof Cinnabar, C.D.X.) —GSP's first triple-titleholder, in that he has been successful in all three venues of competition: show, field and obedience. Owned by Joseph and Julia France, Maryland.

THE SHORTHAIR IN OBEDIENCE

Inherited qualities contribute to the excellent adaption of the Shorthair to Obedience work, in whatever form an owner is pleased to promote. Whether merely in terms of Yard Work for the hunting dog, or whether for the stylized requirements of formal competitive Obedience at licensed shows, this breed is genetically endowed to respond very well to demands made upon it.

The statistical tabulation of the last few years makes good reading. Many owners have turned to this form of competition in order to have *something to do* with their Shorthairs, lacking unluckily the provision of Working Trials such as so many of the other sporting breeds promote for the interest of owners whose dedication (or means) do not carry them all the way to licensed Field Trial competition.

Tabulations available at this present time cover officially a period as from 1964 to 1971, during which time 368 Shorthairs are reported gaining their CDs. 61 made CDX. 19 acquired a UD, and 14 made Tracking. First Shorthair, however, to possess itself of the honor of holding all titles within the gift of the American Kennel Club, was the Maryland owned, Dual Ch. Frei of Klarbruk, UDT, who clinched the last of his titles in 1971.

First to hold the UD title in this country was Van Donk's Kong, 1949, followed in that same year, at a few months' distance, by Lone Star v. Schlesweg. The Tracking Degree was first nailed down in 1965 by Marlee Chocolate Chip Megary. The first Field Trial champion to add the US after his name was Fieldacre Hans, 1965.

The Tracking pattern of the Shorthair is a denial of his hound inheritance in that he carries his head high, sampling airborne scent rather than the foot. One of the most spectacularly interesting exercises to watch in Field Trial competition in Germany is the free running tracks on fur and (separately) feather, in which the dogs follow a scent at the gallop with uncanny accuracy.

A useful asset to the Shorthair headed towards Obedience competition is the "commonsense" mentality of the breed—wherever its purity has been preserved—and the unvarying disposition to please.

Dual Ch. Oxton's Minado v. Brunz (Dual Ch. Oxton's Bride's Brunz v. Greif ex Am/Can. Ch. Sergeville's Happy Holiday. Owned by K. and I. Clody, Calif.—*Photo: Yuhl.*

Dual Ch. Cede Mein Dolly der Orrian (Dual Ch. Zipper der Orrian ex Dual Ch. Erdenreich's Jetta Beckum). The mating of Minado and Dolly has produced a raft of champions—already at time of this compilation, there are two Duals among their get. Minado's grandsire was "Old" Greif. Dolly's was the Greif son, Fld. Ch. Von Thalberg's Fritz II, and her granddam was the famous brood, Am/Can. Ch. Erdenreich Die Zweite, C.D. Owner, Dean Tidrick, Iowa.

Dual Ch. Dee Tee's Baschen v. Greif, a Minado son ex Dolly. Owner, Gary Short, Iowa.

11

Field Trials for German Shorthaired Pointers in America

WORKING towards his title of Field Trial Champion, a German Shorthair may run in the A.K.C.-licensed trials promoted for his breed alone, or in many of those promoted within the same official bracketing: Pointers, Setters, Weimeraners, W.H. Pointing Griffons, W.H. Pointers, Viszlas, Brittany Spaniels. Trials usually occupy a two-day weekend, with the A.K.C. National most recently expanded to three days in order to cope with the large entry.

Competition is also available under the rules of the American Field, though wins under these rules do not count for an A.K.C. Championship. However, this organization was the first to promote Field Trial competition for the German Shorthaired Pointer, and, interestingly, also first in the promotion of many events that now have become national classics, such as the first National Championship in 1952, the Regional Championships, and a Futurity. Under the sponsorship of this body, too, an annual National Retriever

Championship is promoted in which carefully drafted rules seek out the most the German Shorthaired Pointer has to give in this form of competition. In 1961, there was further inaugurated a National Amateur Championship for German Shorthaired Pointers. Between these National events and the many events separately staged by the 14 affiliated Member Clubs across the nation, the world of breed competition under American Field rules is wide indeed.

Rules governing the conduct of the A.K.C.-licensed Field Trials are clearly set out in the manual familiarly referred to as "The Orange Book" (*Registration and Field Trial Rules and Standard Procedures*), published and copyrighted by The American Kennel Club. It is to be considered a must for novices with Field Trial competition aspirations, and is to be secured on application from The American Kennel Club, 51 Madison Ave., New York, N.Y. 10010.

Field Trials are defined and classified in this Rule book as follows:

"*A MEMBER FIELD TRIAL* is a F.T. at which Championship points may be awarded, given by a club or association which is a member of The American Kennel Club.

"*A LICENSED FIELD TRIAL* is a F.T. at which Championship points may be awarded, given by a club or association which is not a member of The American Kennel Club, but which has been specifically licensed by The American Kennel Club to give the specific Field Trial designated by the license.

"*A SANCTIONED FIELD TRIAL* is an informal F.T. at which dogs may compete but not for Championship points, held by a club or association, whether or not a member of The American Kennel Club, by obtaining the sanction of The American Kennel Club."

Within this trio of Trials can be found a catering for every kind of competition, from the greenest novice to the most sophisticated champion status.

Competition is further arranged according to age and performance. Again quoting the Orange Book (material has been reprinted by permission of The American Kennel Club, 1971), the divisions are as follows:

"*OPEN PUPPY STAKE* for dogs six months and under fifteen months of age at the first advertised day of the trial.

"Puppies must show desire to hunt, boldness, and initiative in covering ground and in searching likely cover. They should indicate the presence of game if the opportunity is presented. Puppies should show reasonable obedience to their handlers' commands, but should not be given additional credit for pointing staunchly. Each dog shall be judged on its actual performance as indicating its future as a high class Derby Dog. . . .

". . . if the premium list states that blanks will be fired, every dog that makes game contact shall be fired over if the handler is within reasonable gun range. At least 15 minutes and not more than 30 minutes shall be allowed for each heat."

"*OPEN DERBY STAKE* for dogs six months of age and under two years of age on the first advertised day of the trial.

"Derbies must show a keen desire to hunt, be bold and independent, have a fast, yet attractive style of running, and demonstrate not only intelligence in seeking objectives but also the ability to find game. Derbies must point but no additional credit shall be given for steadiness to wing and shot. Should birds be flushed after a point by handler or dog within reasonable gun range from the handler, a shot must be fired. A lack of opportunity for firing over a Derby dog on point shall not constitute reason for nonplacement when it has had game contact in acceptable Derby manner. Derbies must show reasonable obedience to their handlers' commands. Each dog is to be judged on its actual performance as indicating its future promise. At least 20 minutes and not more than 30 minutes shall be allowed for each heat."

"*GUN DOG STAKE (OPEN OR AMATEUR)* for dogs six months of age and over on the first advertised day of the trial."

"*LIMITED GUN DOG STAKE (OPEN OR AMATEUR)* for dogs six months of age and over on the first advertised day of the trial which have won first place in an Open Derby Stake or which have placed first, second, third or fourth in a Gun Dog Stake. A field trial-giving Club may give an Amateur Limited Gun Dog Stake in which places that qualify a dog have been acquired in Amateur Stakes only."

The two Stakes above mentioned are bracketed in terms of required performance as follows:

"*GUN DOG AND LIMITED GUN DOG STAKES.* A Gun Dog must give a finished performance and be under its handler's control at all times. It must handle kindly, with a minimum of noise and hacking by the handler. A Gun Dog must show a keen desire to hunt, must have a bold and attractive style of running, and must demonstrate not only intelligence in quartering and in seeking objectives but also the ability to find game. The dog must hunt for its handler at all times at a range suitable for a handler on foot, and should show or check in front of its handler frequently. It must cover adequate ground but never range out of sight for a length of time that would detract from its usefulness as a practical hunting dog. The dog must locate game, must point staunchly, and must be steady to wing and shot. Intelligent use of the wind and terrain in locating game, accurate nose, and style and intensity on point are essential. At least 30 minutes shall be allowed for each heat."

"*ALL-AGE STAKE (OPEN OR AMATEUR)* for dogs six months of age and over on the first advertised day of the trial."

"*LIMITED ALL-AGE STAKE (OPEN OR AMATEUR)* for dogs six months of age and over on the first advertised day of the trial which have won first place in an Open Derby Stake or which have placed first, second, third or fourth in any All-Age Stake. A field trial giving club may give an Amateur Limited All-Age Stake in which places that qualify a dog have been acquired in Amateur Stakes only."

"*ALL-AGE AND LIMITED ALL-AGE STAKES.* An All-Age Dog must give a finished performance and must be under reasonable control of its handler. It must show a keen desire to hunt, must have a bold and attractive style of running, and must show independence in hunting. It must range well out in a forward moving pattern, seeking the most promising objectives, so as to locate any game on the course. Excessive line-casting and avoiding cover must be penalized. The dog must respond to handling but must demonstrate its independent judgment in hunting the course, and should not look to its handler for directions as to where to go. The dog must find game, must point staunchly, and must be steady to wing and shot. Intelligent use of the wind and terrain in locating game, accurate nose, and style and intensity on point, are essential. At least 30 minutes shall be allowed for each heat."

An *AMATEUR OWNER OR HANDLER* is defined in the Rule Book as "a person who, during the period of two years preceding the trial, has not accepted remuneration in any form for training or handling dogs in any form of dog activity, and who at no time in the past has for any period of two years or more operated as a professional trainer or handler of field trial dogs."

A German Shorthaired Pointer owner with ambition to make his dog a Field Champion, must compete within the framework of these A.K.C. rules. In addition, there are rules that govern entry. Entries will be received only in respect to purebred dogs registered or "listed" with The A.K.C. and must be in the name of the actual owner who must, further, be a person in good standing with The A.K.C. The dog must be free of communicable disease and not have been in contact with any dog suffering from such a disease. Bitches in season are not allowed on the ground. There are also strict rules relating to judging a dog that has been in any way under the care of the judge of any stake in which it runs.

Actual competition is conducted under rules long tested. Usually, the course is divided into two parts, a back course and a bird field. There has been, of late, increasing tendency to try out what is called a continuous course, with birds distributed throughout. Dogs run in bracings of two, chosen at drawings held a specified time before the date of the Trial. The only exception to this prior drawing is in the case of the Limited Stake. Drawings for this are usually made on the ground just before the Stake is run. The Limited, of course, is the Stake for the Stars, where the best work should be seen. Many hold this to be the only Stake in which to run the Champions, but no rule enforces this, so in practice most of the Champions also run in the Open, the Gundog, the Amateur, or in any Stake on the day the owner feels he has a hope to win. Pros and Cons: Running a champion in Open, etc. could perhaps hinder other dogs' chances of earning *their* points. The opposite view holds that an aspiring champion should be able to gain his title over finished champions if he is good enough. This argument will likely go on to the end of time unresolved.

Bracing (running the dogs in pairs) is for convenience, for saving time, and for allowing the judges to see the dog's manners towards a running mate. In A.K.C. competition, heats last most usually for half an hour—22 minutes in the back course (except when a continuous field is used), and eight in the bird field. Many Stakes are lost or won in the back course, where the judges penalize things done and things not done, a wide range from pottering to chasing fur.

Official gunners, appointed by the Trial-giving Club, shoot the birds flushed over the dogs' points.

For its Field Championship a dog must win a total of ten points in regular Stakes in at least three Licensed or Member Club Trials. The only short cut is to win the annual National Field Trial Championship, a route that is as steeply tough as it is short. Of the ten points necessary, three must have been won in one three-point or better Open All Age, Open Gundog, or Open Limited All-Age Stake. Puppy or Open Derby Stakes can count only two points, and Amateur Stakes to four. Points are based on the number of dogs competing, and are scheduled by the Board of Directors of The A.K.C. from time to time, according to the number of dogs usually competing in the various parts of the country.

Water Test: It is now mandatory for a Shorthair (and a Wirehair, or a Weimaraner) aspirant for title honors to be certified by two approved judges to have passed a Water Test at a licensed or member field trial held by a Specialty Club for one of these three breeds.

NATIONAL CHAMPIONSHIP FIELD TRIALS. Two such trials are sponsored annually, one under American Field, one under A.K.C. license. American Field was first to promote such competition, in 1952, when however no dog was held to have shown merit sufficient to be crowned National Champion.

National German Shorthaired Pointer Assn. Inc. Champions
(American Field)

Year	Dog	Owner
1952	No Champion Named.	
1953	Field Ch. DIXON'S SKID-DO	Russell Dixon, Michigan
1954	Field Ch. FRITZ V. STRAUSS	Carl Kemritz, Illinois
1955/6	Field Ch. DIXON'S SHEILA	Russell Dixon, Michigan
1957	Field Ch. KAY STARR	Frank Summers, Michigan
1958	Field Ch. DIXON'S SUSY Q	Howard Confer, Michigan
1959	Dual Ch. KAY V.D. WILDBURG (imp. Ger.)	Walter Kogurt, Canada
1960	Field Ch. BROWNIE'S GREIF MCCARTHY	Laurence McCarthy, California
1961	Field Ch. INMAN'S SWISS JAGER	H. & L. Inman, Michigan
1962	Field Ch. REX V. WAGGER	Luther Shockley, Illinois
1963	Dual Ch. BARON FRITZ V. HOHEN TANN	R. Bauspies, Illinois
1964	Field Ch. SUSAN V. HOHEN TANN	T. & M. Schwertfeger, Illinois
1965	Field Ch. DE LONG'S POINTING GABBY	Robert DeLong, Indiana
1966	Field Ch. BUCKSKIN	Claude Butler, Illinois
1967	Field Ch. FIELDACRES SIR JAC	Vincent Laramie, Michigan
1968	Dual Ch. TELSTAR DIRECT	Ralph Laramie, Michigan
1969	Field Ch. MOESGAARD'S VON SCHMIDT	William Moore, Ohio
1970	Dual Ch. LUCY BALL	Dr. L. Kline, Florida
1971	Field Ch. PATRICIA V. FRULORD	G. & E. Laird, Washington

Field & Nat'l Ch. Dixon's Sheila. Sheila had a record of three Nationals—two under American Field rules, and one under AKC (1958). Here she is shown with Field Ch. Lotte v. Heidelberg. Sheila is remembered with pride by her owner-breeder, Russell Dixon of Michigan.

Field Ch. Dixon's Sheila made history, but is not the only Shorthair to take both Nationals. The achievement is shared by 1961 Am. Field Nat'l Ch., Rex v. Wagger that, with a name change to Shockley's Pride was A.K.C. Nat'l winner in 1964. 1971 saw the double-barreled win subject to yet another record performance. Field Ch. Patricia v. Frulord (Dual Ch. Gert's Duro v. Greif ex Juliana v. Frulord whose two grandparents were Old Greif and son Yunga) took both titles the same year. Six-and-a half years old! It is the pride of a good Shorthair to carry years lightly.

Other Dixon-bred dogs to be successful in this National event include Field Chs. Dixon's Skid-Do, Dixon's Susy-Q and Kay Starr.

Nationally known early on, Russell Dixon came into hunting from the time his father used to stand him on a stump to shoot after quail. He still carries in his mind the measure of a good hunting dog as his father defined it: "Short-coupled, with big heads and mouths to retrieve, none of those small heads with long noses that can't pick up a pheasant, and none that run nose to ground, slow-gaited, and have no class on point. If a dog went over the same ground twice, my Dad got rid of it—fast! The first Field Trial ever I saw, the men took out their dogs and bet who could find the most covey. Boy! Hot times and good fights!

"The first German Shorthaired Pointer I saw working on pheasant I liked, so I went and bought one. Did I get stuck! Inbred, not a brain in its head! I shipped it to my Dad to train for me while I was in the service. In a month he wrote—this dog has killed two hogs and some turkeys. So, I was out 25 bucks and you can guess what happened to the dog. So, I went shopping again, and this time it was Dixon's Belle, later Champion. Bold she was, and full of fire, with the head I wanted, and the body. My father trained her on quail, and she made up to the best all-round dog I ever owned. The average Shorthair doesn't make a good quail dog, too slow, you do more walking than the dog. But Belle was good. A good brood too. Dixon's Starlite, Sheila's dam, is out of Belle. And if I'm sure of anything, I'm sure it's you've got to have good bitches. Old Starlite was mated to 7 different studs during her long producing life. Every litter got top hunting dogs and several became famous."

Russell Dixon's breeding is conducted minus theory, and with no respect for titles, only for the performance of a dog in front of his own eyes. "To breed my bitches, I have to see a dog run in the Field," he says. "I've seen Field Champions I wouldn't give a dime for."

Gauging his successes, Russell Dixon's method may have much to recommend it, but it is certainly not for those lacking his ability to assess the working worth of a dog—also lacking, perhaps, the Dixon luck. From Belle and Starlight also stem such as Field Ch. Dixon's Skid-Do, in his own turn a useful stud, his get including Field Ch. Caudle's Leader, Field & National Ch. Dixon's Susy-Q, Field & National Ch. Kay Starr, and Field Chs. Dixon's Sinbad the Sailor and Dixon's Sheiloh Star and Sheiloh Sky (ex the great

Sheila), and proudly, Dual Ch. Skid-Do's Bonnie Karen.

Yet, of course, the Dixon dogs are not the whole story of American Field National history. Other fine-performed dogs have won the honor. The winner in 1954 and runner-up in 1958 was a very meritorious dog in Field & National Ch. Fritz v. Strauss, owned by Carl Kemritz, of Illinois. The 1959 Champion, runner-up in 1961, was Field & National Ch. Kay v.d. Wildburg, a German import owned by Walter Kogurt, of Canada, at the time of his win, and now American-owned by Joseph Eusepi, of New York, and Richard Johns, of Pennsylvania. The 1960 champion introduces the pride of West Coast bloodlines in the Field Ch. Greif v. Hundsheimerkogel son, Field & National Ch. Brownie's Greif McCarthy, owned by Laurence McCarthy, of Burbank, California, and sired when his amazing forbear was batting on for his twelfth year. In 1961, competition swung again in favor of the mid-West, when Michigan's Field & National Ch. Inman's Swiss Jager, owned by Helen and LaVern Inman, of Muskegon, headed Kay v.d. Wildburg in exciting competition.

To qualify for entry to this National Championship Stake, it is necessary for a dog to have won a first place in a Derby or better in any recognized American Field Trial. Major differences exist between the conditions of this Stake and the conditions imposed in respect to the A.K.C.-licensed National. In the qualifying heats of the First Series, which are of an hour's duration, the dogs are shot over with a blank pistol. In the Second Series, dogs called back at the judges' discretion face a Shoot-to-Kill and must make an acceptable retrieve. The Rule also makes plain that the winner is to be a finished dog charged with no errors, one that displays all the characteristics of class, including style, pace, drive, bird sense, and obedience. "However," the Rule continues, "a brilliantly performing dog charged with some error or breach of manners may be named Champion over other contestants with no mistakes but not showing outstanding bird-finding ability." (From: "Rules—Ninth Annual Running, National German Shorthaired Pointer Championship, 1961." Pub. The National German Shorthaired Pointer Assn., Inc.)

Many keen American Field supporters feel that anything less than an *hour* on *wild game* is no test fit to name a Champion, and view the shorter running of the A.K.C. National as an inconclusive

179

test of a first class Pointing dog. However, the A.K.C. National has also found many quality dogs to hold the title, though the success of Dual Champions in the first two years was not continued into our present time. Location is in a different State each year, coast to coast, and the host club in whose area the Stake is being run takes care of the promotional work for that year. This roster of sites is doubtless the reason for the wider geographical location of winners of this event as compared to the American Field National, with its permanent home in Ohio.

Just as the Dixon strain dominated early American Field Nationals, so onward from his 1957 A.K.C. National, Bobo Grabenbruch Beckum dominated that Stake, first through his son, 1961 winner, Field & Nat'l Ch. Von Saalfield's Kash, and subsequently through his daughters, Field Chs. Mitzi and Patsy Grabenbruch Beckum. In matings with Field Ch. Von Thalberg's Fritz II, these provided winners of 1965–67–68 Nationals, and several placings as well.

National German Shorthaired Pointer Field Champions (A.K.C.)

Year	Dog	Owner
1953	Dual Ch. DANDY JIM V. FELDSTROM	Dr. Clark Lemley, Michigan
1954	Dual Ch. WENDENHEIM'S FRITZ	Frank Nuzzo, Illinois
1955	Field Ch. GUNMASTER'S JENTA	James M. Howard, Ohio
1956	Field Ch. TRAUDE V.D. WENGENSTADT	Oliver Rousseau, California
1957	Field Ch. BOBO GRABENBRUCH BECKUM	Dr. W. Schimmel, California
1958	Field Ch. DIXON'S SHEILA	Russell Dixon, Michigan
1959	Field Ch. OLOFF V.D. SCHLEPPENBURG (imp.)	Roy J. Thompson, Illinois
1960	Field Ch. DUKE V. STRAUSS III	Steve Molnar, Wisconsin
1961	Field Ch. VON SAALFIELD'S KASH	Walter Seagraves, California
1962	Field Ch. MOESGAARD'S DANDY	Dr. L. L. Kline, Florida
1963	Field Ch. MOESGAARD'S ANGEL	D. Prager, California
1964	Field Ch. SHOCKLEY'S PRIDE (previously Fld. Ch. Rex v. Wagger)	L. Shockley, Illinois
1965	Field Ch. ONNA V. BESS	R. G. Froelich, California
1966	Field Ch. FIELDACRES BANANZA	H. & J. Dowler, Pennsylvania
1967	Field Ch. RIP TRAF VON BESS	M. Bess, California
1968	Field Ch. THALBERG'S SEAGRAVES CHAYNE	D. Miner, California
1969	Field Ch. BLICK V. SHINBACK	Cal. Rossi, Jr., California
1970	No Champion Named	
1971	Field Ch. PATRICIA V. FRULORD	Gladys & Fred Laird, Washington
1972	Field T. Ch. WYATT'S GIP V. SHINBACK	W. Palmer
1973	NFC & Fld. Ch. PATRICIA V. FRULORD	Gladys & Fred Laird
1974	Field Ch. CEDE MEIN GEORGIE GIRL	R. A. Flynn & W. P. Troutman

180

Fd. & Nat'l. Ch. Shockley's Pride won Am. Field National, 1962 and AKC National, 1964. His distinguished career began very late. Owner: Luther Shockley, Illinois.

Dual Ch. Kay v.d. Wildburg (imp. Germany), added the Nat'l Ch. title to his record under the handling and part-ownership of Richard Johns, Pennsylvania.

GSHP AKC National Field Trial Championship, 1968—1st, Nat'l Field Trial Ch. Thalberg's Seagraves Chayne; 2nd, Dual Ch. Richlu's Dan Oranian; 3rd, Dual Ch. Bo Diddley v. Hohen Tann; 4th, Dual Ch. Tip Top Timber. The placing of three Dual Champions in National Field Trial competition constitutes a record to that time, deserving the flattery of imitation.

The National Associations also do valuable work in the promotion of *Futurities* calculated to encourage the breeding of first-class litters. Entry requires the enrollment of a dam within 30 days of breeding, and the recording of her litter at whelping. Fees are payable at her enrollment, the recording of the litter, the entry to the Futurity Stake, and at Starting. This money is divided percentage-wise between the breeder and the owner of the winning dog after the expenses of conducting the Stake have been deducted. As only dogs nominated via this procedure are eligible to compete, the advantage of enrolling a dam, and the advantage of buying a youngster eligible to compete, are plain.

The new rule of the Orange Book requires an aspirant to a Field Trial title to pass a modest Water Test. It represents first move towards recognizing inbred utility inheritance. Many owners resented the new rule, being satisfied with the status quo, and perhaps distrustful of training skills to foster other than merely a running dog. Some owners may have been anxious as to the hindering effects of possible Pointer cross behind stock that did not resemble Shorthair type. There were threatened defections to American Field competition—a pettish threat to Pick Up Marbles and Go! Yet, of course, American Field has long sponsored a Water Retrieving Championship for Shorthairs, this requiring far more of a dog than merely the bringing of a bird from the water on his own initiative (*Orange Book. p. 36*)

"The Water Test shall be judged by two of the judges of the Field Trial. The dog shall retrieve a live or dead game bird from water after a swim of about 20 yards to the bird. The handler shall stand 6 feet from the water, and the dog must demonstrate its willingness to enter the water, to swim, and to retrieve, at the direction of its handler without being touched or intimidated. Style shall not be considered. The dogs shall not be placed but shall either pass or fail. The judge shall certify on the judging sheets provided the particulars of each dog that passed the test."

Dissenters are reminded that if the easily-satisfied Saturday/Sunday casual/field trialler finds no use for water skill, practical hunting men do. The more important aspect is that inherited skills be preserved by breeders. If Water Testing helps screen away dogs of suspect cross-breeding and no taste for cold water—Good! If a proportion of owners find pleasure in so working their dogs, that too is

Good! They might even seek other venues of competition, such as the increase of opportunity represented by the N.G.S.P.A. Retriever Championships, held in the mid-West, with Open All-Age stake open to all Utility Breeds, Poodles included, and also the National Retriever Championship for Shorthairs only. Requirements are stiffer than for the qualifying A.K.C. Water Test, including retrieve through decoys, and handling from behind blinds, etc.

An organization making steady way in the sporting dog scene, attracting owners with interest to do more with their versatile Shorthairs than has been usual in the past is the North American Versatile Hunting Dog Association, NAVHDA, dedicated to active promotion of all hunting skills. Trials are much to European pattern, water and land. Such an organization caters for the increasing number of owners bored with the pattern of stylized field trial competition, and promises the possibility of winning more and more adherents as the modern population explosion shrinks the acreage available to running dogs. NAVHDA sets no greatest value on the horizon runners, and one would not expect to find in reports of this body's competitive occasions such wordage as "So-and-So ran a great race," or "Such-and-such was out-raced by his bracemate."

As a newer generation of dog owners takes over, demanding possibly much more in terms of sport, per se, from their stock, there could possibly come (even if belatedly, being LONG overdue) a catering by the Parent Club responsible for Shorthair interest some form of Working Certificate promotion to the same pattern as the Weimaraners, and several other sporting breeds, currently promote. Such promotion, already it appears being discussed within the breed, could be paralleled also by Fun and Picnic Trials such as bring together in sporting amity the adherents of other breed interests within the Sporting Group. Undoubtedly, the promotion of such enjoyable occasions will be hindered by the objections of the reactionary side of competitive interest, but may it not be that the reactionary in sport *also* comes under the blanketing of that chill reminder given by the young of this world: "More of them die every week and more of us are born!" Those who arbitrarily and ignorantly harnessed the Utility Sporting breeds into the narrow shafts of the Bird Dog vehicle, and closed the gate in the face of those who would have fostered the utility skills, are not going to live forever, and such as Shorthair Dual Champion One Hundred is the guarantee for owners and breeders of a future time that the instincts bred into the European Utility Breeds as from a century past are still safely stored within the genetic inheritance.

Field Trial Judging: The best Field Trial judging—like the best Show judging—is based on the recognition of virtues rather than on the mere penalizing of faults, though, of course, mistakes have to be evaluated when summing up the performance of a dog. This country as yet provides no equivalent of the German performance sheet which the judges mark, duty by duty, as the dog dispatches it. These sheets become part of the dog's record, and are often passed over with his papers when he is sold.

In this country, local practices vary. Thus, in some areas judges do make their marking slips available at a place where the owners can collect them after the trials. This is the opposite pole from another recognized procedure, in which the judge fends off dissatisfied owners with a brusque: "That's the way I saw 'em, and that's the way I placed 'em." As a matter of strict fact, there is no official obligation imposed upon a judge to discuss his placings if he does not wish to do so. Incompetents sometimes take refuge under such protection. The philosophy is expressed by the judge who said he knew he placed the dogs right, but if he started giving out reasons, his reasons could possibly be all wrong! So far as the owners are concerned, gracious acceptance of decisions marks not only the good sportsman, but the wise one. He saves his breath to cool his porridge, knowing that there will be another day, another judge, another chance.

Field Trial judges are not subject to licensing by The A.K.C., as Show judges are. It is necessary only that they have their names submitted beforehand by the Trial-giving club for official approval, and that they be persons in good standing with The A.K.C. It is their privilege to run their own dogs in any Stake they are not judging on the same day, with the exceptions to this provided for in Special Rules applying to certain breeds.

A famous handler, who also does his share of judging, recently summarized the responsibilities of a Field Trial judge for the author: "He will forget his friends and his enemies, and any considerations of breeding. He will look for style and class, the way a dog runs the back course. He won't admire a pottering dog, nor one that continually checks back to its handler. He will let handlers make their own pace, ride back of them, never come between the handler and the dog. He will take account of the way a dog searches for game, and also consider the time of day, well knowing that the first and last braces are often in better luck than those running, say, between 11 A.M. and 3 P.M., and make allowance for it. He must remember the Shorthair is a pointing breed, required at all times to be lofty and penalized when not. A judge forgetting that Field Trials are run to improve the breed is not doing his job. It should never be club policy to let two inexperienced judges be braced together. Nor does holding an official position in a club constitute a sufficient reason to consider a person a competent Field Trial judge."

The well-understood requirement in other countries that the dogs should drop, bears hard at times on adult trained dogs imported here from other countries, especially from Germany. Experience seems to vary from dog to dog. Some adapt easily; some never do. The observations of famed trainer Richard S. Johns, of Pennsylvania, who has been associated with many good imported dogs, are valuable in this connection.

"I have imported a good number from Germany and one from France, and experienced difficulty with only one," he advises. "While in Germany, I purchased Nanny v. Lüchseck as a fully trained dog and shot over her for a year. Nanny was trained to stand up on feathered game, but would drop on a hare. Sepp (K.S. Sepp v. Grabenbruch) did not drop to wing and presented no problem, but a bitch I imported from Germany as a trained dog could not be got over dropping to wing and shot. I had no difficulty with the language difference, and all of my imports quickly learned commands in English. However, I no longer import trained dogs from Europe, only pups, and it is my feeling that the majority of people too would be far better off with puppies or early Derby age dogs from Europe. Present National Ch. Kay v.d. Wildburg, imported at Derby age, was not taught to drop in Germany, is very lofty on point, to shot and kill. The Germans, of course, put no pressure on their Derby age dogs, seeking to this age only the proof of inherited working qualities and desirable conformation."

Some owners and trainers have waged terrific, unpublicized battles to re-train adult German dogs to the American style. Stern pressure exerted has too often failed of its aim, resulting only in the complete ruin of the bewildered dog, undergoing heavy punishment for what he was originally taught was the right thing for him to do. The unedifying sight of a once-competent dog false-pointing all

185

over, and going down as soon as he hits scent of any kind, could be as good a text as any for a sermon on the advantages of importing dogs before they have been taught what they do not need to know in this country.

The Germans have always allowed young dogs the privilege of being young, and even some chasing is allowed a Derby there, provided he doesn't turn it into that little bit that is just **TOO** much. Many of the best American trainers are also of the opinion that all work and no play makes as dull a dog as it makes a boy. If a dog is having fun he'll show it in his eager intensity of style and movement. If he is merely discharging a duty because his ribs will hurt from correction if he doesn't, well. . . .

Bob Holcomb, West Coast trainer, has a useful observation to make: "You cannot force a dog to go find and point a bird *if he does not want to!*" On the opposite side of the country, Joe Murdock, who has trained many great ones, likes to tell his clients who are taking home their promising youngsters he has worked lightly to Derby status: "Go have fun with him for a season or two. Then, when he's grown up, bring him back, all he'll need then will be steadying."

All regular Field Trialers have seen the wreckage imposed on promising youngsters by pressure too early applied. From such are recruited the "mechanicals," the "blinkers," the "false-pointers," and all that go in plain fear of punishment—than which no less edifying sight exists—the sad roster of those from whom Too Much was expected Too Soon.

Style: By temperament and by anatomical construction, the truebred German Shorthaired Pointer is of less spectacular working habit than his cousin, the Pointer. He makes, preferably, a cautious approach to his bird rather than a dramatic slam, another characteristic that often involves some grief here now for trainer and for dog. Then, too, there is the proved truth that the working habit of a shrewd German Shorthaired Pointer is influenced by the kind of game on which he is customarily worked. Old Itchy-foot, the pheasant, can develop a foot-scent trailing habit in the local dogs, enough to drive all the trainers crazy, the dog working the bird as his instinct directs. Where the varieties of game tend to stay stolidly put, the dog works more steadily, with a higher stance. Good judges need to know these things as well as the trainers do.

186

All such hereditary and environmental factors influence style. Most present-day compilers, seeking to define style, take refuge in the definition published in the Gaines Booklet, *Standards of Judicial Practice:*

"*Style:* Loftiness is a desirable characteristic of a dog on point, but intensity is the more desirable characteristic of the pointing dog, and is far more important than the position of head and tail.... Joy in hunting is a most desirable characteristic and should always be looked for. This is sometimes indicated by merriness, sometimes by other physical attributes of a dog in motion, but it is always unmistakeable. Nor should there be any distinction in the desirability of Style in groundwork or on point between Derby, All-Age, or Championship contenders. . . ."

Joy in hunting! There's your true style! Which takes us back to Bob Holcomb's belief. If the dog is having his fun, it's any odds you can name that he is also showing those "desirable physical attributes of a dog in motion." If he is not having fun, it matters little how he has been schooled, or what brand of electronic collar is on his neck, or how the trainer insists he shall carry his head and his tail.

All the truly great dogs of the breed, their records gleaming brightly in the tables of performance, have been great stylists. It is also true that many useful ones, whose performances never carried them to the giddy heights of National fame, have also had such an eye-catching joy in working as to fix them in the memory of those who have seen them. Such dogs are immediately recognized at a Trial, and their years of competition are often very long, extended into their old age because of the joy they take in running and the joy their owners take in just watching them. Such a dog will be noted by the critics long after its best years are behind it, and whether it makes a win or not. Field Ch. Scott's Pride could serve as an example, his prime long passed but his joy still keeping him out there; or such a one as Field Ch. Zitt v. Sellweide, the big import, owned and now mourned by Col. Keeth, of Virginia. Zitt had his good days and his bad days, but ran always with what an onlooker who enjoyed him describes as "that indefinable ingredient known as color. Like Babe Ruth, who looked as good striking out as when hitting a home run, Old Zitt sometimes looked his best when he was cutting his throat. There was something about the way he covered the ground, slammed into a point—and even something about the way he would occasionally bust a bird and go with it to the next county. . . ."

The world of German Shorthaired Field Trial competition knows many such dogs, counts 'em by the dozen. And no matter *what* that proverb has to say about The Woman, The Dog, and the Walnut Tree (The More You Beat 'Em, The Better They Be!), style is one ingredient (and there are others!) that cannot be beaten into a dog. Style, like the Good Woman of Price Above Rubies, is where you find it. Like gold, too ... First, it has to be *there*—which means good breeding. Then it must be *brought out,* and the best bringing-out power of all is that fueled by Joy-in-Work.

Dual Ch. Fritz of Sleepy Hollow, distinguished East Coast performer in both spheres, also successful sire. Owner: Fred Z. Palmer, New York.

12

Physical Constitution
of the German
Shorthaired Pointer

THE vigorous constitution of the German Shorthaired Pointer, the gift of long life, the tremendous powers of
recuperation, are as much a breed pride as any other attribute already discussed. The many veterans of great performances already
mentioned in these pages are certainly not freaks. Many a grand
old sporting companion lives out a long life in sheltered obscurity
at home. Some gain mention later, such as Ch. Kraut v. Schwarenberg, who won the breed specialty in Minnesota in 1947, when he
was already eight years old, and was reported still hale and hearty
in his home kennel in Nebraska in 1954. Ch. Sportsman's Dream,
first B.I.S. winner in 1940, was B.O.B. at the Intermountain K.C.
show in 1947. Imported K.S. Franco Beckum, an American champion, wh. 1947, was still competing in Field Trials, National at that,
in 1955. Old Field Ch. Butcher v. Schlossgarten ran that year, too,
wh. 1946. Count along with him Butcher's daughter, Frita v.

Schlossgarten, also that year a competitor in the National, just 18 months after she had survived five terrible days held in a trap during a Nebraskan winter freeze. She did her National running minus half a right rear foot, a left foot so mutilated that only the single back pad was usable, a right foot lacking the forepart and several toenails! Sandy's Fritz, first winner of the Water Retrieving Stake when this event was still being promoted by the German Shorthaired Pointer Club of America, Inc., served his owner, John K. Weichmann, seven years straight on Blue Bills in Northern Wisconsin during late Novembers. In ice, or in heavy waves, Fritz worked as well as he did in North Dakota on pheasants. This dog's owner would be surprised to be told that German Shorthaired Pointers are not suited to water work—as surprised as any German breeder would be, hearing the same tale!

The story to end all stories of breed endurance is reported in a 1955 issue of *German Shorthaired Pointer News*. Vicki, owned by J. Krause, of Elizaville, New York, was taken on a fishing trip to Alaska. In a sudden squall, she was washed overboard. Forced to let the boat run on, it was two and a half hours later that her owner returned, quartering 45 miles of open water in hopes of finding her body. He found her still swimming in waters where a man's life expectancy is counted at about ten minutes, and she survived to go home again to Elizaville.

Those who suffer brainwashing, especially from possibly over-enthusiastic bird dog types, with respect to the presumed inability of the German Shorthaired Pointer to cope with cold and wet, should give attention to a sampling of published reports of conditions under which many German Shorthaired Pointer field trials have been held:

COLD: "High winds made freezing weather seem even colder . . . judges in fur-trimmed coat when the Puppy Stake started at 7:25 A.M. . . ."

"Drifted snow from a blizzard made the uneven stubblefield difficult. . . ."

"Several Shorthairs went through the ice, but steadily broke more ice ahead to reach the fallen birds . . ."

"The Spring Trial was held in the worst weather for 40 years, game area covered with 24 inches of snow, the mercury 6 below . . ."

RAIN: "Swollen streams, flooded fields, water deep in the bird field, pheasants too wet to fly . . ."

The back issues of the magazines report such conditions, month after month, year after year. There is also the other side. . . .

HEAT: "On one of the hottest weekends of many a year, the judges said the heat made good dogs show no poor performance, but it did show up poor dogs the sooner . . ."

But, of course, there is always Spring, even at the Field Trials, where the dogs are expected to run, be the weather what it may. So, there are also the reports of "Warm sun, spring peepers, warbling mocking birds, delightful weather . . ."

"Sumac clumps, multiflora roses, lespadezia fields . . ."

"Four thousand acres of beautiful rolling Georgia land, weather perfect, crisp in morning and late afternoon, balmy during the day, breeze blowing, cover good, birds very good, heavy, top flyers . . . what more could you want?"

What more, indeed! Good or bad weather, your stout-conditioned German Shorthaired Pointer will take it as it comes, and if you take care of him (or her) you can savor the joy of a wise old one for long, long years.

Dual Ch. Biff Bangabird, top-notch, all-round utility hunting dog. Owner: Dr. Charles Gandal, New York.

13

Showing Your German Shorthaired Pointer

A SHOW Dog is essentially a production to delight the eye, a presentation, as is a piece of theatre. While it must be of good basic quality, it must also be well raised, well fed, sufficiently exercised, carefully groomed, handled to its best advantage. Nothing is more sure than that the Show Dog, like the Field Trial Dog, is *produced* rather than merely born to triumphs. The stars in the heavens are not more numerous than good prospective show dogs that have been ruined by poor management.

The belief is held among the owners of long-haired breeds especially that the owners of smooth-haired breeds have no show problems; that all a smooth-hair needs to be ready to show is a bath. Actually, the show smooth-hair presents more acute problems than the long. He has no "bib" to screen such faults as a wide front, loose shoulders, paddling gait; no "bracelets" to mask slack pasterns; no breach "feather" to keep the secret of poor hind movement. If he has faults, the judge can see them. Of course, if he has many virtues those are equally clear and on parade.

The claim that smooth-hairs "don't go out of coat" is just plain nonsense. They have the same seasonal ups and downs. Bitches go through the same cycles as do longhairs, their coats go out and their coats come in as their hormones dictate. Early in your show experience you should learn to recognize the "out-of-coat" condition in your German Shorthaired Pointer, male or female. This isn't merely a matter of a few loose hairs on the living-room rugs. The entire jacketing of an "out-of-coat" dog becomes harsh and dry to the feel. All-liver, or liver-patched, coloring bleaches out as a rusty, spilt-iodine shading.

What sometimes escapes the novice is that when the coat is "out" the dog's body tone, flesh and muscle, and also its spirit are influenced as well. When the coat comes back, the flesh firms, the muscles harden, the dog is gayer. Renewal is usually from for'ard to aft—the head, neck, shoulders, will be sleek with new hair while the loins and quarters are still harsh and dryly covered with jacketing thin enough to let the daylight through. The important truth to cling to is that this condition will pass.

The bitch usually suffers much more noticeably than the dog. Smooth-hair or long, she will likely start her shedding about fourteen weeks after the onset of season, the time corresponding to that of pregnancy and lactation—whether she has been bred or not. If expensively doctored, she will get a new coat in due course. If not expensively doctored she will also get a new coat in due course—and as soon. No doubt, some veterinarians have gained reputation and bought Cadillacs on the strength of this predictable cycle. Susy comes to the office, out of condition, shedding, maybe scratching the irritation of loosening hair. The doctor prescribes this and that. In a few weeks, Susy's flesh is firm, her spirits lift, her coat comes new and shiny. Wonderful doctor—wonderful treatment! The point is, she'd have her coat new and shiny if she'd never gone to the office, and dabbings of camomile or some such soothing application had taken care of the local irritation. The best treatment of all is to get rid of the old hair as quickly as possible, either by brush or by hand massage. (There are, of course, pathological conditions quite different from the mere cyclical shedding, and these need professional attention!)

This cycle is well understood by the experienced. They learned the hard way, learned to watch for the spearing of the new coat as it makes, and to keep away messy potions, to work with nature.

193

They learned, too—also the hard way—that taking Susy to shows in her "down" period was merely wasting entry money to win points for someone else. One of England's most respected dog authorities, Vernon Hirst, has wrapped up a lifetime of experience in his direction: "If your dog is out of coat, there is nothing you can do but wait till it grows again."

The glow of a top-conditioned German Shorthaired Pointer's coat is not merely a matter of spraying on hair-oil. It is best produced by the combined factors of top condition (cyclical), good keeping in terms of food, housing, exercise, and the work of your own two hands. Following regular daily brushing, nothing puts on such a finish as hand massage. Your dog will love the attention, look forward to it, relax under it, and the actual work can even do something for your own waistline as well. One way is to stand behind the dog, bend forward, stroke rapidly and rhythmically with both hands down from the occiput, along his neck, back, flanks. Five minutes is plenty, which is usually all your wind will stand, anyway. A wipe over with a slightly-dampened rag before beginning the massage brings up even a brighter glow. This procedure does wonders for any smooth-haired breed.

Even with such regular daily conditioning, you will want to wash your dog before the Big Day. The best way is to do it a couple of days early, to allow natural oils time to seep back into the coat. *Where* you bathe him depends, of course, on facilities available. If you have no prejudice, the family bath tub will do. The tiled walls and floor make mopping up so much easier. One argument against the family bath tub is the crick that locks your spine after you've been bending down at the job—especially if more than one dog has to be washed. The old-style, waist-high laundry tubs were great—but who has them any more? (Large kennels, as a rule, have such a back-saving installation.) Automatic washing-machines are not recommended. This compiler has a recollection of helping get seven English Setters ready for a country show in Australia. All were dunked successively into the family's backyard washboiler, a big copper container over a slow coal fire that kept the water comfortably tepid. Which brings us back to where we came in—you use what comes handiest.

Any shampoo good enough for you is usually good enough for your dog. He will need very thorough rinsing to be sure all the

Ch. Sportsman's Dream (Astor v. Fischtal, imp. Germany, ex Sieglinde v. Meih-sen), was the first German Shorthaired Pointer to win BIS—in 1940 at Silver Bay K.C., San Diego, California. Judge: the late E. E. Ferguson. Handler: Ben Brown. Owner: V. E. Lantow, Colorado.

soap film is out of his coat. Plug his ears with cotton wool before starting, but don't forget to take it out later and swab the ear canals. A grubby inner-ear won't look well. Watch the soap around his eyes, he doesn't like the sting, either.

Thorough drying is important. Never leave your dog damp, day or night. An electric hair-dryer does the job fastest, but a rough towelling and a final hand-drying often does it better, allowing the coat to lie flat and sleek. Trial and test and your own inclination have to provide the answer here. It takes more energy to hand-dry a dog than to hold a dryer over him—more time, too.

You will trim his whiskers, of course, and if any minor fringing fuzzes his outline you could snip that away as well.

If you have taken care of his teeth there should be no tartar. If there is it needs to be scaled away. His toenails should have been having regular care too, not left till a few hours—or a few minutes!—before he goes into the ring. When they have been cut, be sure to file the sharp edges. Now and again, he enjoys a little scratch, and it is tough on him to be carrying razor-blades at the ends of his toes. Those unfiled toenails can give you a nasty cut too if you happen to bump against them. To leave them to the last minute, then have them guillotined by some hasty operator—you or anyone else—can bring a sound dog into the ring limping. That, of course, may then involve you in the embarrassment of a veterinary examination, called for by the judge. When the toenails have been filed, a dab of oil smoothed over gives them a nice shiny finish. Such a dab can go on a dry nose too—especially if photographs are to be posed.

Select a lead for efficiency rather than for showiness. The less conspicuous a show lead, the better it becomes your dog. A metal choke collar looks glamorous but seldom gives the result achieved by a soft leather show lead handled by someone who knows how to use it—which is loosely. However, your dog can only go prettily on the loose lead if he has been trained to gait. The world of dog shows is full of people who take pride in telling everyone that "this is the first time he was ever on a lead!" One notes, by and large, that such dogs do not figure high in the winning lists. As numerous are the people who talk about a good performing dog being, *of course*, just "a natural shower." To hear these "experts," one would think that the great show stars went unschooled from their whelp-

Ch. Alnor's Brown Mike. Derivation from original Thornton imports of the 1930's backs his and his sons' prepotency. Owners: Mr. & Mrs. A. Stranz.

Ch. Kaposia's Waupun II (BIS). Owner, Mrs. Helen Case, Arizona.

ing boxes. That some dogs have better show temperament than others is quite true, but when the art of the handler is added to such a dog's inclination to show himself, the most important partnership is achieved—and the result brings applause from the watching gallery, and the all-important nod from the judge.

At the ring entrance, you can rub him over to get rid of any last stray specks of dust. Use a soft cloth in a stroking motion. This employment will do marvels for your nerves as well as his. He will come to associate such a pleasant stroking with waiting around the entrance to the ring, and be all ready for what you want him to do. If you watch a good handler, you'll see that he isn't just wasting his time, *just standing there*. He is waiting for the right moment to make his entry. There is no reason why you shouldn't try to do the same. If you have a big-striding, prettily-moving dog that can make a prima-donna's entrance into the ring, hold it back till the judge is looking. Don't waste all that motion on a judge who has his back turned, jotting down the numbers of the last class winners. If some eager beaver jostles to get ahead of you, let him go. But find some way to delay your own entrance a second or two, long enough to let him get ahead so you won't have your good-striding dog falling over his dog's heels. There are ways and ways—you have to work out these things for yourself, play it along by ear. But at one of these shows, stay back to watch the groups, even if your own dog isn't eligible. See how the show-wise competitors time their entrances wherever and whenever they can. They don't blunder after some other dog as a small page-boy after the bride moving up the aisle of the village church. They make sure they get *their* share of everyone's attention—including the judge's. Sometimes you'll hear such tactics criticized by the acid gallerites whose dogs didn't make the group. You can play it much smarter—don't fight the good handlers, join them!

You'll hear it said that the professional handlers know all the tricks, and use them. Granted. If they didn't they wouldn't have much of an income. But the professional can be challenged in the ring by the amateur with a good dog—PROVIDED THE AMATEUR HAS TAKEN THE TIME AND THE TROUBLE TO SCHOOL HIMSELF TO THE PROFESSIONAL'S STANDARD OF GROOMING AND PRESENTATION. Handling showdogs in the ring is not a gift that good fairies give to babies in their cradles.

It is a skill that must be learned—like playing the piano or speaking French. That's what the professional handler had to do—learn.

Your best investment on your way to matching yourself with the professionals could be a big old mirror, maybe one you'll find in a junk shop. Prop it against the wall outside the house and set up your dog in front of it. Looking across his back you will see him reflected exactly as the judge sees him in the showring. You can check up on how he looks, and how you are presenting him. You should be able to see his faults and his good points, and then it's up to you to figure out how, in partnership with him, you can minimize the one and enhance the other. Practice till you are a team, you and your dog. Again, it needs to be only a matter of a few minutes a day.

In setting up a dog it is usually easier to get his front lined up if you lift him up off his front legs, one hand under his jaw, the other under his chest. Watch that his legs are in a naturally straight position, then let him drop down with them so. In this way you can avoid that awkwardly conspicuous "placing" of front legs that most amateurs (and surprisingly many professionals) seem to do. Such "fiddling" with a dog's front is undesirable for two reasons; first, the dog's natural reaction is to pull back his leg from the position in which you are trying to set it, and he can do it because his weight isn't on it while you are moving it; Second, if he has a faulty front, the more you fiddle with it, the more likely you are to draw the judge's attention to it.

A useful trick is to press slightly forward and down on a dog's withers—at the top of his shoulder blades. It tends to "set" him in an attractive, forward-leaning pose. Another trick is to give a slight tap near the base of the tail (not a haymaker, the gallery will think you are walloping him!) to a dog that tenses behind. The tap will relax him sufficiently to let his rear-end muscles slacken, to the benefit of his outline and his rear-end angulation. Tensing of the hindquarters makes many a well-angulated dog look straight as a stick behind, and props his rump in the air quite often as well. This is a tendency your mirror-mirror-on-the-wall-outside should be able to show you, and how your tap on his tailbutt relaxes it.

Of course, you know that one about never getting between the judge and the dog. If you want to get a line on this exercise, stroll over to the junior handling rings and watch. Those kids really

199

work at not getting between the judge and the dog. Some of them revolve like moths around a street lamp. You needn't expend quite so much energy as that, but the general principle is one to observe.

In gaiting, obey the judge's direction. If he asks you to go THERE, and return from THERE, try and do what he asks. He has his reasons. The gaiting of big sporting dogs in tiny indoor rings is usually something of a farce anyway. No big dog can get into his true stride in three-steps-this-way-and-turn, three-steps-that-way-and-turn, and back to the judge. Just do the best you can. *You* know, if the judge doesn't, how your dog can move if only someone would give him a chance and a few extra yards of space. The only chance a big show dog ever has to show his gait is in the Groups, so concentrate on getting your good-mover into that select assembly as quickly as you can.

The important factor in gaiting a dog in a show ring is to move with a rhythm that he can match. If you waddle flat-footed like a duck, or like any one of that group of arthritic old gentlemen who once shared a showring with me and my best-moving English Pointer, to our sad hindrance, hire yourself a handler. A show dog positively cannot move correctly, let alone showily, with a bumble-footed handler. Gaiting is also something you can practice with advantage a few minutes every day. Learn your dog's best speed, and practice those turns at the end of the line. Then your dog knows what you want him to do, and is prepared to make his turns with you.

And one last factor of successful showmanship. In front of that mirror-mirror-on-the-wall, practice how to smile—smile if it kills you! Smile nicely when you win, and ten times more nicely when you lose. As we said at the beginning of this chapter, showing a dog is a presentation, like a piece of theatre. And in the theatre everyone learns to smile, no matter what.

There are, of course, the necessary preliminaries to entering a dog for show. The best way to catch on to these is to give your name to the local show superintendent. Then you will receive premium lists of forthcoming shows, plus entry blanks. The blanks are self-explanatory—you fill in the dog's name, sex, breed, sire and dam, breeder, date of birth, registered number, the class in which you are entering it. Then you sign to the effect that you will not ex-hibit a dog that has had any infectious disease, or has been in contact with any such. You include your check for the entry fee, and that's all there's to it. Some time later, before the show, you will receive tickets and advice as to judging times, etc., from the show superintendent, and your obligation, of course, is to have your dog there at the time specified. In a benched show he will have to stay all day—in some few shows, even two days. In unbenched shows he need be there only in time for his judging, and you can leave as soon as he is no longer in competition; that is, when he has been beaten either in his breed or, later, if he is a breed winner, when he is beaten in his group. If he's a group winner, of course, he stays on for Best In Show competition.

Show equipment can be as elaborate—or as plain—as you care to make it. A crate for your dog is always a good investment. A leash is a necessity, as are brushes and a drinking bowl. For benched shows you will need a bench chain. From there on you can follow your own inclinations. Most dog shops and pet dealers have their shelves and showcases crammed with the most exciting additional wares, and you'll have all the fun in the world browsing and buying.

If possible, get your dog to move his bowels before you leave home. If time does not permit, or if he just won't oblige, consider a suppository—baby-size will usually do the trick. Or, if the show day is to be long, and the road is long to reach the showground, so there's a gap of hours between the time you leave home and the time he goes into the ring, take the suppository with you. Anything, *anything* to avoid having him attend to his function in the ring. It unsettles you, it unsettles him, if he "goes," and if he doesn't "go" when he wants to because his gentlemanly (or her maidenly) instinct tells him it's neither the time nor the place, the restraint will show in his gait. He'll have his mind on other things rather than on the free-striding you know he can command when he's feeling comfortable.

It is also necessary for a dog to have the opportunity to empty its bladder before going to the ring. The desperate dog using its handler's trouser leg as a hydrant is no ring rarity, nor is the bitch that squats to void a pool wide enough to float the Queen Mary. Such performance always draws acid criticism from the gallery, based on speculation as to how long the "poor thing" had been cooped up in its crate without a chance to "go." Professional handlers' dogs seldom offend in this way, it being fairly well understood

201

Ch. Weidenbach Aric Teufel Skerl (Ch. Weidenbach Kamiak Snow Shoe ex Weidenbach Bo Calypso). Owned by S. K. and Barbara Topliss, Calif. *Photo: Bennett Associates.*

Ch. Weidenbach Bridget, type-true, magnificently moving, winning three Specialties, BOS at two more including the 1971 GSHP National, plus 8 BOBs,—and all without any promotion at all, which may count among her items of pride. A great one! Pictured in win under the author, 1973. Owners: N. and M. Revell, California. *Photo: Henry Schley.*

that such exhibition has a tendency to rebound against the good name of the handler concerned. However, professional or amateur, a real headache is represented by the bitch (invariably it *is* a bitch!) that refuses to "go" away from home or on the lead. Such a one is often overtaken by sheer necessity at the most awkwardly conspicuous time. The *miles* we have walked with some like that—the operettas we have whistled all the way through—the cajolings, the prayers, the—Oh, what's the use! She just *won't GO!* To encourage your show bitch, then, to attend to her functions while *on the lead* any time and anywhere you take her to a suitable place for this, is a very important part of her show training. In campaigning her there will be many occasions when it will be impossible to let her run off-lead for the purpose—busy highway areas, or the environs of a city show, for example.

Now you are in there pitchin'. Take in there with you a tidbit to make your dog feel happy—just as the handlers do. Otherwise, what has a dog to feel happy about in a showring? This is standard practice the world over—except in Australia, where they have funny rules on the subject: no tidbits, a dog has to "show naturally." "Naturally" includes being strung out like a lizard, topped and tailed, and having his head set just *so,* often with heavy traction on his lip. But no tidbits or out of the ring you go! Well, you aren't showing your German Shorthaired Pointer in Australia. Anything you can find to make him happy in the ring, slivers of dried liver, cheese, a squeaky mouse, A.K.C. regards with a benign and kindly tolerance. Try, if you can, to take also with you a feeling of confidence in yourself and your dog. That's worth a bushel of tidbits to you both. And keep your ears closed to the "well-wishers" who tell you you can't win with a German Shorthaired Pointer in the showring unless he's oversized and almost white. The list is simply *crammed* with the names of hundreds upon hundreds of German Shorthaired Pointer champions that are neither big *nor* almost white. They include all the colors there are. Every one of them had sufficient nods from sufficient judges to make the grade, dark-ticked ones, liver ones, even the white-and-liver pointer-patterned ones. Whether a dog goes up or down usually depends on factors other than color. In most cases, ascribing the success of a good show dog to its color is merely overlooking all the *other* qualities it brought into the ring. Very often these "other qualities" have in-

cluded superb presentation in terms of conditioning and handling—
and this, for sure, is right where YOU come into the picture with
YOUR dog.

BEST IN SHOW-WINNING GERMAN SHORTHAIRED POINTERS

Ch. Sportsman's Dream
Owner: V. E. Lantow, Colorado
(Astor v. Fischtal, imp.,
ex Sieglinde v. Meihsen)

Ch. Flash v. Windhausen
Owners: C. and S. Nussbaum, Utah
(Ch. Rex v. Windhausen
ex. Lady Waldwinkel

Ch. Sir Michael of Hanson Manor
Owner: L. W. Linville, Colorado
(Ch. Sportsman's Dream
ex Bugle Ann Waldwinkel)

Ch. Pheasant Lane's Storm Cloud
Owner: Mrs. J. W. Gordon, New York
(Ch. Pheasant Lane's Stormalong
ex Ch. Pheasant Lane's Deborah)

Ch. Columbia River Lightning
Owner: L. V. McGilbrey, Washington
(*MULTIPLE B.I.S.*)
(Ch. Pheasant Lane's Stormalong
ex Columbia River Tillie)

Ch. Columbia River Cochise
Owner: B. K. Maxson, Wash.
Washington (*MULTIPLE B.I.S.*)
(Ch. Pheasant Lane's Stormalong
ex Columbia River Tillie)

Dual Ch. Captain v. Winterhauch
Owner: Millard W. Axelrod, Minnesota
(Ch. Oak Crest Rick v. Winterhauch
ex Duchess of Hotwagner)

Ch. Cora v. Winterhauch
(bitch)
Owner: John R. Hutchins, Texas
(Ch. Oak Crest Rick v. Winterhauch
ex Duchess of Hotwagner)

Ch. Gunmaster's Ricki
Owner: Ricaviling Kennels, Ohio
(Dual Ch. Doktorgaarden's Caro
ex Gunmaster's Super Speed)

Ch. Columbia River Ranger
Owners: E. D. and Mrs. Andrews, Ohio
(Ch. Columbia River Lightning
ex Helga v. Krawford)

Ch. Columbia River Jeepers
Owner: L. H. Barnett, Texas
(*MULTIPLE B.I.S.*)
(Ch. Columbia River Lightning
ex Helga v. Krawford)

Ch. Columbia River Vagabond
Owner: L. V. McGilbrey, Washington
(Ch. Columbia River Lightning
ex Ch. Columbia River Princess)

Ch. Buck v. Gardsburg
Owner: D. D. Williams, California
(*MULTIPLE B.I.S.*)
(Ch. Red Velvet
ex Zukie v. Gardsburg)

Ch. Erdenreich's Beau v. Gardsburg
Owner: Mrs. J. Greer, California
(Ch. Buck v. Gardsburg
ex Can/Am. Ch. Erdenreich die Zweite)

Ch. Ricefield's Jon
Owner: Miss Camilla Lyman, Mass.
(Ch. Beaver of Hollabird
ex Ch. Ricefield's Brown Bomber)

Dual Ch. Hans v. Eldredge
Owner: R. S. Eldredge, Wisconsin
(Ch. Baron Strauss II
ex Strauss's Pamela)

Ch. Huntsman's Drumfire
Owners: P. F. and M. Winger, Colorado
(Field Ch. Dan-d Leyba
ex Rocky's Reign)

Ch. Ludwig v. Osthoff
Owners: C. and F. Weckerle, Wisconsin
(*MULTIPLE B.I.S.*)
(Gunar v. Alf
ex Ch. Ermgard v. Osthoff)

Ch. Strauss's Happy Go Lucky (BIS). Owned by Serakraut Kennels, Wisconsin.
—*Photo: Twomey.*

Dual Ch. Hans v. Eldridge holds an all-breed BIS. The honor, shared currently only with Dual Ch. Captain v. Winterhauch, is very rare in any breed. Owner: R. Eldridge, Wisconsin.

Ch. ROBIN CREST CHIP, C.D.T.
Owners: Robert Crest Kennels, N.Y.
Ch. GRETCHENHOF MOONSHINE
Owners: Gretchenhof Kennels, Calif.
　　　(MULTIPLE B.I.S.)
Ch. COLUMBIA RIVER THUNDERCLOUD
　(Mex.)
Owners: Gretchenhof Kennels, Calif.
NOTE: This B.I.S. was won in Mexico.

RICHLU'S BECKY ORANIAN (bitch)
Owner: W. V. Rawlins, Georgia

Ch. GRETCHENHOF WHITE FROST
Owner: John Hutchins, Texas
Ch. GUNHILL'S MESA MAVERICK
Owner: P. C. Tuttle, Va.
Ch. IRE JA'S STARLITE GUNBEARER
Owner: Irene Stapp, Ohio
Ch. STRAUSS'S HAPPY GO LUCKY
Owner: Serakraut Kennels, Wisc.
AM/CAN. Ch. CEDE MEIN SIR GANDY
　DANCER
Owner: Cede Shorthairs (Reg.), Wash.
Ch. WEIDENBACH ARIC TEUFEL SKERL
Owners: S. K. & B. Topliss, Calif.
Ch. KAPOSIA'S WAUPUN II
Owner: Helen Case, Ariz.
Ch. KAPOSIA'S OCONTO
Owners: Kaposia Kennels, Minn.
Ch. OTTO V. OSTHOFF
Owner: Charles Weckerle, Wisc.
Ch. GRETCHENHOF MOONSONG
Owners: Gretchenhof Kennels, Calif.

Ch. NESSETHAL'S BROWN MIKE
Owners: Mrs. Rose Ann Scukly, New
　York
Ch. BENWICK KRONNENMUHLE BECKUM
Owner:
AM/CAN. Ch. CEDE MEIN CHAT NUGA
　CHU CHU
Owners: C. D. Lawrence, Mill, and
　Davidson, Wash.
Ch. GRETCHENHOF COLUMBIA RIVER
Owner: Dr. R. Smith, Calif.
Ch. ROCKY RUN'S STONY
Owner: R. L. Arnold

(Ch. Alnor's Brown Mike
ex Ch. Montreal Belle)
(Ch. Columbia River Thundercloud
ex Ch. Columbia River Jill)

(Ch. Columbia River Lightning
ex Ch. Columbia River Princess)

(Ch. Richlu's Jeffson
ex Ch. Richlu's Jan Oranian-Nassau)
(Ch. Columbia River Thundercloud
ex Ch. Columbia River Jill)
(Ch. Tasso Fran Hallam
ex Manchaps Alaska)
(Ch. Fliegen Meister's Gunne1
ex Ira Ja's Starlite Kippy Karen)
(Strauss's Viktor
ex Strauss's Teora)
(Am/Can. Ch. Columbia River Moon-
　watcher
ex Zeugencarl's Duchess v. Aho)
(Ch. Weidenbach Kamiak Snoe Shoe
ex Weidenbach Bo Calypso)
(Ch. Kaposia's Otsego
ex Ch. Kaposia's Blue Chinook)
(Ch. Kaposia's War Lance
ex Ch. Kaposia's Star Dancer)
(Ch. Ludwig v. Osthoff
ex Baroness v. Freckles)
(Dual & Nat'l Ch. Baron Fritz v.
　Hohen Tann
ex Ch. Gretchenhof Blue Moon)
(Baba Lin's Ima Fancy Flash
ex Elaine's Ginny)

(Baron Kronnenmuhle Beckum
ex Lucas McCaine's Sue)
(Ch. Cede Brass Badge
ex Ch. Cede Mein Gadabout, C.D.)

(Ch. Gretchenhof Moonfrost
ex Columbia River Della)
(Ch. Adam v. Fuehrerheim
ex Ch. Rocky Run's Poldi)

14

The Standard

As approved for the purebred dog breeds recognized by The A.K.C., Standards blue-print the ideal—the physical, and often the mental, characteristics that distinguish one breed from the other. The breeder should aim to produce dogs as close to this ideal as possible. The judge is obligated to accept its direction, a knowledge of the Standard being, of course, a prerequisite to gaining a license.

To support such an aim, such an obligation, there must be Rule. Briefly, and to quote: "When the banks are removed, the stream becomes a swamp." (Mary Gilmore, D.B.E.) In any activity, the alternative to Rule is chaos. In dogs, specifically, it is degeneration.

The present Standard for the German Shorthaired Pointer was compiled by the Parent Club (The German Shorthaired Pointer Club of America, Inc.) and approved by the Directors of the American Kennel Club in 1975. Though there has been considerable agitation over many years for overhaul, the actual work was belatedly undertaken only in the later 1960s, when some clarifying language was grafted to the original, imposing no drastic changes but attempting a clearance of obscurities, defining aims and, where possibly

K.S. Blitz v. Ovila, DK 3855, wh. 1957, Austrian Sieger for 1961. Accomplished in show and field. Owner: Dr. Julius Duy, Vienna.

some adverse trends were recognizable, in drawing up remedial requirements to help the judges. The better compiled of modern breed Standards, incorporating the scientific findings in respect to dog movement, specifically those of the late McDowell Lyon (*The Dog In Action*), have prompted also an interest to define Shorthair Gait, merely skimmed over in the original compilation of 1946.

Whenever a modern-day revision is undertaken, there is necessarily a good deal of work involved. Inevitably, there must in such cases be clashes of interest; especially as most regional groups tend to put most emphasis on the problem recognized as most acute within their own territory. That, of course, means compromise—as all Committee work necessarily must mean compromise. Yet, however involved may have been the processes by which these various Standards were modernized, wherever the work was attended to, high aims seem to have been favored. Best brains are hopefully enlisted and basic attention paid to the breed's reason for existing.

Lebensraum problem coming up!

THE BREED STANDARD OF THE
GERMAN SHORTHAIRED POINTER
(As approved by the Board of Directors of the American
Kennel Club, to be effective January, 1976.)

*The Shorthair is a versatile hunter, an all-purpose gun dog capable
of high performance in field and water. The judgment of Shorthairs in the show ring should reflect this basic characteristic.*

GENERAL APPEARANCE: (A.K.C. Standard)
*The overall picture which is created in the observer's eye is that of
an aristocratic, well-balanced, symmetrical animal with confirmation
indicating power, endurance and agility and a look of intelligence
and animation. The dog is neither unduly small nor conspicuously
large. It gives the impression of medium size, but is like the proper
hunter, "with a short back, but standing over plenty of ground."*

*Tall leggy dogs, or dogs which are ponderous or unbalanced be-
cause of excess substance should be definitely rejected. The first impression is that of a keenness which denotes full enthusiasm for work
without indication of nervous or flighty character. Movements are
alertly coordinated without waste motion. Grace of outline, clean-
cut head, sloping shoulders, deep chest, powerful back, strong
quarters, good bone composition, adequate muscle, well-carried
tail and taut coat, all combine to produce a look of nobility and
an indication of anatomical structure essential to correct gait which
must indicate a heritage of purposefully conducted breeding. Doggy
bitches and bitchy dogs are to be faulted. A judge must excuse
a dog from the ring if it displays extreme shyness or viciousness
toward its handler or the judge. Aggressiveness or belligerence toward another dog is not to be considered viciousness.*

SYMMETRY: (A.K.C. Standard)
*Symmetry and field quality are most essential. A dog in hard and
lean field condition is not to be penalized. However, overly fat or
poorly muscled dogs are to be penalized. A dog well-balanced in all
points is preferable to one with outstanding good qualities and
defects.*

210

AUTHOR'S COMMENT: If the novice in the breed up and asks that "unduly small" and "conspicuously large" be rather more exactly defined, he deserves at least a hearing. If he mentions the requirement that the dog should "give the impression of medium size," he is probably within his rights when he asks: "Medium size, as compared, say, with what?" And in a day when the automobile rules the road, not everyone that reads a dog Standard really gathers the import of the long-familiar, older-day comparison with the "proper hunter, with a short back, standing over a lot of ground." It's dollars to doughnuts that many who read that for the first time picture the "hunter" with two legs, not four, and wonder what exact gymnastic exercise the guy is actually up to, by golly! As for the opening sentence of the second paragraph, think how much wordage could be saved by just setting down that fat dogs are out—period. Cold-blooded analysis can find more excess wordage, but for now, let it go.

We are all on much firmer ground when reviewing the demand for "an aristocratic, well-balanced, symmetrical animal with conformation indicating power, endurance, agility . . ." The best minds within the breed, from the great German experts, such as Dr. Paul Kleeman, to the most knowledgeable of our own judges, have always applied such a measure to the German Shorthaired Pointers that come within their sight. They ask for a dog that looks right because it is built right to move right. Mere flashiness may catch the judges who don't know—"mug-catchers," we call dogs of such a flashy description where I hail from—but it never catches the ones who do know. The ones who know look for elegance in all-over appearance, the sloping shoulders that shape the short back, the long upper arms that facilitate movement, the rib cage that makes place for heart and lungs, the clean legs that provide the movement, and the sound, thick, arch-toed feet that carry the load. They look for the kind, wise eyes of a temperamentally sound dog, and the tail that emphasizes what the eyes have said. These indicators, fore and aft, are the proof of "intelligence and animation."

Dr. Kleeman has pointed out that the rules of structural engineering are also the rules of nature. To work right, a dog must be built right. To be built right, it has first to be born right. Mighty simple, if one comes to think of it. . . .

GOOD HEADS
"A" AND "B"

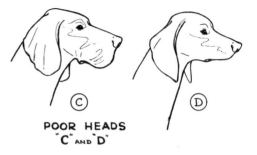

POOR HEADS
"C" AND "D"

"B"

"C" HAS A COARSE EAR, TOO MUCH CHOP AND A FLEWY LIP.

"D" HAS EARS THAT ARE TOO LONG AND POINTED, A POINTED SNIPY MUZZLE, IS TOO ROUNDED IN SKULL AND HAS A POOR EYE SET.

BOTH LACK BALANCE, ARE SHORT IN MUZZLE, HAVE TOO MUCH STOP.

GOOD FOOT

HEAD: (A.K.C. Standard)

Clean-cut, neither too light nor too heavy, in proper proportion to the body. Skull is reasonably broad, arched on side and slightly round on top. Scissura (median line between the eyes at the forehead) not too deep, occipital bone not as conspicuous as in the case of the Pointer. The foreface rises gradually from nose to forehead. The rise is more strongly pronounced in the dog than in the bitch as befitting his sex. The chops fall away from the somewhat projecting nose. Lips are full and deep, never flewy. The chops do not fall over too much, but form a proper fold in the angle. The jaw is powerful and the muscles well developed. The line to the forehead rises gradually and never has a definite stop as that of the Pointer, but rather a stop-effect when viewed from the side, due to the position of the eyebrows. The muzzle is sufficiently long to enable the dog to seize properly and to facilitate his carrying game a long time. A pointed muzzle is not desirable. The entire head never gives the impression of tapering to a point. The depth is in the right proportion to the length, both in the muzzle and in the skull proper. The length of the muzzle should equal the length of skull. A pointed muzzle is a fault. A dish-faced muzzle is a fault. A definite Pointer stop is a serious fault. Too many wrinkles in forehead is a fault.

AUTHOR'S COMMENT: In the practical sense, as is to be observed, the variation of head type within the German Shorthaired Pointer breed is extremely wide, not only in American-bred dogs, but also in the dogs imported from overseas. There appears here to be a variation from the widest of "Pointer" skulls to the finest of "Setter"—to quote the extreme opposites. Between, one finds every possible variation on those themes, adding up to the reasonable belief that head type in the breed is not as yet exactly fixed, and that each line-bred strain tends to favor a head type of its own. Actually, most heads seem to sit suitably on the front ends of the dogs that own them, so that the vagueness of the opening sentence of the Standard, as it applies to this part of the dog, reasonably caters to them all. "Neither too light nor too heavy, in proper proportion to the body" . . . "skull should be reasonably broad," leaves much to the discretion of a judge. How little is "too light"? How much is "too heavy"? What is "reasonable breadth"? In the listing of the faults, further along, heads are held less desirable if they are "too large, with too many wrinkles in forehead, dish-faced, snipy muzzle." But how *many* wrinkles are too many? How large *is* too large? Certainly, such wordage presents some good arguments for the compilation of dog breed Standards in a pictorial medium rather than in words.

With the head the seat of character and intelligence, inevitably it can make or mar a dog. It is the first thing looked at, by the buyer in the yard, the trainer at the kennels, the judge in the show ring. If the head displeases in that first going-over, the rest of the dog may even be dismissed without any great amount of further consideration—it happens. The bitterest wrangling of the pioneer German breeders was in respect to the head the developing utility breed should have. The first direction to prevail was for a head described as "Grecian" in profile, as near as could be a straight line, nose to occiput. In the view of many strong supporters of this type of head, it was considered to favor trailing-keeping (which meant hound) abilities, as distinct from the dished profile of the high-scenting Pointer. Many of the best of the early-day dogs, pillars of the breed such as Wodan Hektor II v. Lemgo, and Tell aus der Wolfsschlucht, had definitely Roman-nosed heads. The tendency to a "bump" on the bridge has come down the generations with a persistency that not even the disapproval of the original Standard here has been able wholly to thwart. One still sees many a German Shorthaired Pointer with the same bumpy profile as, say, K.S. Michel v.d. Goldenen Mark had in his prepotent day. Such inheritances are not lightly scotched.

Over the years intervening since such dogs as Tell and K.S. Michel, there came to be emphasis on the signs of working qualities, such as a skull really broad enough to contain brains and the ole-factory (scenting) nerves; a lower jaw long, deep and strong enough to bite to kill when necessary, as well as to bear heavy weights over long-distance carries. It is just such a head that the present-day Standard seems to define, the good honest head of a useful working dog. However, the wording could possibly be made clearer for the novices. One useful way would be to delete references of comparison with the Pointer. The modern American field trial Pointer is not the familiar sight in Shorthair competition that he was when the first breed Standard was compiled in 1946. Many novice Shorthair owners may never actually have seen a true Pointer-type head, though modern resurgence in show competition has brought many classic examples to the fore. But the average Pointer seen at Field Trials may have a head in which any resemblance to classic breed type is purely coincidental. For these reasons, the comparison as worded provides little help in making the definition clear to German Shorthaired Pointer novices.

EARS: (A.K.C. Standard)

Ears are broad and set fairly high, lie flat and never hang away from the head. Placement is just above the eye level. The ears, when laid in front without being pulled, meet the lip angle. In the case of heavier dogs, the ears are correspondingly longer. Ears too long or fleshy are to be faulted.

AUTHOR'S COMMENT: Now, *there's* some dog Standard writing at its very best. Every word means exactly what it says, and no confusing comparisons dragged in—nor any comparisons needed.

The Germans, perhaps still influenced by the preoccupation of the pioneer breeders with ear shape, spell the requirements right out—ears shall be neither too thick nor too fine, and lower ends shall be blunted and round. Well, the A.K.C. Standard takes care of that description as well, bracketing it in the fault column, spelling out exactly what German Shorthaired Pointer ears shall *not* be.

Closer to home, a writer in the A.K.C. *Gazette* has truthfully described the ear as "the one part of the dog that cannot tell a lie." In many animals, as a matter of fact, the ears are the barometers of emotion. Who doubts the message conveyed by the flattened ears of the horse, or those of the family tomcat? Similarly, the dog can convey his feelings by the movement even of such pendant lugs as grace the heads of the sporting dogs as a group.

Ears in this breed, as in all smooth-coated, pendant-eared breeds, are cruelly vulnerable. Flaps suffer in cover, get chewed in fights, are prey to flies. Absence of feather helps the entrance of grass seeds, foreign bodies. Blows can produce painful, bulging hematomas, and allergic reactions do the strangest things. I am reminded of a fine young bitch greeting me one morning with her ears swollen literally inches thick through, and heavy as lead—a condition (oedema) that vanished as rapidly and as mysteriously as it came, within a few hours.

215

Looking over the ears of the German Shorthaired Pointer breed, one may discover them to be as varied in type as heads—ears long, ears short, sometimes even folded. However, the Standard directions are excellently plain, so no confusion should be experienced by breeder or by judge as to how those ears *should* be.

EYES: (A.K.C. Standard)

The eyes are of medium size, full of intelligence and expressive, good humored and yet radiating energy, neither protruding nor sunken. The eye is almond shaped, not circular. The eyelids close well. The best color is dark brown. Light yellow (Bird of Prey) eyes are not desirable and are a fault. Closely set eyes are to be faulted. China or wall eyes are to be disqualified.

AUTHOR'S COMMENT: The Germans are more detailed in their definition of German Shorthaired Pointer eyes. They ask for as little as possible—none at all they hold better—of the conjunctiva tumica showing, not wanting the haw of the hound. They reject a deepset eye, and define a "bird of prey" eye as light yellow. No doubt, a German breeder could not visualize, even in nightmare, a "china" or "wall" eye coming up. There does not seem to be, in the purebred German Shorthaired Pointer, any source from which such an eye could legitimately be derived. Breeds permitted such an eye—such as harlequin Great Danes, say, or the varied breeds of merle or "dappled" color—just don't seem to have come into allowable genetical contact with the dog from Germany—in its purebred representation, at any rate.

Otherwise, in Germany as here, breeders have their troubles keeping to a desirable dark eye. In the Summer, 1961, issue of *Kurzhaar Blätter,* the German breed magazine, a judge's critique of the *Sonderausstellung* (Specialist Show) of the *Südwestdeutscher Klub Kurzhaar,* in June, 1961, is spotted through with two complaints: loose elbows and light eyes. Both faults meet the judges here, too. However, many new imports from Germany to the United States *are* bringing in nice dark eyes.

In the breed monograph, *Deutsch Kurzhaar,* on pages six and seven, the famed German expert, E. v. Otto, makes an interesting observation concerning problems of eye color. He points out that in the early days the brown coat color, with or without white, was held to be the only genuine color for a Kurzhaar (judges who penalize solid livers please note!), and a too-close adherence to this belief resulted in a loss of pigmentation and the prevalence of ugly, light, staring eyes. As a counter-measure, experimental breeding was undertaken, using black pointers from England, notably Killian v. Kanatsche, bred by Wm. Arkwright, and the bitch, Beechgrove Bess. These founded strains of black-brindled (or dark gray) dogs, that for a time were given a seperate registration in Germany as "Prussian Shorthairs." From these there was gained an improvement in eye color throughout the breed generally, and they no longer have a separate registration.

American breeders with stubborn problems of light eyes in their strains can take no hope from this experimentation of fifty years ago. First, where would they find their black pointers? Well, Scandinavia has some still but in any case, prevailing American registration rules would not sanction such cross-breeding, and the Standard, as we shall presently see, lists any black pigmentation as a fault. Those fortunate enough to gain dark eyes through some of the newer German imports here should perhaps budget to take good care of them, for they are so easily lost in all breeds!

One other thing is necessary to know about eyes: what particular *shade* of light eyes does a puppy have? In English Pointers, for example, the greenish-yellow eye of a pup will remain undesirably light for the lifetime of the dog. The honey-yellow eye, on the other hand, continues to darken as the dog matures, so that at two years of age, the light-eyed pup will have a nice hazel eye. It is an observable process, the pigment darkening inward from the iris rim to the pupil. Breeder-trainer Bob Holcomb was told in Germany that a well-bred, dark-colored German Shorthaired Pointer pup does not get his true eye color till two years. The same rule, then, would seem to apply in this breed as in Pointers. German breeders also hold that the lighter colored a well-bred German Shorthaired Pointer's jacket is, the darker should be those well-pools of his spirit, his eyes.

This German teaching holds well with what prevailed in the old-time requirement for English Pointers here. Long-time breeders will recall the one-time requirement of the Standard in America that an orange-and-white Pointer should have—well, didn't the Standard actually ask for a *black* eye? Only the liver-and-white was permitted a hazel eye by the old Pointer Standard, now discarded for a 1968 revision. This wiping-out of a rigid eye-color requirement could be a coming to terms with the realities of the present day, the once-desirable eye-color having become virtually lost to the breed. The new Pointer Standard requires of an eye only that it be "the darker the better." This could represent a compromise to which the German Shorthaired Pointer Standard might never be reduced if breeders take care with keeping eyes right. Worth mentioning here is the observation that experience in sporting breeds generally opposes what one often hears at the ringside: "Maybe his eyes *could* be a bit darker, but I wouldn't call them *light*—they match his coat." In truth, such eyes *are* light. The requirement seems to be rather that the lighter the jacketing, the darker the eye. Pointers, Springers, English Setters, etc., all come within this rule, as well as German Shorthaired Pointers.

Also widely held, is the belief that light-eyed dogs are uncertain of temperament. Experiment and experience do not support the belief. In English *Dog World* (February 24, 1961), E. Sandon Moss points out that eye color is unimportant in Border or Working Collies, the only breeds that rely on their eyes to impress or force the dominance of their personalities. "Contrary to general belief, one can rarely estimate character, fidelity, or any other quality in the dog by the expression of its eyes," he writes. "It would be difficult for Labradors, or Spaniels, for example, whatever their feelings, to convey anything but ready and willing compliance and abounding good nature by their eyes alone. Other breeds . . . have a consistently hard expression that is certainly no real indication of their frame of mind or attitude to life generally."

Mr. Frank A. Longmore, of the kennel-governing Executive of Victoria, Australia, also had a most important observation to make concerning eyes and the dog. Dogs, he held, can suffer severely from eye-strain—"the strain of your eyes and mine!" he clarified. "Often, when judging, I find it necessary to turn my eyes away from a dog under review, finding it restless, even resentful, under a too-concentrated stare."

Based on wide judging experience, Mr. Longmore's is an observation to be digested by the type of judge who makes a performance of "going through the motions" in the show ring. Such often stand and stare at a dog, acting the part of being in the deepest judicial thought. Presently, visibly, the dog goes to pieces. Some back away. Some glare in resentment, ready to defend their persons against such psychological intrusion.

NOSE: (A.K.C. Standard)

Brown, the larger the better, nostrils well-opened and broad. Spotted nose not desirable. Flesh-colored nose disqualifies.

AUTHOR'S COMMENT: Nothing there that doesn't make best sense. The German view seems to be that the outward sign of good scenting is a big, moist nose with flaring nostrils, prominent, movable. Those among us with interest in history know that one of the features of the Old Spanish Pointer was that "double nose" the engravers always depicted so faithfully at the end of his face. "Double," of course, merely describes the visual effect—as of two circles, back to back.

TEETH: (A.K.C. Standard)

The teeth are strong and healthy. The molars intermesh properly. The bite is a true scissors bite. A perfect level bite (without overlapping) is not desirable and must be penalized. Extreme overshot or undershot bite disqualifies.

AUTHOR'S COMMENT: The "scissors bite," as the Standard asks, is a neat fitting of the front teeth of the upper jaw over the front teeth of the lower, with no space between. Any variation of this pattern is not desirable. An *overshot* (or pig) jaw is one in which the upper teeth protrude beyond the lower. An *undershot* jaw is one in which the bottom teeth protrude beyond the upper. Either fault, if at all severe, makes a dog's head look wrong, especially in profile. In their more serious manifestations, such malformations make it hard for a dog to pick up an object. Cosmetic considerations apart, hunting men will not want a dog so handicapped.

In assessing puppies' mouths, it should be remembered that the lower jaw grows out more than the upper. If a youngster shows you his erupting second toothy-pegs with the top ones jutting out a bit in front, don't start worrying for a while. In most cases, natural jaw development takes care of it, and at maturity such a pup will usually have a good scissors bite. But if the *lower* jaw

The neck elegance of the prepotent pioneer import, Arta v. Hohreusch, has come down as inheritance to her Dual- and BIS-winning descendants.

sticks out beyond the upper, chances are not usually good. The lower jaw will likely grow out further still and the mouth of the mature dog will look worse than that of the pup.

Many dogs have a completely level mouth, upper teeth sitting neatly on top of the lower in front. Owners tend to be annoyed if a judge looks hard at a mouth of this kind and, indeed, most judges let it pass. Yet experience shows it to be less than desirable. Those "riding" teeth on top wear down the lower. Long before such a dog is middle-aged he will have a mouth full of ground-down shards. Some breeders of wide experience also hold that level "riding" mouths of this pattern can in one generation be the source of really faulty undershot mouths in the next. Then, of course, there is the school of thought that believes faulty feeding practice, rather than inheritance, imposes bad mouths. That, of course, is only to be proved by a carefully controlled experiment that is beyond the hope of an ordinary breeder to put into practice.

NECK: (A.K.C. Standard)

Of proper length to permit the jaws reaching game to be retrieved, sloping downwards on beautifully curving lines. The nape is rather muscular, becoming gradually larger towards the shoulders. Moderate houndlike throatiness permitted.

AUTHOR'S COMMENT: Anatomically, there are the same number of vertebrae in the neck of a dog that appears short-necked as in that of a dog that appears long-necked. The factor of length, then, is something of an illusion. It is wholly influenced by lay of shoulder. The steep-fronted dog's shoulder blade imposes the "start" of the neck inches further along the string of vertebrae than does the shoulder blade that is desirably and obliquely sloping.

Reasonably, one may believe that correct shoulder assembly and a general front-end flexibility count for more in making it easy for a dog to retrieve game than any mere illusion of length his neck may present to view. (If he has this correct anatomical construction, then of course his neck *does* look desirably long.) Something along these lines may possibly be given consideration as expressing the requirement rather better in terms of strictly practical breeder concern. After all, the recognized retriever breeds, all whizzes at scooping up game, are not usually considered remarkable for swanlike length of neck. But they ARE, in all their A.K.C.-recognized varieties, required to have good sloping shoulder assembly wherein, the anatomists tell us, are located those mechanical aids that favor the designated work. The dog with the tied-in, straight shoulder, his short upper-arm forming with that shoulder a straight line that runs right down his leg to his toes, as one sees quite often, is the dog likely to have his troubles getting his jaws down to his game. And the apparent "length" of his neck, plus or minus, has no more to do with his awkwardness than the length of his tail, also plus or minus.

It is beyond argument that an elegant neckline sloping into correctly-placed shoulders benefits not only the show dog, but the field dog as well. Nothing contributes more style to the stance of a dog on point. Nothing furthers the beauty of a show pose so unmistakeably.

CHEST: (A.K.C. Standard)

The chest in general gives the impression of depth rather than breadth; for all that, it should be in correct proportion to the other parts of the body with a fair depth. The chest reaches down to the elbows, the ribs forming the thorax show a rib spring and are not flat or slabsided; they are not perfectly round or barrel-shaped. Ribs that are entirely round prevent the necessary expansion of the chest when taking breath. The back ribs reach well down. The circumference of the thorax immediately behind the elbows is smaller than that of the thorax about a hands-breadth behind elbows, so that the upper arm has room for movement.

AUTHOR'S COMMENT: The requirement of an oval, rather than a round, chest formation has been long understood in the case of dogs required to exert themselves in action. As the Standard points out, round ribs hinder expansion for extra breathing needs. The reason is mechanical—a circle cannot be further expanded. The relationship between round (barrel) ribs and a wide (bulldog) chest; the forcing apart of upper-arms that are oftenest short, and shoulder blades ditto; the bull-neck coarseness imposed by the wide gap between the tops of the shoulder blades—all are clearly demonstrable. These are very commonly seen anatomical faults in the German Shorthaired Pointer. Dogs come into sight with such a width between their shoulder blade tops that one may be pardoned for

Connie v.d. Arriërvelden (imp. Eng. from Holland). Owned by Wittekind Kennels, Eng. Why the Standard asks for "the circumference of the breast to be slightly less just behind the elbows." There must be clearance for the shoulder mechanism to function.

guessing a cup of coffee could be balanced there, as on a table, with no trouble at all!

Oval ribbing facilitates the expansion imposed by stress in breathing, thus helping endurance. It is most often matched anatomically by long upper arms and long shoulder blades lying with their tops desirably close. Instead of the bulldog front of the barrel-chested dog, with the awkward far-apart placing of the front legs that imposes a choppy gait, the oval-chested dog will be able to stand on legs much closer together, to stride out cleanly. This is the forechest formation, as just mentioned, that lets a dog get his nose down. Herr v. Otto, as quoted by Dr. Kleeman, draws attention to the ability of Foxhounds, big-bodied as they are, to get their noses down, even at the gallop, because their legs are set well beneath them in the proper forehand assembly. (Check back to Columbia River Tillie, Chapter 6.)

That the circumference of the chest should be slightly less just behind the elbows is also easy to understand. There has to be clearance for the upper-arm, working along the same lines as the
piston-rod of a railway engine. In the round-ribbed, wide-fronted
dog, the upper-arm get forced right out, and awkward movement
results. In the tied-in shoulder, equally undesirable, the opposite
prevails, with equal effect on easy gait. The pointing breeds, caught
by the camera racked-up on a bird, can usually provide a good
object lesson in respect to the inter-relationship of rib and front
assembly generally.

The wide front too often seen in the German Shorthaired Pointer,
unwelcome as it is, has been with the breed rather too long. It is
not only a local problem. It has caused concern to breeders in most
parts of the world, perhaps as successfully as anywhere in England
where high popularity has brought experienced breeders into the
Shorthair interest and considerable attention has been paid to elim-
ination of defects of coarseness.

BACK, LOINS and CROUP: (A.K.C. Standard)
*Back is short, strong and straight with slight rise from root of tail
to withers. Loin strong, of moderate length and slightly arched.
Tuck-up is apparent. Excessively long, roached or swayed back must
be penalized.*

AUTHOR'S COMMENT: In the dog, where length of body sufficient to contain the vital organs is asked for in the same breath as a
short back, the length of back is measurable from the highest point
of the withers to the first of the lumbar vertebrae. The back is the
member that spans the distance between the forehand assembly and
the hindquarters as a bridge, supports the head and the neck, the
weight of the down-hanging ribs, the body organs contained below.
For this, it needs to be taut and strong. For this, most judges look
away from swampy-backed (dippy-backed) dogs with their back-
bones sagging between shoulders and hips like a garden hammock
between two trees. The opposite curve, known as a roach, is also
undesirable and usually penalized, though preferable to a dippy-
back as less suggestive of a structural weakness. Old engravings
seem usually to depict the Old Spanish Pointer as roached, but
modern breeding practices have long since done their best to elim-

inate this not-so-handsome outline from German Shorthaired Pointers.

As does the neck, the back owes its "length" or, in this case, shall we say its "shortness," to the lay of shoulder. Again, there are the same number of vertebrae in a long-backed dog as in a short. Thus, a steep-shouldered dog will appear longer in back than one with a correctly placed shoulder. An interesting game to play with a view to understanding this is to place an imaginary saddle on the dog's back, as though he were a horse. If the saddle rides up towards his ears, his shoulders are steep, his back is long (and his neck correspondingly short). If the saddle sits where saddles on horses are supposed to sit, the dog is shortbacked, with correct shoulder placement.

The Germans, who will not countenance a long-backed German Shorthaired Pointer, ask for a taut back to further such energetic movements as, say, jumping. In loin, they ask for a short, slightly-curved area, holding that too strong an arch here hinders action and speed.

FOREQUARTERS: (A.K.C. Standard)
The shoulders are sloping, movable, well-covered with muscle. The shoulder blades lie flat and are well laid back nearing a 45° angle. The upper arm (the bones between the shoulder and elbow joints) is as long as possible, standing away somewhat from the trunk so that the straight and closely muscled legs, when viewed from the front, appear to be parallel. Elbows which stand away from the body or are too close indicate toes turning inwards or outwards, which must be regarded as faults. Pasterns are strong, short and nearly vertical with a slight spring. Loose, short-bladed or straight shoulders must be faulted. Knuckling over is to be faulted. Down in the pasterns is to be faulted.

AUTHOR'S COMMENT: In connection with the Standard's requirement of an upper arm to be as long as possible (how long IS possible?), Dr. Paul Kleeman has also observed in his German discussion that the further back a dog can move its elbows, the more easily it will be able to drop its torso between its upper shoulder-blades. Seeking the dog that can take its elbows furthest back, he directs, look for the one with the longest upper-arm, and to find

225

it, look in turn for the dog with the longest shoulders and the most usefully developed withers.

The ability to drop and elevate the body between the shoulder-blades, especially while in motion, has served the best hunting dogs for centuries, maybe since the beginning of time. It is a first instinct, carried along from the era when men hunted birds with nets, when the dog's low-to-ground creeping was in the essential nature of its work. It is amazing with what tenacity the instinct clings within the mentality of the sporting breeds, as may be rapidly learned of most dogs themselves when they have not been receiving training to be lofty. Present-day field trial performance in America, of course, definitely discards much movement; the drop-to-shot requirement of the European and English trials is not permitted here. However, practical hunters in any part of the world, including here, seldom quarrel with it, the movement having its useful application to their service. On the other hand, to eradicate it can cost a field trial trainer plenty of sweat when some individual dog, otherwise a good field trial prospect, makes up a stubborn mind that the way his fore-bears hunted clear through the centuries, feather or fur, is good enough for him.

HINDQUARTERS: (A.K.C. Standard)
The hips are broad with hip sockets wide apart and fall slightly toward the tail in a graceful curve. Thighs are strong, well-muscled. Stifles well bent. Hock joints are well angulated and strong, straight bone structure from hock to pad. Angulation of both stifle and hock joint is such as to combine maximum combination of both drive and traction. Hocks turn neither in nor out. A steep croup is a fault. Cowhocked legs are a serious fault.

AUTHOR'S COMMENT: Here, too, the Standard presents an exact word-picture of what is required in the after-end of a good German Shorthaired Pointer. It disallows narrow, weak-looking hips and the straight-stick back legs increasingly seen. In the show-ring, by the way, there are times when a judge should exactly satisfy himself whether the apparently straight, stuck-out hindleg of a dog is the result of poor construction or showring tenseness. Many a correctly-built dog will mulishly or nervously straighten out his backlegs in the showring, and no amount of persuasion on the part of his handler can coax him to relax and stand normally. (A sharp

226

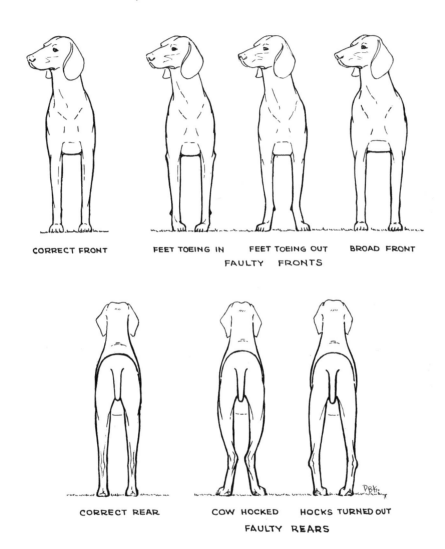

CORRECT FRONT   FEET TOEING IN   FEET TOEING OUT   BROAD FRONT

FAULTY FRONTS

CORRECT REAR   COW HOCKED   HOCKS TURNED OUT

FAULTY REARS

little tap near the tail-butt will effect the relaxation in many cases, perhaps operating on a nerve-center. Don't know why, but it seems to work.) On the other hand, it is also necessary for a judge to discover whether the dog with a sharply-sloping topline (which the Standard doesn't ask for, anyway!) really is as over-angulated as he appears, or whether his handler is contriving a crouching pose in the interests of outline. Pulling the legs unnaturally far back will correct a "dippy" back at times—till the dog moves. Spreading the legs wide apart at the rear will counteract a tendency to "high behind." Both methods are used consistently by handlers in posing dogs in the show ring, but the contrivances do not work when the dogs are required to move. The "dippy" back shows, and so does the "high behind." A "high behind" is also masked quite often in action by a good handler who will bring back a dog in an exact straight line to the judge in gaiting—then the head and neck mask the fault. All these smart tactics are fair in love and war, so far as the show ring is concerned, but they do not help in producing good pups in the breeding pen. Old Mother Nature is never bamboozled by such.

The requirement that hocks shall turn neither in nor out is also clear. No uglier sight exists than the cow-hocked dog, especially in tall breeds. The term applies to hock joints that lean in together, as opposed to equally faulty hocks that lean out the opposite way and turn the back legs into a pair of parentheses, as viewed from behind.

FEET: (A.K.C. Standard)
Are compact, close-knit and round to spoon-shaped. The toes sufficiently arched and heavily nailed. The pads are strong, hard and thick. Dewclaws on the hind legs must be removed. Dewclaws on the forelegs may be removed. Feet pointing in or out is a fault.

AUTHOR'S COMMENT: Here is another paragraph of the Standard that may possibly lend itself better to pictured explanation than to that of words. What is a novice to make of "sufficiently arched"? Sufficiently for what? The description of the foot itself as "round to spoon-shaped" could also bother anyone not versed in some elementary knowledge of a dog's foot construction. Taking for granted that the "round" foot refers to what most dog folk call the "cat" foot; that the "spoon-shaped" refers to the "hare" foot, obviously the Standard is here saying that any shape of foot goes. For, presumably, as boys and girls are the only two kinds of babies the stork can bring, "cat" and "hare" are the only kinds of sporting-dog feet. These are recognized also in Pointer and Setter breeds, with those who don't like a "cat" foot on the Pointer charging it to the inheritance from the Foxhound. Well, for the German Shorthaired Pointer, any shape of foot. . . . No problem.

The Germans add a further requirement that the dewclaws be removed. This is usually done at a very early age in the pup, within a few days of birth. The removal guards against one annoying form of hunting field accident. Front leg dewclaws are very susceptible to laceration, they catch on this or that out in the field, causing ugly tearing wounds. Also, when the nails on dew claws are left untrimmed, as so often they tend to be, it can often be the *owner* that suffers a nasty tearing wound when the friendly dog reaches over to give his boss a love pat.

There is no lack of those, among the old-time Field Trial men especially, who are strongly opposed to the removal of dewclaws. As one expressed it not so long ago, he holds these dewclaws to be necessary to the German Shorthaired Pointer. Necessary for what? "For climbing trees!" he claimed in all possible seriousness. Cats, yet! But even cats don't use dewclaws to climb!

In general, the toenails of sporting dogs—of *all* dogs!—deserve more care than they usually get. While hard-run dogs tend to grind their own, a little extra help is seldom amiss. Nothing destroys the "compact, close-knit" formation of the German Shorthaired Pointer foot so completely as do neglected nails that enforce a loose spreading of the toes. Kenneled dogs especially need regular toe-nail care. Often such dogs present a grievous sight to dog-minded visitors, which reminds the author of two German Shorthaired Pointers once seen in a kennel—the matron with her toenails left so long they were curving back under her feet! On the other hand, there is no need to go to the extremes being currently practiced among many of the poodle fraternity, where even the handlers themselves often feel a little squeamish over the close guillotining imposed on their charges. "One starts it, and the rest of us have to follow," is the limp explanation for bloodied little feet. Perhaps, in this connection, the forthrightness of an overseas judge is worth recalling. He eliminated one of the nation's top-winning sporting dogs from his

229

final consideration for B.O.B. for just such closely-guillotined nails. Speaking of this later, following the judging, he spread his own hands on the table. "If my fingers were chopped right back to the first knuckle, would you call this a sound hand?" he asked, not unreasonably.

The desirable state of a sporting dog's foot pad is that of hardness and strength, as the Standard requires. To the searching fingers of the experienced judge, the sandpaper roughness of a pad tells an agreeable story of good conditioning. Nothing, but NOTHING, feels worse than a foot composed of thin pads, slippery smooth as rubber.

COAT AND SKIN: (A.K.C. Standard)

The skin is close and tight. The hair is short and thick and feels tough to the hand; it is somewhat longer on the underside of the tail and the back edges of the haunches. It is softer, thinner and shorter on the ears and the head. Any dog with long hair in body coat is to be severely penalized.

AUTHOR'S COMMENT: The German Standard makes specific

objection to any extra length of hair on the underside of the tail. Any resemblance to a "brush" is also rated a fault with them as, too, it would be rated here. However, it is interesting to turn back to the picture of the Talbot Hound (p. 17). If his tail were to be lopped where a German Shorthaired Pointer's tail is nowadays lopped, he would be going his way with a tail much as the present Standard describes—with the hair a little longer on the underside. He has that hair on the back of his haunches as well. No comment. Merely an observation.

That the skin be close and tight-fitting is most important. Nothing looks less attractive than a German Shorthaired Pointer whose tailor has done nothing for him, his coat slopping loose on his frame.

TAIL: (A.K.C. Standard)

Is set high and firm, and must be docked, leaving 40% of length. The tail hangs down when the dog is quiet, is held horizontally when he is walking. The tail must never be curved over the back toward the head when the dog is moving. A tail curved or bent toward the head is to be severely penalized.

AUTHOR'S COMMENT: A thick tail is also held objectionable in the same way as is a dewlap, or loaded shoulders and thick ears, faults that seem to lean together.

Cutting the tail of a German Shorthaired Pointer pup is not much as surgical operations go, but it requires doing with the very greatest of care. It involves estimation of the eventual size of the dog, and what will be an eye-pleasing, balancing length for him to carry aft. The majority of opinion would seem to hold that leaving the tail a mite long is better than cropping it a mite short. A smidgin could be shaved off later if necessary, but no one has yet worked out a way to stretch an extra inch onto a tail that's too short. Many a good German Shorthaired Pointer's appearance has been improved by re-docking an overlong tail. As Dr. Kleeman has pointed out, this can provide an illusion of strengthened hindquarters. He quotes the horse-dealer practice of bundling up a tail to provide a like illusion.

Apart from looks, a reason for docking the sporting dog is to save it from injury. Not only in the field, either; long wagging tails in the house, or in the kennel, can do themselves dire hurt against the walls, and such tail-tip injuries are stubbornly resistant to healing. Dr. Thornton, in his early-day Kennel Brochure, gruesomely warns of the injuries that can result from uncut tails. He also adds another reason for docking: "It adds greatly to the appearance of the dog, as most of them have large, heavy tails carried over from their hound ancestors. Docking serves to remove this hound appearance." Which sets us to turning back the pages here again to have another look at the tail on that Talbot Hound!

One thing more before leaving the subject of German Shorthaired Pointer tails. Just turn back the page and read again the Standard's description of the placing of a tail—*down* when the dog is quiet, *horizontally* when he is walking, *never* turned over the back! The breed could use some firm-minded judges who will walk over to a German Shorthaired Pointer being ring-posed like a Boxer, in respect of his tail, and require the handler to allow the tail to assume its natural position. Such a judge might even then discover a long back that otherwise he might easily have missed.

BONES: (A.K.C. Standard)

Thin and fine bones are by no means desirable in a dog which must possess strength and be able to work over any and every country. The main importance accordingly is laid not so much on the size

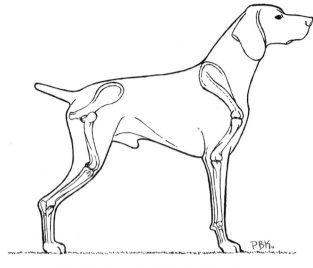

GOOD ANGULATION

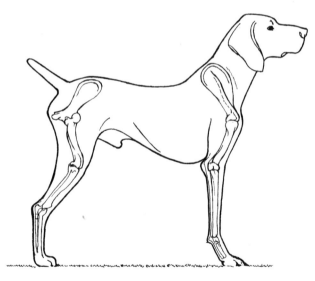

POOR ANGULATION

of bone, but rather on their being in proper proportion to the body. Bone structure too heavy or too light is a fault. Dogs with coarse bones are handicapped in agility of movement and speed.

AUTHOR'S COMMENT: The German Standard further points out that when breeding is carried on with the breed's advancement in view, the skeletal shape will be refined, its bone texture become closer and firmer, as opposed to the porous, spongy texture of bone that is too bulky. Checking *puppy bone,* it should be remembered that it *is* porous and spongy. Anyone acquainted with the fantastic rate of growth in well-reared pups in the larger breeds within their first six months, understands this very well. The pup that has flourished like a green bay tree stalks around on leg bone that looks—and is—enormous. It is also full of air cavities because of its quick growth. As the pup matures, the spongy baby bone consolidates into a good hard strength to support him for the rest of his life. So, if your otherwise promising six-months' pup is stomping around on young tree trunks rooted in enormous feet—don't sell him down the river for that. The one to discard would be rather the one with the fine underpinnings. Fine bone in a pup consolidates into finer bone still in the adult.

WEIGHT AND HEIGHT: (A.K.C. Standard)
Dogs, 55 to 70 pounds. Bitches, 45 to 60 pounds. Dogs, 23 to 25 inches. Bitches, 21 to 23 inches at the withers. Deviations of one inch above or below the described heights are to be severely penalized.

AUTHOR'S COMMENT: There has always been squabbling on the subject of height, especially, and there have always been those fanciers who would like to see a disqualification clause added, it seems, specifically to control *the show judges,* against some of whom is held a belief in their tendency to lean towards overlarge dogs. Such disqualification clauses do operate in several breeds, including some within the sporting group. Where a disqualification clause applies, a judge *must* check the measurement where it seems to be necessary. Certainly, most will do so only where such an obvious necessity does exist, though there is always the chance that some disgruntled exhibitor will over-readily employ that bane of show superintendents and officials generally—the protest. It can even happen that in the hurly-burly of the showring confusion, a very good dog can be tossed out over the chance of a fraction of an inch incorrectly measured against him. It can also happen that judges subconsciously penalize a dog that is possibly close-up to a standard size burdened with a disqualification because of reluctance to make waves or bring about delay caused by necessity to measure.

Doubtless, it is just such a consideration that has influenced compilers of some modern revised Standards to shy away from including any such disqualification clause, realizing that good dogs come in a range of sizes. The Irish Setter Standard (revised, 1960), for example, is one such, holding that over-all balance is a more important consideration than inch-fraction measurement. The exact same reasoning could possibly be behind the reluctance of many German Shorthaired Pointer breeders to support any revision in terms of disqualification for reasons of height and/or weight.

In the current clamor, by the way, it is notable that the most noise and heat seem to be generated in field trial circles where, so far as it is possible to establish, such a disqualification, based on measurements up or down, would have no bearing. Dogs in field trial competition would not expect to be measured. Therefore, the claim that agitation for "locking up the Standard" in terms of disqualification clauses governing height and weight is being made to "protect the breed" would seem to ring rather hollowly. By and large, the show exhibitor breeds with an eye close to the requirements of the Standard, his dog being judged by these. The field trial owner is subject to no such discipline. If, then, the claims arising in these quarters for imposing height and/or weight qualifications are honestly advanced for the benefit of the breed, it should be required that the measurements be applied to dogs within both spheres of activity, and that measurings operate in both directions, up *and* down. ("Sir!" thundered Dr. Johnson. "Your levellers always want to *level down*—they never want to *level up!*"—*Boswell*.)

In breeds that possess varieties distinguished by size, as in Poodles, Beagles, Dachshunds, etc., a measurable Standard requirement is, of course, arbitrary. But where no such division applies, there could be a case made for finding good in the big ones *and* the little ones, one tendency counterbalancing the other. Breeders opposed to "locking up" the Standard, hold the view that the most important qualities in a German Shorthaired Pointer are those of sound conformation plus the desire to hunt. An inch or two, or a pound or

234

two, more or less, makes no great matter, these feel. Be that as it may, and even granting that there may be danger in over-size or under-size, in actual and practical breeding, these qualities appear to cancel each other out. Most German Shorthaired Pointers seen in the showrings and the field trials fit very nicely into the (desirable) middle range. Those predicting ruin to the breed when a big one (or small one) has a win in their area do not have statistics on their side. The only persons competent to assess the true trend would be the busier judges that officiate clear across the country. To date, none seems to have been moved to air an opinion or to forecast the prospect of breed ruin.

To draw again on the wisdom of the German breeders, it is also understood by these that size and weight are often relative, influenced by other factors. A dog with a bulky skeleton and sloppy-fibred fleshing may weigh less than a dog of smaller build with firm flesh and muscle.

COLOR: (A.K.C. Standard)

The coat may be of solid liver or any combination of liver and white such as liver and white ticked, liver spotted and white ticked, or liver roan. A dog with any area of black, red, orange, lemon or tan, or a dog solid white will be disqualified.

AUTHOR'S COMMENT: Wide color tolerance of Shorthair color and patterning is restricted in the USA only by a disallowance of blacks and tricolors. As elsewhere in the world, the tick-patch dog is the most numerous, hair-for-hair stitching of brown and white, with or without patches. Lightly-ticked dogs are liked in the show-ring and the hunting field, mainly for being more conspicuous. Solid livers have many friends and the color has often been carried by exceptionally good dogs of versatile worth. The field trial scene here accepts a proliferation of clear white-brown Pointer-patterned which the rest of the world does not favor. The main criticism of such color is that it can serve to cloak possible irregular breeding practice.

German Klub Kurzhaar recently published color analysis in that country: Liver-ticked, 66%; Solid liver, 28.4%; Black-ticked, 4%; Solid Black, 0.6%; white-brown patched, 0.4%. (*Kurzhaar Blätter, May 1971.*)

One does not see clear white-brown patched in Germany. Black-ticked are few. Two appeared under my eye at 1967 Solms and one at the Kleeman (1968). The two at the Solms (Dortmund) were sired by Maniz v.d. Forst Brickwedde, a strong source of modern black factor. The Kleeman K.S., Anke v. Ichenheim was ex a black-tick dam also carrying Brickwedde, by Esser's Chick, the Axel v. Wasserschling son. No solid blacks appeared anywhere I gallery-sided.

In May, 1966, Dr. Byhain, then president of Klub Kurzhaar, reported club concern over a young solid black male at the breed Specialty. He asked through *Kurzhaar Blätter* pages, that persons that could throw any light on this dog's background factors to please pass this on to Herr F. Bollhöff, who dealt with statistics in this realm. A percentage of solid black breeding still to report in 1971 suggests a channel of conveyance still exists in Germany.

It is then entirely possible that a *legitimate* black-ticked whelp could crop up in a purebred Shorthair litter in the U.S., but one would reserve judgment in respect of solid black. Almost a century ago, German experimentation introduced black Pointer in hope to darken pigmentation, eye color especially. The strain resultant, known as *Prussian Kurzhaar,* was for a time given separate stud book recording, but the practice fell into disuse long since—Short-hairs are Shorthairs! However, the circumstance of the black Ark-wright Pointer introduced for this purpose has been used for decades since as justification of any black that crops up in Shorthair litters. USA is the only country where anyone really worried about a black-ticked, but solid black is a dog of another color, literally as well as figuratively.

Of course, not only black Pointer blood put such ticking into Shorthairs ages past. Many European Pointing types (universally known as Braques) carry the blue-tick (i.e. black-speckled).

In any "patched" breed, a very good show dog can occasionally be handicapped by markings in an unfortunate location. Thighs and necks are especially vulnerable. A ticked dog with an elongated solid patch on his thigh bordered by ticking can, at a slight distance, especially if the lighting is poor, appear to have a thin, stringy thigh that the judge will hold against him. Patching that runs the length of the neck can similarly make it appear thin and scraggy. This is one of the things an owner may discover while practicing by posing his dog in front of a mirror. Once discovered, it is up to him to figure out how to show his dog to counteract such a disadvantage.

It seems to be the perversity of fate that such undesirable markings are usually located on the "judging side" of a good dog. Within my own experience, my own best show Pointer was so handicapped, a slash of solid liver down one side of her neck being bordered by white, top and bottom. From a distance, especially in a poor light, her neck looked ewe. Her "other side" was clear white, showing the correct and elegant shape that took her to several B.I.S. awards. Figuring that no K.C. rule, in any country, says that a dog MUST stand with head pointed in any particular direction, I made it a rule to pose her first-up with her "good side" to the judge. So, he received his first so-important impression to her advantage. Turned the "other side" he may quite likely have gained a totally different one. All her ring-photos show her standing the opposite way to the rest of the class. This was an extremely good bitch, well deserving of her many wins. It would have been a sad waste to sacrifice her quality and show career to what is, after all, a convention.

If the mirror-mirror-on-the-wall shows your German Shorthaired Pointer similarly handicapped, consider turning it around in the ring. The judge may wonder why you stand the dog so. Even if he asks you to turn it the same way as the others (which many do not bother to do, as my experience showed), he will have gained his first impression usefully, and then of course will understand why you turned your dog about. His function is to find the best dog in the class. Anything that will help towards that end deserves his appreciation.

GAIT: (A.K.C. Standard)
A smooth lithe gait is essential. It is to be noted that as gait increases from the walk to a faster speed, the legs converge beneath the body. The tendency to single track is desirable. The forelegs reach well ahead as if to pull in the ground without giving the appearance of a hackney gait, and are followed by the back legs which give forceful propulsion. Dragging the rear feet is undesirable.

Field & National Field Ch. Patricia v. Frulord (Am/Can. Dual Ch. Gert's Duro v. Greif ex Juliana v. Frulord). Patricia made GSP history by taking both Nationals in 1971, and the AKC National again in 1973. Owner, Mrs. Fred W. Laird, Wash.

Centa v. Bornefeld (imp. Ger.), K.S. Vito v.d. Radbach daughter, a useful producer. Owner, Don Miner, Calif.—*Photo, Dr. Marlowe Dittebrandt.*

Caesar v. Bomberg, DI; SIa; m.S, Formwert V. Distinguished modern German stud. Pictured here in 1969 at 11 years. Owner: Hansjörg Hüggenberg, Germany.

Danish Ch. Fangel's Rolf, sire of Dual Ch. Doktorgaarden's Caro, imp. Well-performed, well-constructed SHP to type and color conformity of Denmark's bests in the breed.—*Photo, courtesy of C. Carlson.*

15

Breeding Your German Shorthaired Pointer

To breed for less than the best is to waste time, trouble, money, and the birthpangs of the bitch. The new breeder might heed the warning that the current winner is not necessarily the best mate for his bitch. This one's name might sell you a pup or so, but cannot guarantee their quality. Many big winners—in any breed—become so because of wide campaigning across the country with top handlers. Such winning records prove no prepotency. The measure of a stud is still that applied by the great Dutch geneticist, Hagedoorn: "The value of a stud is proved only by the quality of his get."

Since cross-country campaigning costs lots of money, many spanking good dogs never get an opportunity to compete coast to coast. There could be such a one in your own area—one with much to give the breed. Among the top-producing studs in German Shorthaired Pointers, many are known to us less by their own winnings than by the brilliant comet's tail of their get. Such was Field Ch. Greif v. Hundsheimerkogel. Treu v. Waldwinkel was never shown. Timm v. Altenau, with 15 champion get, did not finish for his title.

239

Fd. Ch. Von Thalberg's Fritz II (left), owned by D. Miner, California, overlooks the style of his get, (l. to r.) Fd. Ch. Marga v. Bess, Fd. Ch. Mitzi's Bo Jack v. Bess, and Fd. Ch. Onna v Bess. Missing: Fd. Ch. Missy v. Bess.

Dual Ch. Albrecht's Baron Cid with his distinguished dam, Fd. Ch. Albrecht's Countess Tena (front). Owners, M. & L. Albrecht, Kansas, are dedicated to the cause of the Dual GSP.

Ch. Rick v. Winterhauch, though a successful winner, was no circuit star. This, of course, is matched with the other side of the picture. Ch. Buck v. Gardsburg, several times top winner for the year in the breed, very widely shown, proved a very fine sire. So, Dr. Hagedoorn's measure yet applies—what has a dog produced?

Great dogs, as the various tables in this book attest, can come from competitively obscure but demonstrably good parents. Horses, too. The 1961 Derby winner, Carry Back, got heart and speed from an unfashionable sire and a dam seemingly valued at little more than on-the-hoof value as meat, yet the qualities must have been there. Perhaps Europeans come near the truth in describing breeding as an art, and the clever breeder as an artist. Such can always explain the use of a sire: "He suited my bitch."

Several reasons for using a stud do not stand scrutiny. One is using him because he happens to be *there*. In other words, you own him or he's a close auto drive away. Your own dog may be your heart's pride and a good winner. That doesn't necessarily make him the right mate for your bitch. Both may have the same faults—wide front, say, or short, thick heads. Another poor reason for using a stud is that he happens to be owned by a friend. Equally bad is by-passing the right dog because you don't like the guy who owns him. So you don't like the guy? You pay your check to get what you may possibly need—the complementing qualities to help your bitch.

What "complementing qualities" means is that you hope to gain from the dog something your bitch may lack. If your strain lacks something, the only way to get it is to go out for it. It won't generate spontaneously. In the same way, if your strain is plagued by a persistent fault, you must by-pass your dog, his parents, his get. It can involve time and leg work, or a few more gallons of gas, but results often justify all this.

The strangest things happen in breeding, which is why the graph-and-chart characters so often come to grief. Take litter brothers— one's a fine producer; the other, maybe with more opportunities, maybe the better winner, show or field, in production is a nothing. It happens in all breeds. Hagedoorn's research, of course, was carried out in the sphere of farm animals where aims were limited to milk and/or meat. Flock and herd owners listened because they knew they had to be practical. Such do not become emotionally

241

involved with herd or flock sires as do dog owners with their kennel prides. The breeding duds go to the butcher, their faults thus siphoned away. *Raus mit!*

Many dog breeders go by the opposite rule. They cull *nothing!* They breed *everything*, faults and all. Kennel blind, they blink at the stud reproducing his own faults—they will even breed him to his daughters! The bitch unsuited to show or field will "do" for a brood!

Ringside, or at the trials, one hears: "Who's he by?" Less often: "Who's he out of?" Yet many a stud owes his reputation to the luck of linkage with one or more great producing bitches. Never embark on the heartbreaking process of "grading-up" from a poor bitch. Even to screen out one fault can take years. The only shortcut is to buy the best bitch you can afford from the best-bred strain available to you. Long experience seems to have made clear that even a moderate one from a good strain is a better buy than a flyer, chance-got from a poor. In buying the best bitch you can afford from the carefully bred stock of a successful strain, you make your start at the point at which the breeder has arrived after years of hard work.

For such a bitch, your responsibility to pick the best mate becomes heavy. One wrong mating throws you back to where that good breeder started, perhaps ten or fifteen years ago. The view of breeding as *continuity* is a valuable one. The best expressed view of this I ever heard was that of a Great Dane breeder who started with moderates and had reached the commendable heights. Praised for this, he observed thoughtfully: "Yes, I've come a long way. But there's still a ways further to go. *I've got to run the pups through a few more bitches yet.*" With each breeding, he hoped to make his strain a little better, and a little better still.

It is poor breeding practice to attempt the cancellation of a fault by introducing its opposite. Two wrongs make no right in breeding, either. If your bitch is straight behind, breeding her to a grotesquely overangulated dog only multiplies your problems. You then have *two* kinds of poor rear ends instead of only one. A big, coarse, football of a head is not corrected in the next generation by introducing the equivalent of Minnie Mouse's. Short legs in your bitch will not be stretched in her produce by a sire too tall. It is much safer to use the dog that is as close to the Standard as you can find

—and try to discover if his parents are as well. Nor should you hope to correct all faults in a single mating. You, too, will likely have to "run the pups through a few more bitches yet" to reach your ideal.

When your stud is chosen, come to an agreement with his owner. Reserve a booking, give an idea when you expect her in season. When she shows signs, such as swelling of the vulva, the presence of color, notify the stud's owner. Don't appear on his doorstep unannounced, claiming your bitch to be ready right now! It could even happen that the dog has an engagement for that same time. What financial arrangements you make are between you and the stud owner. If it's anything more than handing over a check, have the agreement in writing. If you give choice of litter, have a written agreement as to when the stud's owner is to make his choice. Otherwise, you could find yourself holding the litter weeks and weeks past the best selling time. The older the pups when he makes his pick, the better end of the deal he gets, even if only in terms of board and lodging. Choice of litter can involve other disadvantages. It takes experience, as a rule, to discover them.

If your bitch misses, the stud owner usually extends the courtesy of a repeat mating—to the same bitch. Actually, this *is* a courtesy, not any legal obligation. You buy a mating, you don't buy pups. Some stud owners do advertise "Pups guaranteed," and that could ensure your free return service. However, sometimes the most guarantees issue from the owners of the least desirable studs. A guarantee is fine—good pups are better.

The owner of a good bitch (maybe even a not-so-good bitch!) will sometimes be approached by the owner of a stud looking for business, show or field. As you gather in your winning bitch after an event, you may find this character at your elbow. You should *breed* that bitch, you really should, he'll tell you. You should breed it to his champion! He'll leave his card. Very often—VERY OFTEN—he owns the one stud you should by-pass for your good bitch. The aftermath of such salesmanship can be seen in several breeds: a much touted—therefore much used by novices—stud, who has put his own faults through and through the breed in some certain locality. Novices are this promoter's all-time prey. He seems able literally to smell them out. Brush off such promotion. Take your time. Look around. Talk to everyone. Learn and observe. Seek out the best opinions available to you. Nothing but the very best is ever right for that good bitch you took so much care to select in the first place.

If you own a good, well-bred male, you doubtless hope he will have opportunity at stud. An owner of a stud has, of course, different problems from those of the owner of a bitch. Yet, basically, he, too, has grave responsibilities if he has the welfare of his breed at heart. He will at times recognize that his dog is not suited to some proposed bitch with whom, perhaps, he shares a fault of some gravity. Where, for any reason, you feel a mating may not help your dog's reputation, it would be wise to refuse his service.

Experience seems to prove the advisability of some early matings for a dog intended to use for stud, choosing, where possible, an older, experienced bitch to help him learn the Facts of Life. Breeding kennels seem to prefer to use a dog at least once before he is a year old. The most harrowing tales of frustration seem to come from those breeders who seek to get the co-operation of some middle-aged dog that has till then lived a bachelor life. Often enough he has the desire, but just doesn't know the drill.

Often times the tendency, in such cases, is to seek the boon of artificial insemination. Here, by the way, the novice with a good dog might accept a word of warning. Be wary of the "modern-minded" owner of a bitch that is inclined to think artificial insemination is *the* way to go about the contrivance of a mating. Give nature a chance first, being sure that the bitch is actually ready for service. Especially, if your dog is a proved stud, view with reservation the owner who comes to you and says "his bitch can only be mated artificially." Quite often this is not strict truth, but opinion derived from attempts to mate a bitch before she is ready.

However, there are certainly times when some artificial aid may be needed, and if so, be very sure of the capacity of the veterinarian who is entrusted with the job. Some glaring examples of mishandling in this respect are seen from time to time—male dogs who have resented the means by which semen was taken, and thereafter retain some deep suspicions of any person (especially strangers) who may put a hand near their after parts. So far as a show dog is concerned, it could mean the end of his career if he will not allow a judge to handle his rear end. It has happened.

As the function of a breed definitive book cannot possibly be considered the equivalent of—or the substitute for—a stud book, the requirement of selection immediately faces any compiler who must tailor coat to cloth—or records of production to space available. Selection there had to be, and the one basis for selection that made any sense at all was in terms of the dogs and bitches that had proven themselves able to provide stock that could win recognition in the sphere both of conformation and of performance. That is, in brief, stock that could acquire field *and* show titles. In many lands it is not necessary to spell out this requirement as a "champion" (per se) is automatically a dog that *has* proven itself both in terms of bodily conformation and working ability.

There have been many fine producing studs and broods that have operated here in but one sphere of endeavor—this of course not necessarily by *their* decision, but by that of the owners. Often enough, in the case of the get of some one dog shining *only* in show sphere, this is because those who owned his stock had no interest in the work sphere. In the case of the working dog it may also be that the interest to have assessment of conformation is lacking. These reasons for one-sphere performance are entirely valid, but for such a work as this present edition of the breed definitive book, where some measure *must* be applied to fit material between the covers, the restriction of the tabulations to the dual-sphere producers has proved mandatory.

However, in assessing production, must *also* be taken into consideration the time factor—the time in which the studs and broods were active. Thus, in the period prior to AKC licensing of Field Trials for Shorthairs, there was no chance for any stud to be honored with F.T. Ch. get. In an earlier time still, say that of the great bitch import, Arta v. Hohreusch, there was not even any recognizable show venue for the breed.

Further, the factor of registration figures adds also to the difficulty of assessing the production records of Shorthairs over the decades. Thus when F.T. Ch. Greif v. Hundsheimerkogl was compiling *his* record, Shorthair registrations were down under 5000 annually, and the interest in the production of Dual Chs. was scattered and somewhat lukewarm. Now, such an aspirant to the crown of production

245

versatility as the late F.T. Ch. Lutz v.d. Radbach (among others!) is free of the production figures of near enough 15,000 per annum—and an ever-growing aspiration of owners towards the distinction of the Dual title. Over and over have been heard the expressed aims of stud owners to have their dogs compile a record "to beat Greif's." It would take a better mathematical brain than that of your present compiler to assess figures in accurate relationship to the differing numerical status of the breed of the '70s as compared with the '50s.

No breed definitive work can omit the productions of the early studs and broods that in their competitive venues made the fame of the Shorthair in this country. Their influence still sits in back of so many of our very best contemporary dogs, as the Dual Champion tabulations accurately portray. Even when subjected to less than wise management, even at times to deplorable waterings down with less valuable contributions, the genes seem to have the ability again and again to assert themselves. The Germans have a proverb about "the Apple that Never Falls Far From the Stem." Apples and Shorthairs, Cabbages and Kings, the same rule would seem to apply. So, let's honor the Old 'Uns. But for the luck of their introduction to the United States at a difficult time in the history of this old world we might well be lacking those great qualities they sped on and down into this time that is momentarily our own.

First, then, some of the numerically-strongest of the producers of the 1940s, by which time competition in the show-rings had built up from the fairly general one-dog-to-a-class, and three, maybe four dogs to a breed, of the 1930s. Let us start with Treu v. Waldwinkel and Fritz v. Schwarenberg, and please don't overlook the presence of the mama they shared:

TREU V. WALDWINKEL
Breeder: L. C. Cori, New York
Owner: Joseph Burkhardt, Minnesota
  Ch. Searching Wind Bob

  Ch. Thalbach Waldwinkel Hans
  Ch. Searching Wind Cita

  Ch. Fritz v. Schlossgarten

(*Hallo Mannheimia ex Arta v. Hohreusch*, German imports both)
(*ex Maida v. Thalbach—his grand-daughter*)
("   "   "   "   )
(*ex Dual Ch. Schatz v. Schwarenberg*)
(*ex Bessie v. Winterhauch—a Fritz v. Schwarenberg daughter*)

Ch. Glanz v. Winterhauch	(" " " " " " ")
Ch. Senta v. Waldwinkel	(ex Feldjager's Grisette (German import)
Ch. Prince v. Waldwinkel	(" " " " " ")
Hans v. Waldwinkel	(ex Berg's Choice—ex Arta v. Hohreusch)
Ch. Heinrich v. Karlwald	(ex Senta v. Karlwald)
Ch. Jack v. Schoen	(ex Susie Dee Waldwinkel)

Ch. Fritz v. Schwarenberg	(Bob v. Schwarenberg ex Arta v.
Breeder: Joseph Burkhardt, Minnesota	Hohreusch, his half-sister. Ger-
Owner: Jack Shattuck Jr., Minnesota	man imports both)
Dual Ch. Shatz v. Schwarenberg	(ex Helga v. Schwarenberg)
Ch. Tell v. Schwarenberg	(" " " ")
Ch. Kraut v. Schwarenberg	(ex Lena v. Dreschler)
Ch. Trae v. Schwarenberg	(ex Hun v. Dusseldorf)
Ch. Sporting Butch	(ex Braunne v. Schmeling)
Ch. Dreaming Sweetheart	(ex Jäger's Pagina—German import)
Ch. Pagina's Young Lover	(" " " ")

Now, see Mars v. Ammertal and his Dual Ch. son, Rusty v. Schwarenberg, a brace adding wealth to the tally of studs and broods to be found in the pedigree hinterlands of many best dogs of later years.

Ch. Mars v. Ammertal (German import)	(Heros v. Ammertal ex Asta v. Rohrhalde)
Owner: Jack Shattuck Jr., Minnesota	
Dual Ch. Rusty v. Schwarenberg (first SHP Dual Champion)	(ex Vicki v. Schwarenberg, she ex Feldjager's Grisette imp. Ger.)
Ch. Cora	(ex Vicki v. Schwarenberg—above)
Ch. Rex v. Brecht	(ex Senta v. Karlbach)
Ch. Madchen v. Karlbach	" " " ")
Ch. Karl v. Schwarenberg	(ex Dixie v. Schwarenberg)
Ch. Heidi v. Ammertel	(ex Heidie v. Schwarenberg)

Dual Ch. Rusty v. Schwarenberg	(Mars v. Ammertal ex Vicki v.
Breeder/Owner: Jack Shattuck, Jr. Minnesota	Schwarenberg)
Ch. Hal	(ex Dutchy v. Schleswig)
Ch. Hanover Hills Hansel	(ex Hanover Hills Kitrena)
Ch. Rusty of Min o'Wash	(ex Heidi v. Ammertal)
Ch. Iron v. Schwarenberg	(ex Bess v. Schleswig)
Ch. Thor v. Schwarenberg	(ex Sue v. Schwarenberg)
Ch. Vesta of Penray	(" " " " ")
Ch. Pixie v. Ritter	(ex Dixie v. Waldwinkel)
Ch. Pheasant Lane's Schnapps	(ex Ch. Four Winds Gretchen)

Ch. Jo Jo v. Schwarenberg	(*ex Waldewinkel's Mahogany Flash*)
Ch. Rex v. Forst Ammertal	(*ex Heidi v. Forst Ammertal*)
Ch. Tustav v.d. Schwarzwalder	(*ex Lady Golden Mark*)

Ch. Pheasant Lane's Schnapps, of course, made a name as a producer with his son and grand-daughter Duals. Ch. Cora, the daughter of Mars, founded the Winterhauch line. Iron v. Schwarenberg, in a more modest way, was a valuable promotional force and early-day stud on the West Coast.

Though he did not finish to his title, Timm v. Altenau, a grandson of the great German prepotent, K.S. Kobold Mauderode-Westerholt, by way of the Kobold son, imported Donn v. Sulfmeister, provided a tremendous influence that survives down to our time, to be found behind many distinguished Duals. He was out of Dr. Thornton's breeding entirely, and his virtues have been preserved by clever management of close breeding by his owner.

TIMM V. ALTENAU (9 points) *   (*Donn v. Sulfmeister (imp. Ger) ex*
Breeder: Dr. Charles Thornton, Mont.   *Dreizenheim v. Brickwedde*)
Owner: William Ehrler, Michigan

Ch. Bella v. Rheinberg	(*ex Distel v. Rheinberg*)
Ch. Hilda v. Rheinberg	(" " " ")
Ch. Karl v. Rheinberg	(" " " ")
Ch. Tillie v. Rheinberg	(" " " ")
Ch. Timmy v. Rheinberg	(" " " ")
Ch. Treu v. Rheinberg	(" " " ")
Ch. Madel v. Rheinberg	(*ex Dixie v. Rheinberger—sister to Distel above*)
Ch. Treff v. Rheinberg	(" " " ")
Ch. Bea v. Dee	(" " " ")
Ch. Ford v. De	(" " " ")
Ch. Alsedda	(*ex Tillie v. Rheinberg Distel daughter, as above*)
Ch. Rita v. Rheinberg	(" " " ")
Ch. Sweet Tillie Too	(" " " ")
Ch. Rhoda v. Rheinberg	(*ex Wanda Gale Altmark, dam of Distel and Dixie. Wanda is a granddaughter of John Neuforsthaus, first Thornton stud of pioneer note*)
Ch. Loal's Dot	(*ex. Zest v. Horstig*)

* As Timm did not finish his title in those days of little interest in show competition, neither did his son, Duke v. Rhenberg (ex Wanda Gale Altmark) who later sired Dual Ch. Valbo v. Schlesburg. Timm's strong bitch production tally has operated to lace so much K.S. Mauderode-Westerholt inheritance into early-day American Shorthair stock that still serves so usefully.

Mention of imported Donn v. Sulfmeister, the K.S. Kobold-Mauderode Westerholt son, brings us also within hail of his grandson, Ch. Davy's Jim Dandy, and here we are pitchforked again into the heart of Dr. Thornton's Missoula enterprise.

Ch. DAVY'S JIM DANDY	(*Fritz ex Freda v. Waldhausen*)
Owner: L. McGilbrey, Washington	
DUAL & NAT'L FIELD Ch. DANDY JIM V. FELDSTROM	(*ex Joan v. Stolzenfels*)
Ch. Pheasant Lane's Stormalong	(*ex Krautina v. Stolzenfels*)
Ch. Jim Dandy v. Roger	(" " " ")
Ch. Sistie Frau	(" " " ")
Ch. Hunter's Moon Jemima	(*ex Boots Etta v. Schwarenberg*)
Ch. Cupid Casador	

Now, in strict and tidy sequence, we look first at Dual & Nat'l Ch. Dandy Jim v. Feldstrom and then at Ch. Pheasant Lane's Stormalong, which adds up to being busy for the next few minutes. First the Dual . . .

DUAL & NAT'L FIELD Ch. DANDY JIM V. FELDSTROM	(*Ch. Davy's Jim Dandy ex Ch. Joan v. Feldstrom*)
Breeder/Owner: Dr. Clark Lemley, Michigan	
DUAL Ch. Fritz of Hickory Lane Farm	(*ex Am/Can. Ch. Susanna Mein Liebchen*) *
DUAL Ch. Gustav Mein Liebchen	(" " " " " ")
Sth/Am Dual Ch. Jaime Mein Liebchen	(" " " " " ")
Ch. Gentleman Joe of Crescent	(*ex Dark Pattern of Crescent*)
Field Ch. Grand Discovery of Crescent	(" " " " ")
Field Ch. Eric v. Zelon	(*ex Bee-Coo of Zelon*)
Field Ch. Gussie v. Feldstrom	(" " " " ")

* Am/Can. Ch. Susanna Mein Liebchen, C.D. is also the dam of DUAL Ch. Marmaduke Mein Liebchen, to a mating with Ch. Fieldborn Tempo II, a Timm v. Altenau grandson, a legacy shared by Susanna, who was all Old American breeding, at long range. The concentration of the Donn v. Sulfmeister blood is here very strong.

Still with the descendants of imported Donn v. Sulfmeister, through son Fritz and grandson Ch. Davy's Jim Dandy, we have Ch. Pheasant Lane's Stormalong who slips under our barrier requirement of versatility of production with a Field Champion plus the great producing bitches that helped him make the pioneer impact he did.

AM/CAN. Ch. PHEASANT LANE'S STORM-
ALONG   (*Ch. Davy's Jim Dandy ex Krautina
Breeders: Mr. and Mrs. W. H. Warren,   *v. Stolzenfels*)
     S. Dak.

Ch. Columbia River Lightning (B.I.Ss)	(*ex. Columbia River Tillie*)
Ch. Columbia River Cochise (B.I.Ss)	(" " " ")
Ch. Columbia River Chief	(" " " ")
Ch. Columbia River Princess	(" " " ")
Ch. Rena Cazadora	(" " " ")
Ch. Grand Columbia Chilli	(" " " ")
Ch. Pheasant Lane's Storm Cloud (B.I.S.)	(*ex Ch. Pheasant Lane's Deborah*)
Ch. Pheasant Lane's Tomahawk*	(" " " " ")
Ch. Pheasant Lane's Lightning	(" " " " ")
Ch. Pheasant Lane's Liesel	(" " " " ")
Ch. Mustang v. Derer	(*ex Ch. Heddy v. Holly Lane*)
Ch. Pheasant Lane's Treu	(*ex Ch. Four Winds Gretchen*)
Ch. McElroy's Cates	(*ex Pat v. Cates*)
Ch. Cates' Pat of Millvale	(" " " ")
Ch. Dutchess Beverly	(*Ch. Hedda of Hollylane*)
Field Ch. Schlosser's Dusty Jack	(*ex Spottie v. Brickwedde*)

* Sire of 9 show champions.

The Stormalong tabulation provides prelude to a sequence of distinguished producers that relayed his prepotency. Predominantly, this is a show strain, but the inclusion of Dual and exceptionally high-rated obedience titleholders passes our requirement of versatility. Herein, the K.S. Kobold inheritance is braced with the K.S. Artus Sand inheritance through Columbia River Tillie. The Stormalong/Tillie weld was rich in productive sons, Chs. Columbia River Lightning, Cochise, Chief. Lightning sired sixteen show champions, seven of them ex Helga v. Krawford (Ch. Rex v. Krawford ex Lady Golden Mark). Cochise sired ten show champions and a field champion. Chief sired only two show champions, but proved himself the most important in the long-term sense—that to be described as More by his Good Luck and Enterprise than by anyone's Good Management. He found Helga v. Krawford one day before his brother, Lightning the nominated stud. The result of that happy accident—which was likely deplored at the time—was a neat, beautifully constructed bitch, later Ch. Columbia River Jill. With the assist from a full brother to her sire (Ch. Columbia River Thundercloud) Jill really started something. So, first to look at her produce and then what stems from it:

Ch. Columbia River Jill
Breeder: L. McGilbrey, Washington
Owners: Gretchenhof Kennels, California
Ch. Gretchenhof Moonshine

Ch. Gretchenhof Cinnabar, C.D.X.
Ch. Gretchenhof White Frost
Ch. Gretchenhof Stormy Weather
Ch. Gretchenhof Tally Ho
Ch. Gretchenhof Snowflake
Ch. Gretchenhof Thunderbird
Ch. Gretchenhof Cimarron
Plus non-ch. producers, Gretchenhof
Tradewind and Gretchenhof
Thunderbolt

(Ch. Columbia River Chief ex
Helga v. Krawford)

(by Ch. Columbia River Thundercloud)
("   "   "   "   ")
("   "   "   "   ")
("   "   "   "   ")
("   "   "   "   ")
("   "   "   "   ")
("   "   "   "   ")
("   "   "   "   ")

The channeled prepotency provided by Jill must be regarded with highest respect. Daughter Ch. Gretchenhof Moonshine compiled a record of 15 BIS and 50 Groups that stood for her lifetime as indeed the *combined* wins of Shorthairs from her retirement in 1964 to her death in 1973 never did reach this figure. She ended the quiet tenor of her life in retirement by falling asleep one morning beside her owner's couch, and took her great record safely with her. It was then her great-grandson's turn. Ch. Gretchenhof Columbia River in 1973 did pass her record. She was bred once, and one daughter, Ch. Gretchenhof New Moon figured as top showdog in the breed in 1967, but the channelling of Jill's inheritance came down by another daughter, Ch. Gretchenhof New Moon that, picking up the pioneer inheritance of bloodlines through Dual Ch. Baron Fritz of Hohen Tann, provided a son to mesh presently with the old Columbia River strain, and provide another remarkable showdog.

Moonshine was not the measure of Jill's entire contribution. The record is readily available of such as the several Jill bitches compiled.

Ch. Gretchenhof Cinnabar, CDX
Breeders: Gretchenhof Kennels, Ca.
Owners: Joseph & Julia France, Maryland
Dual Ch. Frei of Klarbruk, U.D.T.

Ch. Heide of Klarbruk, U.D.T.
Jillian of Klarbruk, U.D.T., Nat'l
Obedience winner, 1968. Spayed.

(Ch. Columbia River Thundercloud ex Ch. Columbia River Jill)

(by Dual & Nat'l Ch. Kay v.d. Wildburg)
("   "   "   "   ")
("   "   "   "   ")

251

| Ch. Moonshine Sally of Runnymede | ("   "   "   "   ") |
| Ch. Neckar v.d. Klarbruk, U.D.T. | (by Radback v. Lowin, he by K.S Ulk v.d. Radbach, Ger. imp.) |

GRETCHENHOF TRADE WIND	(Ch. Columbia River Thunder-
Breeders: Gretchenhof Kennels, Ca.	cloud ex Ch. Columbia River
DUAL Ch. Hochland Jaeger's Titel-	Jill)
halter	
Ch. Cede Brass Badge	(by Mars v.d. Radbach)
Ch. Cede Mein Featherbedder	(by Ch. Cede Mein Gandy Dancer)
	(by " " " " ")

In the East, Gretchenhof Tally Ho in repeated matings with the very prepotent Ch. Adam v. Fuehrerhein, had at last available count 8 champion produce that included 1968 show Shorthair of the year, Ch. Whispering Pines Tally Hi. Ch. Gretchenhof Snowflake, mated to Field Ch. Tip Top Timmy provided Bruha prefix with four show champions. Several others of Jill's children—Chs. G. White Frost, Cimarron, Thunderbolt, also added to the eventual breed pool.

In 1968 the original powerhouse gave out a belated rumble, and the Columbia River strain name was again news. Once again it was by way of the Stone That the Builders Had Rejected, Ch. Columbia River Chief. Chief had gone long to his rest, but Lance McGilbrey still had a Chief daughter, Columbia River Della, she ex Ch. Columbia River Sweet Betsy, sister to C.R. Thunderbolt. It was straight down the line from old Columbia River Tillie, and represented closely adherence to the K.S. Kobold-Mauderode-Westerholt line through the imported Donn v. Sulfmeister of Thornton's. Della mated to Moonshine's grandson, Moonfrost, linked in the Mauderode-Westerholts again through Panther II of that greatest of German strains of the 1930s. Also shackled to this mating was the proved show inheritances of Ch. Pheasant Lane's Stormalong and Helga v. Krawford. The resultant type had been well-recognized by the 1950s—big handsome fleshly fellows pictorially strutting their stuff. Judges invariably found them, forgave the many with rigid pasterns (if those with this tenacious inheritance had been horses one would feel nervous to ride them, and as shock absorbers in hard field work such endowment would fail a dog!) and forgave too those with the Columbia River Tillie inheritance of low-set ears (German judges will not have this a mark of the hound) recognizing that all dogs have faults but not all show dogs have such spectacular style and handsome coloration.

The placid ghost of old Ch. Columbia River Chief may have been pleased when the 1970s fellow began to make such impact in the rings. Chief is to count among the Dogs-of-the-past it has been this compiler's luck to see in the flesh, nudging for attention when Tillie was being posed for the camera. And *because* Tillie, then aged 16, *had* survived to be photographed, we can pin-point the origin of the tenacious, low-ear-placement endowment. So, as the saying goes, *who* beats the percentages in terms of dog breeding? However, counting down the many generations from Tillie, even though her ear placement will out in the inbred strain, it is also true that the tremendous gifts of prepotency, of strength, of magnificent movement and showmanship, provide recompense that few judges would be inclined to miss. How far the Moonshine great-grandson will go, who at this time of compilation would care to guess. But this compiler is very glad that the record of the great bitch that in the most literal sense put the Shorthair breed on the show map was not passed during her own lifetime.

Ever since breeder interest has been stirring in the production of dogs, hopefuls have seized upon some demonstrated success of close inbreeding and plunged to match this with belief in the mere mechanics of putting parent to get. Bare accumulation of names in each generation has never provided of necessity the delivery of good stock. While knowledgeable (and lucky?) inbreeding is behind some of the great dogs of this wide world, the magic of such directed prepotency in successive generations has always stemmed from well-proven, outstandingly good individual basics. Failures are much more common than successes—the rate of difference is geometrical (as in astronomy!) but success siphons in tremendous breed gain.

The initial requirement, of course, is to find the vehicle of prepotency that produces gains, not losses. There have been times when the discovery of such prepotents have been accidental—as in Ch. Columbia River Chief, with that one chance mating providing greater boon to his breed than have the activities of his much-used litter brother. This of course is not unique to the Shorthair breed, that one brother may prove a producer of enormous value, the other merely average or so-so.

Trouble is, the value of a stud or brood is too often measured in terms of competitive successes and promotional advertising, neither

253

of such activities influencing actual production. Too much of dog-breeding success then is in terms of happenstance—Chief snatching his brother's bride—Greif having the interest of a field trial trainer to rustle a backyard dog a few bitches. Many valuable inheritances fritter away from lack of promotion. Speaking of his Dual & Nat'l Ch. Kay v.d. Wildburg recently, Dick Johns noted wryly that it had been his expectation that Kay's reputation would not require additional promotion of his value as a stud. "For that reason Kay has had less work than he should. Dual Ch. Blick v. Grabenbruch too. We didn't protect this strain with a wide-enough breeding base. Blick should have had more bitches; I should have used Dual Ch. Valkyrie more as a brood and less of a trial and Nanny v. Luckseck should have been bred to her best son . . . All now over the dam. Now I have only my Inge, the last in-and-in bred Grabenbruch, and a great joy she is to me when the hills start to color and the woodcock moon is in full and the flights start down from the north. She is the witch of the white beech hillside, and black alder swales— but then, why wouldn't she be . . ."

The Grabenbruch name here is one of the many strain names borrowed out of Germany from whence, after World War II, Dick on service in Germany had managed to buy little K.S. Sepp. One Dual, two show champions, was all the short-lived little fellow left behind him. The strain name here was made instead by his son, and mighty has been the contribution in terms of background stock to find in so many of our present-day compilations.

DUAL Ch. BLICK V. GRABENBRUCH	(K.S. Sepp v. Grabenbruch, he by
Breeders/Owners: Grabenbruch Kls, Penn.	K.S. Odin v. Weinbach ex Leda v. Grabenbruch)
DUAL Ch. Valkyrie v. Grabenbruch	(ex Ch. Katrina of Sycamore Brook, C.D., she by Ch. Dallo v.d. Forst Brickwedde)
DUAL Ch. Junker v. Grabenbruch	(" " " " " ")
Field Ch. Dirk v. Grabenbruch	(" " " " " ")
DUAL Ch. Grousewald's Blitz	(ex Debby v. Hollabird)
Field Ch. Tricia v. Baab	(ex Asta v.d. Schwarzwaldforte (imp))
Field Ch. Dax v. Heidebrink	(ex Betsy v. Heidebrink)
Ch. Dixie v. Heidebrink	(" " " ")
Ch. Donar v. Schlangenberg	(ex Susie v. Schlangenberg)
Ch. Tuxa v. Schlangenberg	(" " " ")
Ch. Gamecock Hallmark	(ex Adda v. Assegrund (imp))
Ch. Sue v. Krupp	(" " " " ")

254

The years of the early 1950s, providing the introduction of National Field Trial competition under American Field and American Kennel Club rules, generated increasing interest in the German breed, with the production lists of studs and broods mirroring this with faithful precision. Early in the public eye during this decade were the well-performed field trial dogs of Dixon breeding. This strain provided three National Field Trial champions over a very short span of years, all out of Dixon's Starlite (Shot v. Falkenhorst ex Field Ch. Dixon's Belle). They were the Field & AmField National champions Dixon's Skid-Do and Kay Starr, and the immensely brilliant Dixon's Sheila who collected the title in both spheres of competition under both American Field and A.K.C. license. The honors of further production went to Skid-Do, and the quality that permitted him the honor of siring a Dual seems also to have skipped a generation as some of his grandchildren have come up in show entries under me, one at least to the WD placing in the sizeable entry of the 1968 Specialty of the Buckeye Club in Ohio—now-Champion Don's City Slicker, by Skid-Do's Skeeter.

FIELD & NAT'L FIELD (Am. Fld) Ch. *(Meadow Mickey v. Reichenberg ex*
  DIXON'S SKID-DO *Dixon's Starlite)*
Breeder/Owner: Russel Dixon, Michigan
  DUAL Ch. Skid-Do's Bonnie Karin *(ex Field Ch. Dixon's Bonnie)*
  Field Ch. Caudle's Leader *(ex Ladie II)*
  Field Ch. Dixon's Shiloh Star *(ex Field & Nat'l Field Ch. Dixon's Sheila)*
  Field Ch. Skid-Do's Shiloh Sky *("   "   "   "   "   "*
  Field Ch. Dixon's Sinbad the Sailor *(ex Dixon's Tula)*
  Field Ch. Skid-Do's Bee *(ex Audy Girl)*

Two other studs with both the honor of Dual get and influence on later breedings belong to this period: Ch. Bill's Linzer Boy, by the Dual Ch. Rusty v. Schwarenberg son, Ch. Pheasant Lane Schnapps and Ch. Rex v. Krawford who provided the breed not only with the fantastically prepotent Helga v. Krawford, but also a Dual Ch. bitch (Big Island Spook) that made a considerable reputation in her time.

Ch. BILL'S LINZER BOY *(Ch. Pheasant Lane's Schnapps ex*
Owner: Lt-Col. W. A. Wolcott, Washington *Sun Valley Queen)*

255

DUAL Ch. Riga v. Hohen Tann	(*ex Ch. Bella v. Hohen Tann (imp)*)
Ch. Linzer v. Hohen Tann	(" " " " ")
Ch. Faust v. Hohen Tann	(" " " " ")
Ch. Jerry v. Hohen Tann	(" " " " ")
Ch. Juliana v. Hohen Tann	(" " " " ")
Field Ch. Ardy's Judith v. Hohen Tann	(" " " " ")
Field Ch. Linzer Boy's Little Heidi	(*ex Jean's Amanda*)
Ch. REX V. KRAWFORD	(*Schnapps v. Waldwinkel ex Katrina*)
Breeder: John F. Crawford	
Owner: W. A. Olsen, Minnesota	
DUAL Ch. Big Island Spook	(*ex Graff's Lady Lou*)
Ch. Baron v. Fuehrerheim	(*ex Gretchen v. Fuehrerheim*)
Ch. Senta v. Fuehrerheim	(" " " ")
Ch. Waldwinkel Lisa	(*ex Roxy v. Waldwinkel*)
Ch. Waldwinkel's Nutrena Heini	(*ex Judy of Ettendorf*)
Ch. Will o' the Winds Greta	(*ex Sandra*)

Also properly to this period may have been placed German import K.S. Ulk v.d. Radbach, with his high reputation made in Germany, and his inability to change over to the entirely different requirements of American field trial rule requirements. His legacy in Germany was a fine one through sons and grandsons, but little used here his qualities were in degree lost.

K.S. ULK V.D. RADBACH	(*Kay v.d. Schrummer Heide ex Ruth v.d. Radbach*)
Breeder: Herr Bleckman, Germany	
Owner: Dr. Kenworthy, Vermont	
Ch. Wag-ae's Zit v. Radbach	(*ex Dual Ch. Wag-Ae's Snowflake, CD*)
Field Ch. Wag-Ae's Helga v. Radbach	(" " " " " ")
Field Ch. Freya v. Beckum	(" " " " " ")
Field Ch. Erika Radbach v. Greif	(*ex Ch. Lisa v. Greif*)
Ch. Toni Radbach v. Greif	(" " " " ")
Ch. Becky Radbach v. Greif	(" " " " ")

The adjustment to American conditions of competition that plagued Ulk seem to have bothered rather less his predecessor in the same ownership, Am. Field Ch. K.S. Franco Beckum. This dog, living to a great age, had been also a fine performer in Germany, and is historically represented by a prepotent son in National Field Ch. Bobo Grabenbruch Beckum. Subscribers to our same unshakeable belief, that the Good Ones Come from the Other Good Ones, will not overlook that Bobo's dam, Kenwick's Diana Beckum, was by Ch. Tell v. Grabenbruch, a Franco Beckum son ex Dual Ch. Valkyrie v. Grabenbruch, which serves again to emphasize Grabenbruch influence behind successful later day strains. The Von Bess line that made history in National Field Trial competition in the 1960s, stems down from Bobo bitches bred to a Greif v. Hundsheimerkogl son.

FIELD & NAT'L FIELD Ch. BOBO GRABENBRUCH BECKUM	(*K.S. & Am.Fld. Ch. Franco Beckum ex Kenwick's Diana Beckum*)
Breeder: Dr. Kenworthy, Vermont	
Owner: Dr. Wm. Schimmel, California	
DUAL Ch. Bee's Gabby v. Beckum	(*ex Field Ch. Skid-Do's Bee*)
Field Ch. Bee's Beau v. Beckum	(" " " " " ")
Field Ch. Rebecca Grabenbruch Beckum	(" " " " " ")
Field & Nat'l Fld. Ch. Von Saalfield's Kash	(*ex Von Thalberg's Belle*)
Field Ch. Von Saalfield's Jill	(" " " ")
Field Ch. Stutz Beckum	(*ex Thornton's Princess*)
Field Ch. Mitzi Grabenbruch Beckum	(*ex Becky v. Luven*)
Field Ch. Patsy Grabenbruch Beckum	(*ex Duchess of California*)
Field Ch. Michael Kane of California	(" " " ")
Field Ch. Gretchen Grabenbruch Beckum	(*ex Pacific Wind Penny*)
Am/Can. Ch. Rappa Ringo Feldstrom Beckum	(*ex Field Ch. Gussie v. Feldstrom*)
Ch. Tammy Grabenbruch Beckum	(*ex Flikker v. Windhausen*)
Ch. Rocky Road v. Jonesdorff	(*ex Feldunbach Von Sue Ann*)
Ch. Von Flecki's Bo Beckum	(*ex Miss Pepperoni v. Sudwald*)

The tremendous pioneer strength of the Minnesota import bloodlines was running steadily through many fine dogs as from the 1940s onward. A representative stud with ability to produce field and show dogs into the '50s was Ch. Oak Crest Rick v. Winterhauch, a very fount of versatility and prepotency. His get includes three Duals and a bitch that was first of her sex in Shorthairs to take a Best in Show.

Ch. OAK CREST'S RICK V. WINTERHAUCH	(*Ch. Glanz v. Witnerhauch ex Chimes Girl who were respectively grandson and granddaughter of Arta v. Hohreusch*)
Breeder: Dr. E. Berg, Minnesota	
Owners: J. & M. Deiss, Minnesota	

DUAL Ch. Lucky Lady v. Winter- hauch*	(ex Hephizibah Holzman)
DUAL Ch. Captain v. Winterhauch (BIS)	(ex Duchess v. Hotwagner)
DUAL Ch. Able v. Eltz	(" " " ")
Ch. Oak Crest Cora v. Winterhauch (BIS)	(" " " ")
Ch. Northern Flights Cash v. Eltz	(" " " ")
Am/Cub/Mex. Ch. Clipper v. Eltz	(" " " ")
Ch. Blitz v. Oak Crest	(ex Smocky v. Treuberg)
Ch. Tell v. Lowin	(ex Heidi v. Lowin)
Ch. Oak Crest's Arno v. Winterhauch	(ex Maida v. Thalbach)
Ch. Rudolph Ammertal	(ex Velvet v. Ammertal)
Ch. Wag Inn's Mistress	(ex Miss Lace the Ace of Windy Hill)

* Dual Ch. Lucky Lady v. Winterhauch was dam of Dual Ch. Kaposia's Firebird.

The legacy that is the double endowment of the great Arta v. Hohreusch in the above compilation carried on also in Dual Ch. Captain v. Winterhauch and also in due course in Ch. Oak Crest Cora v. Winterhauch, both slanting towards show stock in the main. However, Captain's Dual Ch. daughter, Miss B'Haven v. Winterhauch represents a very early example of that always impressive happening, a Dual with Dual parents—her dam having been the German imported Dual Ch. Alfi v.d. Kronnenmuhle, whose sire line stems from her grandfather, great prepotent German stud, K.S. Axel v.d. Cranger Heide.

Ch. Pardner, CD, also provides an example of the successful combination of Old Pioneer American and modern German import welding, being honored by his Dual Ch. son, Jones Hill Friedrich (ex Ch. Wilhelmina v. Kirsche, CD) and four show champions.

A different pattern began increasingly to be woven, however, as the continued infiltration of Danish breds came to be in turn combined with the best of Old American. An outstanding example of such is Ch. Sobol's Pointing Jay Mer, whose get includes no Dual Champion but titled dogs in both field and show spheres.

Ch. SOBOL'S POINTING JAY MER Breeder/Owner: Oscar Sobel.	(Skriver's Jens (Danish imp.) ex Cocoa Queen)
Field Ch. Sobol's Pointing Pepper II Field Ch. Sobol's Pointing Argus II	(ex Sobol's Pointing Snow Ball)
Field Ch. Marko v. Lindenwald	(ex Am/Can.Ch. Fraulein Gretel v. Lindenwald)

258

Am/Can. Ch. Katrina Radbach v. Lindenwald	(" " " ")
Am/Can. Ch. Kristen Radbach v. Lindenwald	(" " " ")
Can. Ch. Jens Radbach v. Lindenwald	(" " " ")
Ch. Our Gal Sally v. Grabenbruch	(ex Our Sal)
Ch. Gruenweg's Binger	(ex Gretchen Gruenweg)
Ch. Kristi v. Lohengrin	(ex Heidi v. Lohengrin)
Can. Ch. Colonel Dennis Moflame	(ex Fieldborn Heinrich Villaricos)
Ch. Sobol's Pointing Jens	(ex Gunmaster's Sohio Supreme)
Ch. Gruenweg's Minda	(ex Ch. Tessa v. Abendstern) *
Ch. Gruenweg's Graf	(" " " " ")
Ch. Gruenweg's Emilie	(" " " " ")

* Ch. Tessa v. Abendstern is further the dam of Dual Ch. Gruenweg's Dandy's Dandy and Can. Ch. Gruenweg's Ib, both by Dual & Nat'l Field Ch. Moesgaard's Dandy, representing a doubling of Danish blood as Tessa was a grand-daughter of Ch, Skriver's Jens, and her maternal line stemmed clear back as a great grand-daughter of the first Danish imported dog to here, Gelsted's Bob. Bob's mating to a Treu v. Waldwinkel daughter, ex Bessie v. Winterhauch, however, provided a powerful addition of Old American bloodlines to balance the Danish.

Perhaps this is as good a place as any to examine the record of that truly magnificent bitch, Am/Can. Ch. Erdenreich die Zweite, C.D., that stubbornly held her high place so long in the tabulation of modern producing bitches. This one owed as good as nothing to modern importation. Her background stems solidly from Old American lines, no import closer in her pedigree than the fourth generation where we find imported Aar v.d. Wengenstadt in a mating with that magnificent Old American solid liver prepotent, Little Gretchen's Brownie.

AM/CAN. Ch. ERDENREICH DIE ZWEITE, C.D.	(Ch. Yankee Tim's Kurt ex Ch. Yankee Sal)
Breeder:	
Owner: Miss Irene Pauly, California	
DUAL Ch. Erdenreigh's Eartha	(by Erdenreich's Able v. Yankee, he by Ch. Yankee Tim, double grandsire of Die Zweite)
DUAL Ch. Erdenreich's Jetta Beckum*	(by Field Ch. Stutz Beckum)

* Dual Ch. Jetta Beckum is in her turn dam of Dual Ch. Cede Mein Dolly der Orrian (by the Greif grandson, Dual Ch. Zipper der Orrian). Then to carry the matter a generation further, Cede Main Dolly der Orrian is currently proving a tremendous prepotency, her litter of 6 champions to a Greif grandson already productive of two Duals.

259

Ch. Erdenreich's Beau v. Garsburg (BIS)	(by Ch. Beau v. Gardsburg)
Ch. Erdenreich's Buck v. Gardsburg	(" " " " ")
Ch. Erdenreich's Bea v. Gardsburg	(" . " " " ")
Ch. Erdenreich's Jim Dandy Beckum	(by Field Ch. Stutz Beckum)
Field Ch. Erdenreich's Ginger v.d. Yankee	(by Ch. Erdenreich's Aar Von Yankee)

Mention of Little Gretchen's Brownie recalls a necessity to look to her early day produce, her grandget as well as her children.

LITTLE GRETCHEN' BROWNIE Breeder/Owner: T. Hanna, California	(Brown Ace ex Ackerman's Little Gretchen)
FIELD & NAT'L Ch. Traude v.d. Wengenstadt	(by Aar v.d. Wengenstadt, imp.)
Field Ch. Brownie's Pat McCarthy*	(by Field Ch. Adolph v. Edelheit)
Field Ch. Little Brownie's Frieda	(" " " ")
Ch. Helen's Little Ladybug	(" " " ")
Ch. Brownie's Jill	(" " " ")

* Dam of Field & Nat'l Am. Field Ch. Brownie's Greif McCarthy. The untitled Just Penny of the Picts, another daughter of Little Gretchen's Brownie (also sired by Aar v. Wengenstadt), was the paternal granddam of Ch. Erdenreich Die Zweite.

There are still those in California who remember a day when Little Gretchen's Brownie was braced with an old tick-patch import with a jawbreaker name. No one who watched them seems to have forgotten the thrill of the performances. Now Brownie is long ago dead, and so too her bracemate. Brownie lives on in the hinterland of pedigree compilations, but great fame attends the name of her bracemate of that day. Fourteen years after his death in 1958 we still find Old Greif the dog to beat in terms of versatile production and a prepotency that defies the weight of the generations. It is surely time that, in these pages, we took a look at what was in gift of Brownie's obscure bracemate that long ago day . . . Field Ch. Greif v. Hundsheimerkogl, imported Austria.

FIELD Ch. GREIF V. HUNDSHEIMERKOGL Breeder: Viktor Rohringer, Austria Owner: D. H. Hopkins, California	(Alf Gindl ex Berta Spiessinger v. Pfaffenhofen-Ilm)
DUAL Ch. Oxton's Leiselotte v. Greif	(ex Ch. Yunga War Bride)
DUAL Ch. Oxton's Bride's Brunz v. Greif	(" " " " ")
DUAL Ch. Madchen Braut v. Greif	(" " " " ")
DUAL Ch. Schoene Braut v. Greif	(" " " " ")

Ch. Lisa v. Greif
Field & Nat'l Ch. (Am. Field) Brownie's Greif McCarthy
Field Ch. Yunga v. Hundsheimerkogl
Field Ch. Karen v. Greif
Field Ch. Konrad Christenson v. Greif
Field Ch. Katy v. Hundsheimerkogl
Field Ch. Hanne Lore v. Greif

Field Ch. Della v. Hundesheimerkogl
Field Ch. Feld Jager v. Greif
Ch. Baron Rudiger v.d. Heide
Ch. Bissen v. Flieger
Ch. Bote v. Flieger
Field Ch. Von Thalberg's Fritz II

(" " " " ")
(ex Field Ch. Brownie's Pat McCarthy)
(ex Bettina v. Schwarenberg)
(ex Freida v. Schoenweide)
(ex Lily Marlene v. Greif his daughter)
(" " " " " " ")
(ex Hella v. Yunga, his granddaughter)
(" " " ") -
(ex Toni Marlene)
(ex Ch. Royal Victrix v. Kurt II)
(ex Frau Jill)
(" " ")
(ex Von Thalberg's Katydid—his grand-daughter)

First indication of the prepotency extant here was given with the maturing of the oldest son, Field Ch. Yunga v. Hundsheimerkogl, the solid liver, by way of his v. Schwarenberg background.

FIELD Ch. YUNGA V. HUNDSHEIMEROGL

AM/CAN. DUAL Ch. Gretchen v. Greif
Field Ch. Fritzel v. Greif
Field Ch. Kristen v. Greif
Field Ch. Rex v. Hundsheimer

Ch. Chula Hundweise Galli
Field Ch. Carol v. Hohen Tann
Ch. Ricefield's Eric
Ch. Ricefield's Maja

DUAL Ch. OXTON'S BRIDE'S BRUNZ V. GREIF
Breeder/Owner: J. Huizenga, California
DUAL Ch. Brunnenhugel Balder
DUAL Ch. Brunnenhugel Jarl
Ch. Brunnenhugel Brock
DUAL Ch. Oxton's Minado v. Brunz

Ch. Oxton's Liese v. Brunz
Ch. Holiday's Wendi v. Greif
Ch. Holiday's Sieglinde v. Greif
Ch. Aintree Dyna-mite v. Brunz
Ch. Jody Radbach v. Greif
Ch. Greta Radbach v. Greif
Ch. Merry Maker's Extra Special

(Field Ch. Greif v. Hundsheimerkogl ex Bettina v. Schwarenberg)
(ex Field Ch. Karen v. Greif above)
(" " " " " ")
(" " " " " ")
(ex Ch. Freida v. Schoenweide, dam of Karen, above)
(" " " ")
(ex Ardy's Judith of Hohen Tann)
(ex Ch. Ricefield's Brown Bomber)
(" " " " ")

(Field Ch. Greif v. Hundsheimerkogl ex Ch. Yunga War Bride)

(ex Ch. Weidenbach Suzette)
(" " " ")
(" " " ")
(Am/Can. Ch. Sorgeville's Happy Holiday)
(" " " ")
(" " " " ")
(" " " " ")
(" " " " ")
(Ch. Becky Radbach v. Greif)
(" " " " ")
(Ch. Merry Maker's Cherub)

261

Ch. Ricefield's Sohn v. Greif   (*ex Bellshon de Kristine*)
Ch. Oshabere Kibou   (*Dual Ch. Bee's Gabby v. Beckum*)
Ch. Castlecrag Bonnie Lassie   (*Heidi Niedersachsenhoff*)
Field Ch. Hulcy's Bailey v. Greif   (*ex Hulsey's Brownie*)
Field Ch. Oxton's Gretta Lore v. Greif   (*ex Field Ch. Oxton's Hanne Lore v. Greif*)

DUAL Ch. OXTON'S MINADO v. BRUNZ   (*Dual Ch. Oxton's Bride's Brunz v. Greif ex Am/Can. Ch. Sorgeville's Happy Holiday*)
Breeders: John & Gertrude Dapper, Calif.
Owners: K. & I. Clody, Calif.
DUAL Ch. Dee Tee's Baron v. Greif   (*ex Dual Ch. Cede Mein Dolly Der Orrian*)

DUAL Ch. Dee Tee's Bashen v. Greif   ("   "   " "   "   "   ")
Ch. Dee Tee's Buc v. Greif   ("   "   " "   "   "   ")
Ch. Dee Tee's Benedict v. Greif   ("   "   " "   "   "   ")
Ch. Dee Tee's Fanny v. Greif   ("   "   " "   "   "   ")
Ch. Dee Tee's Trey v. Greif   ("   "   " "   "   "   ")
Ch. Dee Tee's Flambeau v. Greif   ("   "   " "   "   "   ")
Ch. Fagon Haag v. Greif   ("   "   " "   "   "   ")
Ch. Blitz v. Greif   ("   "   " "   "   "   ")
Ch. Callmac's Mariah v. Minado   (*ex Ch. Callmac's Victory v. Gardsburg*)

Ch. Oxton's Minado's Mark   (*ex Kleine Flagge v. Greif*)
Ch. Uberaschung v. Greif   (*ex Gina Braun v. Greif*)
Ch. Minado's Doc Holliday   (*ex Ch. Von Flecki's Holiday*)

The "assist" that fine producing bitches provide in terms of bolstering the get of sires that usually get *all* the credit is everywhere apparent in these pages. As old Greif had his Ch. Yunga War Bride and his own grand-daughters; as Dual Ch. Oxton's Bride's Brunz v. Greif had Am/Can. Ch. Sorgeville's Happy Holiday, as in the next generation Dual Ch. Oxton's Minado v. Brunz picked up the family theme from Dual Ch. Cede Mein Dolly Der Orrian, so it has proved out in so many families still to be considered in the pages ahead—such as the continuing "assist" that two great bitches in Ch. Katrina v. Albrecht and her prepotent daughter, Field Ch. Albrecht's Countess Tena gave that strain; as the inbred Field Ch. Moesgaard's Angel gave to her relative F.T. Ch. Moesgaard's Coco, and still staying here with the top Field performances, as the half sisters, Field Chs. Mitzi and Patsy Grabenbruch Beckum gave to the reputation of Field Ch. Von Thalberg's Fritz. One could run on a long way in terms of great producer-bitches within the various strains, but a leafing over of these successives includes most all of them and so no real need to recapitualte.

Can. & Am. Ch. Erdenreich die Zweite, C.D., distinguished show bitch and unique producer (left). When this was taken, only one of her two Duals had finished, but the entry includes here a Dual, a BIS, two show champions (one with a C.D. additionally), a bitch with 8 FT points, and a puppy.

Dixon's Starlite was fifteen when she posed for this picture at home with her well-known, prepotent son, Field & National Ch. Dixon's Skid-Do, then eleven. Starlite is also the dam of the three-National winning Field Ch. Dixon's Sheila. They are posed with their owner, Russell Dixon, who says: "If I'm sure of one thing it is that you have to have good bitches!"

263

Yet it does seem that owner attention could profitably be directed to the force of the feminine influences. It always intrigues me to remind myself that in the Bruce Lowe world-famous system of thoroughbred horse Stud Book records the entries are classified under the names of the *mares*. And then—this is a bit of a rough one to advance, but historical studies seem to support it—there is that interesting circumstance that the *rarest thing* to find in the pages of biographies of the world's great is a Great that stems from a Great Father. From Caesar to MacArthur—warriors, kings, artists, musicians, politicians, explorers . . . And the commonest is to find that such men stem from remarkable mothers. What about Turberville, writing in the 1500s to the dog owners: "If you would have a Faire Hound you must first have a Faire Bitch . . ."

FIELD Ch. VON THALBERG'S FRITZ II	*(Field Ch. Greif v. Hundsheimerkogl ex Von Thalberg's Katy did)*
Breeder/Owner: Don Miner, California	
DUAL Ch. Zipper Der Orrian*	*(ex Zetta v. Fuehrerheim)*
Ch. Zeugencarl's Elsa v. Ida	(" " " ")
NAT'L Field Trial Ch. Thalberg Seagraves Chayne	*(ex Field Ch. Patsy Grabenbruch Beckum, by Nat'l Ch. Bobo G. Beckum)*
NAT'L Field Trial Ch. Rip Traf v. Bess	(" *Field Ch. Mitzi Grabenbruch Beckum, by Nat'l Ch. Bobo G. Beckum)*
NAT'L Field Trial Ch. Onna v. Bess	(" " " " ")
Field Ch. Marga v. Bess	(" " " " ")
Field Ch. Missy v. Bess	(" " " " ")
Field Ch. Bo Jack v. Bess	(" " " " ")
Field Ch. Rusty Grabenbruch Beckum II	(" " " " ")
Field Ch. Rip v. Bess III	(" " " " ")
Feild Ch. Blitzkreig v. Bess	(" " " " ")
Field Ch. Blitz v. Bess	(" " " " ")
Field Ch. Jake v. Bess	(" " " " ")
NAT'L Amateur Field Ch. Heinrich v. Bess	(" " " " ")
NAT'L Amateur Field Ch. Andora v. Holkenborn	*(ex Centa v. Bornefeld, imp. Germany, a K.S. Vito v.d. Radbach daughter)*
Field Ch. Von Thalberg's Radbach X-cell	(" " " " ")
Field Ch. Von Thalberg's Wurtze Greif	*(ex. Yunga's Heide)*
Field Ch. Fritzi v. Greif	(" " ")

* Sire, in his turn, of Dual Cede Mein Dolly Der Orrian, ex Dual Ch. Erdenreich's Jetta Beckum.

264

Field Ch. Maxine v. Heidelberg	(ex *Field Ch. Schatzie v. Heidelberg*)
Field Ch. Von Thalberg's Greif II	(ex *Patti v. Greif*)
Field Ch. Lucky Ducate	(ex *Hildy v. Beckum*)

Having acknowledged the strength of best feminine influence in the production of fine stock, please not to think we are robbing any of the breed's great prepotent bitches by listing their get under the tabulation of the studs to which they were mated. Merely, it became easier to do it this way—and the repetitive use of the ditto marks (") down the columns catch the eye here as earlier in the record of Dolly Der Orrian's achievements. So, now to the record of Am/Can. Dual Ch. Gretchen v. Greif, first of any breed to hold the Dual title in two countries:

AM/CAN. DUAL Ch. ARRAK V. HEISTERHOLZ (Ger. imp.) *Breeder:* Carlheinz Herwegh, Germany *Owner:* Ralph A. Park Sr., Washington	(*Lummel v. Braumatal ex Astrid v. Grossenverde*)
DUAL Ch. Janie Greif v. Heisterholz	(ex *Am/Can. Dual Ch. Gretchen v. Greif*)
Field Ch. Kreig Heisterholz v. Greif	(" " " " " ")
Field Ch. Heisterholz's Helga v. Greif	(" " " " " ")
Ch. Eckener Heisterholz v. Greif	(" " " " " ")
Ch. Greif v. Heisterholz CD	(" " " " " ")
Bal Lakes Felecka v. Greif, UD	(" " " " " ")
Field Ch. Wolfwiese Radbach Eric	(ex *Mara v. Hanstein*)
Field Ch. Augustine v. Holkenborn	(ex *Heisterholz Shooting Star, she an Arrak g-daughter & Gretchen g-g-daughter*)
Field Ch. Duke Radbach v. Heisterholz	(ex *Tammy O'Shea*)
FIELD Ch. GERT V.D. RADBACH (Ger. imp.) *Breeder:* Ernst Bleckman, Germany *Owner:* Ralph A. Park Sr., Washington	(*K.S. Zeus v. Blitzdorf ex Ruth v.d. Radbach*)
AM/CAN. DUAL Ch. Gert's Duro v. Greif*	(ex *Am/Can. Dual Ch. Gretchen v. Greif*)
AM/CAN. DUAL Ch. Gert's Dena v. Greif	(" " " " " ")
Field Ch. Tarzan v.d. Radbach	(" " " " " ")
Ch. Greif v. Radbach	(" " " " " ")

* Duro is sire of Nat'l Field Trial Ch. Patricia v. Frulord, for whom 1971 was a banner year, she taking both AKC and Am. Fld licensed Nationals in the same season—a record to date.

AM/CAN. DUAL Ch. Radbach's Arko⁺   (*ex Katja v.d. Radbach (Ger. imp.)*
Ch. Radbach's Asco   ("   "   "   "   "   ")
Ch. Ulda Amber v. Offa   (*ex Tamm v. Grabenwald*)

⁺ Arko is sire of Dual Ch. Radbach's Dustcloud ex Anka Niedersachsen (Ger. imp.)

Arrak and Gert were selected out of Germany by Washington Field Trial trainer, Bob Holcomb, doing a hitch with the army in Germany during the 1960s. They brought in gift from the top bloodlines of the period. Not since the days of Dr. Thornton have so many well-breds arrived within so short a period, this brace being presently joined by a tiny baby pup, who in good time became Am/Can. Field Ch. Lutz v.d. Radbach. All were established on the West Coast and no one of the three received any promotion other than in terms of their actual performance records, ballyhoo conspicuously absent. Gert and Lutz were short-lived. Arrak, now a gentleman of advanced age, looks likely to be around yet for quite a while. All are now moving back in the pedigree generations and may well become forgotten, so let us do them justice herein.

AM/CAN. FIELD Ch. LUTZ V.D. RADBACH (Ger. imp.)   (*Xot v.d. Radbach ex Fitz v.d. Radbach*)
Breeder: Ernst Bleckman, Germany
Owner: R. L. Holcomb, Washington

DUAL Ch. Timberlane's Fritz   (*ex Ch. Timberlane's Honey*)
Am/Can. DUAL Ch. Ricki Radbach v. Greif   (*ex Lulubelle v. Greif, she ex Dual Ch. Gretchen v. Greif*)
Field Ch. Arraka v. Greif   ("   "   "   ")
DUAL Ch. Kamiak Desert Sand   (*ex Field Ch. Kamiak Bold Lark, she a Ch. Buck v. Gardsburg daughter*)

Ch. Kamiak Desert Dawn   ("   "   "   "   "   ")
Field Ch. Kamiak White Lightning   ("   "   "   "   "   ")
Ch. Radbach's Karin   (*ex Katja v.d. Radbach (Ger. imp.)*)
Am/Can. Field Ch. Radbach's Chips   (*ex Glucka v. Greif, she ex Dual Ch. Gretchen v. Greif*)

Field Ch. Von Thalberg's Radbach Queen   (*ex Centa v. Bornfeld (Ger. imp daughter K.S. Vito v.d. Radbach*)

Field Ch. Radbach's Kniff   (*ex Wolfsjaeger's Anka*)
Field Ch. Radbach's Luke   ("   "   ")
Field Ch. Radbach's Krip   ("   "   ")

266

Can/Field Ch. Wolfjaeger's Dax v. Spee	(" " ")
Can/Field Ch. Wolfjaeger's Don v. Spee	(" " ")
DUAL Ch. Fritz v. Trekka Radbach	(ex *Trekka v. La Mer*)

This is but one more of the many German imports that, over the decades, have been able to provide get that can work and still aspire of Dual honors in terms of conformation. Another so endowed was the import, later A.K.C. Champion Alvin's Blitz. His spearheading the Big Island and Albrecht strains also provides considerable interest, Dual successes in each generation. In these latter examples, was produced also, as in earlier strains examined, a tremendous female strength.

Ch. ALVIN'S BLITZ (Ger. imp.)	(*Bodo v.d. Jury ex Cilly v. Schwabenburg*)
Owner: George Reudiger, Minnesota	
Field Ch. Albrecht's Conutess Tena	(ex *Ch. Katrina v. Albrecht**)
Field Ch. Sandy v. Albrecht	(" " " " ")
Field Ch. Goodin's Katy Blitz	(" " " " ")
Ch. Albrecht's Rough & Ready	(" " " " ")
Ch. Big Island Spotter	(ex *Field Ch. Big Island Dancer*)

* Ch. Katrina (Ch. Jagor Valor Albrecht ex Susie v. Schwarenberg) was dam also of Field Ch. Albrecht's Count Gustav (by Dual Ch. Albrecht's Baron Cid) and of Ch. Albrecht's Apache Breeze (by Big Island Nixe's Apache) .

Again the picture is of the welding of pioneer American bloodlines with latter-day German imports. Through her grandsire, Dual Ch. Valbo v. Schlesburg, Katrina draws on the thoroughly proved Timm v. Altenau—Donn v. Sulfmeister—K.S. Kobold Mauderode Westerbolt strength. Ch. Big Island Spotter's dam, Big Island Dancer, was ex Dual Ch. Big Island Spook, a daughter of prepotent Ch. Rex v. Krawford whose untitled daughter, Helga v. Krawford, provides such fantastic strength to Columbia River.

Ch. BIG ISLAND SPOTTER	(*Ch. Alvin's Blitz ex Field Ch. Big Island Dancer*)
Breeder: George Reudiger, Minnesota	
Owner: Houston Carter, Missouri	
DUAL Ch. Albrecht's Baron Cid	(ex *Field Ch. Albrecht's Countess Tena*)
DUAL Ch. Albrecht's Baroness Cora	(" " " " ")
Ch. Albrecht's Baroness Cora	(" " " " ")

Field Ch. Albrecht's Baroness Freya	(" " " " ")
Field Ch. Albrecht's Baron Cy	(" " " " ")
DUAL Ch. Dino v. Albrecht	(ex Ch. Albrecht's Apache Breeze)
Ch. Apache Breeze Pride	(" " " " ")
Ch. Apache Belle Starr	(" " " " ")

DUAL Ch. ALBRECHT'S BARON CID
Breeders/Owners: M & L Albrecht,
  Kansas
    DUAL Ch. Rambling Rock
    Field Ch. Albrecht's Ruff & Tuff
    Field Ch. Albrecht's Van Joker
    Field Ch. Albrecht's Count Gustav
    Ch. Cimarron's Cracker Jack
    Ch. Cimarron's Cannonball
    Ch. Baron Cid's Best Bette
    Ch. Zandor Smoki v. Greif

*(Ch. Big Island Spotter ex Field Ch.
  Albrecht's Countess Tena)*

(ex Albrecht's Countess Abey)
(" " " ")
(" " " ")
(ex Ch. Katrina v. Albrecht)
(ex Trudel Turn & Taxis)
(" " " ")
(ex Ch. Fieldwood Britta)
(ex Bebita Lohman v. Greif)

FIELD Ch. ALBRECHT'S COUNT GUSTAV
Breeders: M. & L. Albrecht, Kansas
Owner: Thomas C. Bowman, Kansas
    DUAL & Amtr. Field Ch. Albrecht's
  Tena Hy *(Dual Champion One
  Hundred)*
    Ch. Albrecht's Tena Inky
    Field Ch. Marshall v. Braun

*(Dual Ch. Albrecht's Baron Cid ex
  Ch. Katrina v. Albrecht)*

*(ex Field Ch. Albrecht's Countess
  Tena)*

(" " " " "
(ex Pepper's Pride)

Still within this same family rests also *Dual Ch. Dino v. Albrecht*
(Ch. Big Island Spotter ex Ch. Albrecht's Apache Breeze). Dino
has matched his family inheritance pattern with the production of
a Dual Ch. in Dino's Princess Marta (ex Field Ch. Albrecht's
Baroness Freya). Bred by E. & I. Owens, of Missouri, and owned
by M. & E. Pascal, Maryland, Dino's record additionally counts to
date 15 show champions, from eight separately-backgrounded
bitches.

The consistency of this strain in the production of Dual champions and the versatile titled in both field and show competition,
studs and greatly prepotent broods included, is likely unrivalled
within the breed in USA—which makes all the more satisfying the
accidental fall of the time factors that permitted an Albrecht to slip
into the One Hundred slot in the Dual tabulation.

The comments of the breeders at this period of sustained endeav-
ors is interesting: "We've always preferred the Dual type dog, al-

though in stubbornly persisting with such, have had also to accept the sacrifices that go along with it.

We have found our reward in the holding-up of the strain through the generations. We certainly have not produced the 100% perfect dogs—nor did we expect to. Few have completely satisfied us—and when the perfect animal is produced anywhere, we will be the first to acknowledge it. Our production however has pleased us in terms of *all-over* quality."

Myron Albrecht has never been a professional, but trains, handles, shows all their dogs. His further dedication is to the continued improvement of his strain and the retention of its consistency in reproduction. Beyond those aims, he devotes much time to schooling club members to make the best of their own dogs, conceding that often enough it is harder to train owner than dog. This is a discovery known to the sport as far as a century back.

In the dedication to continuity that such ownerships as this represent, the backbone strength of any breed is to be found.

By turn of the 1950s, it became possible to assess the impact of the earlier Danish imports. First matings with stock from American pioneer strains provided some very good dogs, some of which still exercise influence behind moderns in the field/show spheres. These earlier imports are to be considered apart from the later introductions of a closely inbred, hugely promoted strain that flashed meteorlike through the skies of Shorthair Field trial competition for a space. Many among these showed considerable divergence from world-accepted Shorthair type and this inevitably gave rise to speculation and even some scandal. Cross-breeding was widely discussed as a possibility. However it could also be reasonably true that the fantastic degree of inbreeding, sire to get—in some instances down to four and maybe five generations, imposed this physical change.

The unquiet ghost of suspected cross-breeding keeps rumor flying in the world of the Shorthair, year after year. There have been some finger-pointings and some few registrations cancelled, and some honestly-concerned breeders have beat their heads against walls for quite some time. There offers no cure for the ill-fortune of type confusion other than the long hard one of breeder interest to cull and to carefully assess strain background *before* contriving matings. The only truly effective tool to strain out off-types is that provided by forms of competition suited to the originally blue-printed abilities of the dogs—in ANY breed!

First among the early Danish imports to make impact as a stud was Dual Ch. Doktorgaarden's Caro.

DUAL Ch. DOKTORGAARDEN'S CARO (imp. Den.)	(*Fangel's Rolf ex Holevgaard's Cora*)
Owner: Dr. W. Hartnell, Utah	
NAT'L Field Trial Ch. Gunmaster's Jenta	(*ex Gunmaster's Super Speed*)
Ch. Gunmaster's Ricki (BIS)	(" " " ")
Ch. Gunmaster's Swift	(*ex Gunmaster's Twister*)
Field Ch. Gunmaster's Pacer	(" " ")
Field Ch. Gunmaster's Kurt	(*ex Nat'l Field Ch. Gunmaster's Jenta*)
Field Ch. Skriver's Jello II	(*ex Gunmaster's Super Speed*)

Another valuable importation from Denmark, a good dog in his own right, was Field Ch. Skriver's Jesper. His opportunities were few, but in a mating with a bitch of excellent pioneer American background in Lady Lydia Swift, Jesper got himself a very useful son in Field Ch. Skriver's Streak, who sits quietly in behind some very valuable contributions to the modern breed pool strength.

FIELD Ch. SKRIVER'S STREAK	(*Field Ch. Skriver's Jesper ex Lady Lydia Swift*)
Owner: Carl Schnell, Michigan	
DUAL Ch. Streak's Herbst Versprechen	(*ex Lady Patricia Valbo, double grand-daughter of Dual Ch. Valbo v. Schlesburg*)
Field Ch. Flash v. Johannesburg	(*ex Rosalinda v. Johannesburg*)
Field Ch. Sky v. Johannesburg	(" " " ")
Ch. Val-Valle's Heyoka v. Waidmann	(*ex Ch. Kristi v. Lohengrin*)
Ch. Waidmann's Valdis	(" " " ")
Ch. Tageacker's Sleepytime Gal	(*ex Ch. Gretchen v. Tagaecker*)
Ch. Streak'em Skipper	(*ex De Joie's Trudi*)
Ch. Konrad v. Hohenstaufen	(*ex Butzi v. Berg*)
Ch. Louise v. Mark	(*ex Lillian v. Brock*)
Ch. Boy Howdy*	(*ex Pepsie v. Schnellberg*)

* Ch. Boy Howdy persents us with an interesting exercise in background iden-tification. As the sire of the only Dual to come out of the extensive breeding establishment at "Fieldacres"—a strain that during its years of operation leaned heavily on Danish import bloodlines—Boy Howdy's status as represen-tative of Danish influence allied with strong American pioneer blood is demon-stratively instructive. His dam, Pepsie v. Schnellberg, is down a route arrow-straight from the Thornton-bred Timm v. Altenau. Three of her four grand-parents are direct get of Timm. A Timm grandson, Dual Ch. Valbo v. Schlesburg, is also behind Streak's Dual Ch. son ex Lady Patricia Valbo.

Pepsie's sire, Ch. Coby v. Schnellberg, carried his Timm v. Altenau inheritance

Again and again, reading back pedigrees, one comes upon the proof that the Danish imports meshed most usefully with the produce of the American early-day imports of the 1930s–40s. Examples abound, past and present, as from such a show-dog and versatile producer as Ch. Buck v. Gardsburg, way along to the wonderful woodcock/grouse dog it was my privilege to follow under Dick John's handling in the autumn woods of Pennsylvania in 1972. She was Inge v. Grabenbruch, almost entirely inbred Grabenbruch but for that one contribution from imported Ch. Skriver's Jens (Ch. Bobby of Bjerringbro ex Ch. Kraglunds Ulla) Most instructive of all, perhaps, within the sphere of Danish/American pioneer breeding is to be found in the Field Ch. Moesgaard's Coco tabulation, in which this stud's entire clutch of show champions stems from a magnificently prepotent (and prolific!) daughter of Ch. Buck v. Gardsburg, as will presently be examined.

Ch. BUCK v. GARDSBURG (BIS)	(Ch. Red Velvet ex Zukie v. Gards-
Breeder: A. Alvin	burg, Ch. Red Velvet by imp.
Owner: D. D. Williams, California	Skriver's Sofus)
DUAL Ch. Sager v. Gardsburg*	(ex Ch. Valory v. Gardsburg, with Timm v. Altenau 3rd generation both sides)
Ch. Pepsie v. Gardsburg	(" " " ")
Ch. Erdenreich's Beau v. Gardsburg (BIS)	(ex Am/Can. Ch Erdenreich die Zweite, CD)
Ch. Buck v. Gardsburg	(" " " " " ")
Ch. Erdenreich's Bea v. Gardsburg	(" " " " " ")
Ch. Atun of Janley Acres	(ex Ch. Oak Crest Cora v. Winterhauch, (BIS)
Ch. Briarwyn's Buckskin	(" " " " " ")

into another sphere also proved out as historical. His daughter, Zukie v. Gardsburg, became the dam of Ch. Buck v. Gardsburg, the show-dog of his time—which is around the time my own first interest in the Shorthair breed was being developed.

The Fieldacres Dual champion, F. Katie, was ex a dam of enttirely Danish influence, but lacking Moesgaard. She was ex Fieldacres Geisha, by way of Danish Ch. Doktorgaarden's Fitz; Dual Ch. Doktorgaarden's Caro, Danish Ch. Skriver's Jens.

* Both Sager v. Gardsburg and Kamiak Bold Bark, in their turn, produced Dual champions. Sager's debt to Timm v. Altenau of Thornton breeding has been noted (above). Bold Bark's four maternal grandparents include Dual Ch. Blick v. Grabenbruch, Lucy v. Schwarenberg and two others with strain names that simply scream Thornton origin—Vorstehund and Ockerbach.

Ch. Briarwyn's Bootjack	(" " " " " ")
Ch. Timm v. Lohengrin	(ex Copper's Kam)
Ch. Heidi v. Lohengrin	(" " ")
Ch. Paglo's Frivol	(ex Ch. Paglo's Cindy)
Ch. Konig v. Gardsburg	(Ch. Heidi v. Waldhausen)
Ch. Callmac's Victory v. Gardsburg*+	(" " " ")
Field Ch. Kamiak Bold Bark	(ex Kimlet of Cayest Meadow, CD)
Field Ch. Kamiak Cloudy Weather	(" " " " " ")

Buck's Dual Ch. son, Sager v. Gardsburg, lives on in my mind as one of the best Shorthairs seen in my life. He was a most handsome dog, a smidgin better for size and elegance than his sire, and while most of his life was spent out of the stream of competition, his years as a personal hunting dog were in his old age crowned by one remarkable field trial season as he reached his tenth year. In mid-west trials, running against the top dogs of the time, National champions and all, Sager walked off with a succession of Limited Stakes, and those he didn't win yielded him a place. My luck was to photograph him as a veteran class competitor in a Specialty soon after. He could have won that Specialty paws down! That he was owned away from the competitive stream hindered his opportunities as a stud, but his useful contribution belongs here in terms of proving out his "family" inheritance with a Dual of his own.

DUAL Ch. SAGER V. GARDSBURG Breeders/Owners: R. & L. Sylvester, Pennsylvania	(Ch. Buck v. Gardsburg ex Ch. Valory v. Gardsburg)
DUAL Ch. Richlu's Terror	(ex Ch. Richlu's Jan Oranien- Nassau)
Ch. Richlu's Stormy Gale	(" " " " ")
Ch. Richlu's Tara*	(" " " " ")
Ch. Richlu's Jeffson	(ex Thora v. Assegrund)
Ch. Mobe's Dapper	(ex King's Lady II)
Ch. Waidmann's Ingwer	(ex Ch. Kristi v. Lohengrin)

The Gardsburg influence follows down another generation through the Sager daughter, Ch. Richlu's Jill Oranian, whose son, Dual Ch. Richlu's Dan Oranien, is also compiling a versatile production record.

*+ Victory v. Gardsburg maternal origin may also owe to Thornton breeding as Waldhausen was yet another of the many names that mark the Montana strains.
* Ch. R's Tara was an almost-Dual Ch, being 2 points from her FT ch. when accidentally poisoned.

DUAL Ch. RICHLU'S DAN ORANIEN   *(Ch. Dax v. Heidebrink ex Ch.*
Breeders: R. & L. Sylvester, Penna.   *Richlu's Jill Oranien)*
Owners: C. & S. Carlson, Ohio

   Ch. Shircle's Twig Oranien   *(ex Dual Ch. Richlu's Terror)*
   Ch. Ritzie's Oranien Rocco   *(ex Dual Ch. Ritzie)*
   Ch. Shircle's Dax Oranien   *(ex Alfie v. Braumatel)*
   Ch. Mitchell's Ohio Bell   *(ex Mitchell's Anka)*
   Ch. Crossing Creek Kate   *(ex Ch. Crossing Creek Molly Pitcher)*

   Ch. Bond's Bruno v. Kieckhefer   *(ex Ch. Adelheid v. Fetterell)*
   Field Ch. Betsy v. Braumatal   *(ex Alfie v. Braumatal)*
   Field Ch. Richlu's Hewlett Sandy   *(ex Hewlett's Lady Bess)*
   Can. Ch. E. F. Fex's Fienie   *(ex Field Ch. E. F. Fex's Blind Spot)*

This tabulation will likely be lengthened after this edition goes to press. However the immediate interest is in the proved ability of successive generations down from Ch. Buck v. Gardsburg to throw to both show and field, though he was damned by field trial people on two counts, his size and his record confined to the show ring.

With importation of Field Ch. Moesgaard's IB from Denmark, later than imports already discussed, came a new element in Shorthair production under the sponsorship of the late Ivan Brower of Friday Island, Wash. Mr. Brower always refused any information concerning the development of his strain, and as it is not within my power to make supernatural contact with him, it remains only to discuss Moesgaard as a strain in public presentation. It built up to a fashion quickly, and in many ways paralleled the history of Llewellin Setter imports of last century, this of course having in the setters involved the over-close inbreeding to a strain Llewellin had made from various weldings. In the Moesgaards all previously valued working bird dog abilities were down-graded in the interest of speed. The steady-working type of Shorthair that had made the breed popular in this and other countries was a victim to the sudden yen for dogs that could run out of sight and only too often also out of control. As in the case, again, of the Llewellin, high prices were presently being paid for dogs that in only too many instances exhibited neither the physical appearance nor the working pattern of Shorthairs.

There was no interest at Friday Island to incorporate any steadying influence of bloodlines linked to Germany's greatest dogs of the

1930s, as the early American imports possessed this quality so magnificently. Pedigrees out of Moesgaard provided instead a fantastically close inbreeding—just as did the last-gasp-pedigrees of the expiring strain of "straightbred" Llewellins. And as history (in all spheres of creation) will in same circumstances similarly repeat itself, the inbred produce out of Friday Island has also—even in shorter span of years than that accorded the Llewellins—run itself into oblivion. Only in such cases in which the inbreds were belatedly shackled to stronger, safer strains does this inheritance now have significance. And in a clearly discernible revulsion among the thoughtful in the Shorthair world, operates a realization that the best gift in Shorthair inheritance is not to be measured in terms of mere speed and a complementary dilution of bird and utility sense. The degree of inbreeding may be assessed from the following tabulation:

FIELD Ch. MOESGAARD'S IB (imp. Den) *(Holevgaard's Kip ex Nyberg's Rix)*
Breeder: Niels Hykkelbjerg, Denmark
Owner: Ivan Brower, Washington
  Field Ch. Doktorgaarden's Lucky (imp. Den) *(ex Field Ch. Doktorgaarden's Bunny)*
  DUAL & NAT'L Field Ch. Moesgaard's Dandy *(ex Field Ch. Doktorgaarden's Lucky (above, sire-daughter breeding))*

  Field Ch. Moesgaard's Doktor   ("   "   "   "   )
  Field Ch. Moesgaard's Sis   ("   "   "   "   )
  Field Ch. Moesgaard's Ruffy *(ex Moesgaard's Arta (and she already a M. Ib daughter out of his daughter Lucky))*

  Field Ch. Moesgaard's Lucky II   ("   "   )
  Field Ch. Fieldacres Ib *(ex Moesgaard's Girl (again a daughter of M. Ib and Lucky, as above))*

  Field Ch. Fieldborn Ib *(ex Lady Windsor—she of course outside the above pattern)*

Continually is raised in Shorthair discussion the opinion that a Pointer cross was resorted to at Friday Island, which would—if true —invalidate the above pedigrees. However, no acceptable proof in the legal sense has ever been provided to support the opinion. It may as likely be merely that the admittedly off-type appearance of so many dogs from this breeding, tending to complete negation at times of Shorthair breed appearance represents merely the inevitable degeneration imposed by the mechanics of their production. Where a saving cross of different blood was shackled to Moesgaard inheritance, as in the Dual Ch. get of M. Dandy and the show champion get of M. Coco, some very good dogs resulted.

No other Moesgaard stud has been granted the wide diversity of bitches that have been brought to Dual & Nat'l Ch. Moesgaard's Dandy, and the benefit of such wiser management likely enough ensures this stud a secure place in Shorthair history.

DUAL & NAT'L F.T. Ch. MOESGAARD'S DANDY
Breeder: Ivan Brower, Washington
Owner: Dr. L. L. Kline, Florida

DUAL Ch. Gruenweg's Dandy Dandy	(*Field Ch. Moesgaard's Ib ex Field Ch. Doktorgaarden's Lucky*)
DUAL Ch. Lucy Ball	(*ex Ch. Tessa v. Abendstern, g-daughter of Skriver's Jens plus an Am. pioneer dam line*)
	(*ex Pearl of Wetzler, who stems back to Schlossgarten/Ammertal lines*)
Field Ch. Big Red	(" " " ")
Field Ch. Moesgaard's Judy	(" " " ")
Field Ch. Erdenreich's Major	(*ex Field Ch. Erdenreich's Hecla v. Greif, a Greif v. Hundshermerkogl granddaughter*)
Field Ch. Erdenreich's Maisie	(" " " " ")
Field Ch. Erdenreich's Maxie	(" " " " ")
Field Ch. Von Holster's Calli	(*ex Kay of Hollabird*)
Ch. Moesgaard's Dandy's Old Smokey	(*ex Gunsmoke's Comanche Squaw*)
Field Ch. Moesgaard's Dandy's Mark	(*ex. Babs v. Dakona, his daughter ex Fieldborn Bessie, Danish but not Moesgaard*)
Field Ch. Southview's Count Dandy	(*ex Skriver's Shovaard's Clove*)
Field Ch. Moesgaard's Dandy Ian	(*ex Fieldborn Flighty Sonja (she from Ch. Doktorgaarden's Fiks and Skriver's Jesper get)*)
Field Ch. Moesgaard's Dandy's Buck	(*ex Fieldborn Flighty Glenda*)
Field Ch. Moesgaard's Dandy's Pixie	(*ex Moesgaard's v. Pyroberg Pix a Fld Ch. M.Ruffy/M.Sis daughter*)
Field Ch. Moesgaard's Dandy's Benno	(*ex Moesgaard's Pat (daughter of M/Ib ex M.Girl, she by M./Ib ex his daughter Lucky)*)
Field Ch. Moesgaard's Dandy's Cruiser	(*ex Field Ch. Moesgaard's Lucky II (she by M.Ib ex his daughter Arta)*)
Ch. Moesgaard's Dandy Orlando	(" " " " " ")

275

Possibly the most inbred of all Moesgaard's produce that has made a place in these tabulations was Field & Nat'l FT Ch. Moesgaard's Coco. Coco's impressively long production list was made in the main with the assistance of two amazingly prepotent bitches. His field champions stem in terms of a batch of eleven from the equally inbred Nat'l FT Ch. Moesgaard's Angel, plus a quartette also from inbred Moesgaard's bitches, most of the produce generally swinging wide of classic Shorthair appearance. His show champion production was bolstered by the tremendous strength of one of the great propotent bitches of our time, the Ch. Buck v. Gardsburg daughter, Ch. Callmac's Victory v. Gardsburg, of whom it was said that mate her as one might, she could be relied upon to throw good ones. She honored Coco with no less than eight show champions.

AMT'R NAT'L FIELD Ch. MOESGAARD'S
    COCO
Breeder/Owner: M. L. Sanders, California
    Field Ch. Moesgaard's Alamo

(Field Ch. Moesgaard's Ruffy ex Field Ch. Moesgaard's BIS)

(ex Field & Nat'l FT Ch. Moesgaard's Angel whose 4 g-parents were M. IB (twice) Arta and Lucky.)

Field Ch. Moesgaard's Angel's Peppy	("	"	"	"	"	")
Field Ch. Moesgaard's Alicia	("	"	"	"	"	")
Field Ch. Moesgaard's Angel's Bart	("	"	"	"	"	")
Field & Amtr. FT Ch. Moesgaard's Angel's Bonnie						
Field Ch. Angel's Rambling Danny	("	"	"	"	"	")
Field Ch. Moesgaard's Angel's Dee Jay	("	"	"	"	"	")
Field Ch. Moesgaard's Starlite	("	"	"	"	"	")
Field Ch. Moesgaard's Angel's Tambora	("	"	"	"	"	")
Field Ch. Moesgaard's Kurt	("	"	"	"	"	")
Field Ch. Moesgaard's Baron	("	"	"	"	"	")

Amtr. Nat'l Field Ch. Pentre Bach Coco
  (ex Pentre Bach Pepper, she a Dual Ch. M. Dandy daughter ex pioneer Am. background)

Field Ch. Pentre Bach Erika
  ("   "   "   "   )

Field Ch. Moesgaard's Stylish Ib
  (ex Moesgaard's Pat (M.Ib ex M. Girl, she by M.Ib ex his daughter, Lucky))

Field Ch. Pentre Bach Dolly
  (ex Moesgaard's Ruffy's Dolly)

Field Ch. Moesgaard's Siegfried
  (ex Field Ch. Saxony Sue)

276

Ch. Callmac's Flecken Moesgaard	(*ex Ch. Callmac's Victory v. Gards-burg, she by Ch. Buck v. Gards-burg*)
Ch. Callmac's Frederick Moesgaard	(" " " " ")
Am/Mex Ch. Callmac's Fraya v. Moesgaard	(" " " " ")
Ch. Callmac's Franz	(" " " " ")
Ch. Callmac's Hank Moesgaard	(" " " " ")
Ch. Callmac's Kurt v. Moesgaard	(" " " " ")
Ch. Callmac's Kapitan v. Moesgaard	(" " " " ")
Ch. Charnet's Geronimo	(" " " " ")
Ch. Coco's Candy Cane	(*ex Lady Sandra v. Hohen Tann*)

Mid-west representation of Moesgaard breeding was concentrated mainly in the interest of the Fieldacres strain, since gone out of business. Here ruled as stud, Field Ch. Fieldacres Ib (Moesgaard's Ib ex Moesgaard's Girl). At last count available to me, his get was nineteen field champions, including the 1966 National AKC Field Trial—Ch. Fieldacres Bananza (ex Fieldacres Lesa (M. Ib ex M. Arta). This kennel housed also one of the breed's remarkably prepotent bitches in Ch. Fieldacres Ammy, Danish bloodlined, but lacking Moesgaard. Her sire was Field & Nat'l Danish Ch. Skovmarken's Sep (Jugens Tommi ex Skovmarken's Daady) Ammy's dam, Fieldacres Sheena was a double granddaughter of Dual Ch. Doktorgaarden's Caro.

For future historians remains the responsibility of assessing the long-term impact of the inbreds.

Of course, whether a Shorthair is oriented towards field or show competition is first and foremost a matter of *owner*-choice among alternatives the breed inheritance presents.

The listing of the Dual champions clearly indicated the ability of the Shorthair to "deliver" in both spheres. Nowhere does there appear any equivalent for the inbreeding that stemmed out of the Pacific Northwest, but stubbornly again and again the trail leads back to Montana and Dr. Thornton's imports. Many prospectively good producers, of course, are also overlooked for various reasons, geographical situation being one; lack of advertised promotion, another. This, for example, can be seen in the comparative records compiled by the litter brothers Field Chs. Fritz v. Smidt and Tip Top Timmy. Fritz has his Dual get in Dual Ch. Briarwood's Peppermint Patty. Timmy has an ever-lengthening list, also headed by his Dual.

FIELD Ch. TIP TOP TIMMY	(*Duke v. Jager ex Rexann v. Stolz-*
Owner: Fred Z. Palmer, New York	*hafen*)
DUAL Ch. Tip Top Timber	(*ex Ute Trail Wild Rose*)
Ch. Broha's Mission Flying Wheel	(*ex Ch. Gretchenhof Snowflake*)
Ch. Bruha's Ring Wheel	(" " " ")
Ch. Bruha's Mission Rex Wheel	(" " " ")
Ch. Bruha's Buck v.d. Gwinner-wheel	(" " " ")
Ch. Guerda of Sleepy Hollow	(*ex Hedwig of Sleepy Hollow*)
Field Ch. Tanzer of Sleepy Hollow	(" " " " ")
Field Ch. Tina of Sleepy Hollow	(" " " " ")
Field Ch. Rollo of Sleepy Hollow	(" " " " ")
Ch. Taffy Town Tara	(*ex Duchess of Lorkin*)
Field Ch. Sep-a-Fetchit	(*ex Grousewald's Dot*)
Field Ch. Wylde Wood Gus	(*ex Fizcre's Wendy*)
Field Ch. Tip Top Beau Brandy	(*ex Fieldacres Vesta*)
Field Ch. Fauna v. Stine	(*ex Field Ch. Maltese Wanderer*)
Field Ch. Molnar's Gamble	(*ex Field Ch. Ute Trail Lore*)
Field Ch. Mr. Tuff of Jagershof	(*ex Ute Trail Cocoa*)
Field Ch. Hewlett Engelchen Nutmeg	(*ex Field Ch. Hewlett Girl Greta*)
Field Ch. Timmy's Chocolate Chip	(*ex Ute Trail's Bonnie*)

Imported Dual & Nat'l F.T. Ch. Kay v.d. Wildburg, also built his reputation by successful produce from a wide spectrum of variously bred bitches, benefiting considerably wherever he picked up earlier German import strains. Kay lived a very long life, and it was "a black day in Benton" when he took his leave in January 1973.

DUAL & NATIONAL FIELD Ch. KAY v.d. WILDBURG (imp. Ger)	(*K.S. Pol v. Blitzdorf ex Cora v. Wesertor*)
Owner: Richard S. Johns & Joseph Eusepi	
DUAL Ch. Frei of Klarbruk, U.D.T.	(*ex Ch. Gretchenhof Cinnabar, C.D.X.*)
Ch. Heidi of Klarbruk, U.D.T.	(" " " ")
Jillian of Klarbruk, U.D.T. (spayed)	(" " " ")
Ch. Moonshine Sally of Runnymede	(" " " ")
DUAL Ch. Fee v.d. Wildburg	(*ex Field Ch. My Ritzie fer Gitunburdz*)
Field Ch. Kay fer Gitunburdz	(" " " " " " ")
DUAL Ch. Eastwinds T.K. Dandy	(*ex Field Ch. Tina of Sleepy Hollow*)
DUAL Ch. Eastwinds T.K. Rebel	(" " " " " ")
Field Ch. Eastwinds T.K. Caesar	(" " " " " ")
Field Ch. Eastwinds Bourbon King	(" " " " " ")
Field Ch. Wynyard Apollo Lobreda	(*ex Seydel's Lottchen* (Ger. imp))

278

Field Ch. Maltese Wanderer	(ex Field Ch. Ute Trail Lori)
Field Ch. Trinka Sam's Girl	(ex Field Ch. Xilla Oranian-Nassau)
Field Ch. Budweiser v.d. Wildburg	(ex Field Ch. Albrecht's Baroness Freya)
Ch. R.B.'s Heidi v.d. Wildburg	(" " " " ")
Field Ch. Jinx v.d. Wildburg	(ex Field Ch. Wag-Ae's Helga v. Radbach)
Ch. Kay v.d. Wildburg Bud	(" " " " ")
Ch. Luftnase to Bar-Hardy Kay	(ex Ch. Wag-Ae's Sheba Bruner)
Ch. Luftnase the Caisson	(" " " " ")
Ch. Hope v. Luftnase	(" " " " ")
Ch. Wildburg's Pointriever	(ex Ch. Heity v. Grabenbruch)
Ch. Vermar's Cindy Wildburg	(ex Ch. Richlu's Becky Oranian)

Kay's latest Dual to finish (October 1973) insofar as this compilation is concerned puts this German import well out in front of all production records within the breed as these may be measured in terms of versatility. He was almost a year gone to his rest when his fourth Dual, Eastwinds TK Rebel, sent him over the long-standing record of Field Ch. Greif v. Hundsheimerkogl. Greif's 17 champions were made up of 4 Duals, 4 show champions, 9 field trial champions. Kay's (to date) reads: 22 champions, made up of 4 Duals, 9 show champions, 8 field trial champions, and his record also honors 4 UDT dogs, of which three are included in the champion listing and one of which is otherwise untitled, being spayed after a mishap with a drug hindering her season.

Many studs within the Shorthair breed have produced many more than 22 champions, show or field. The measure, however, in such a breed as this has to be versatility. And versatility is not represented when some stud with many multiples of show champions managed finally to come up with one that scrapes through somewhere in a field trial. In such a case one must incline to feel that the dam of the dual titled dog must have made some considerable contribution. There are several studs still active, or with get still active, that may lengthen the listing of their versatile production—Dual Ch. Minado v. Brunz comes quickly to mind as likely to endure for many a year yet to come—but Kay's record may well stand as long as Greif's had done till it was toppled—1958/1973.

It has already been said elsewhere in these pages that the breed has a magnificent pool of studs and broods. Many come to mind

279

for which there remains no available space in this compilation—such as Dual Ch. Biff Bangabird, with a long list of get that includes Dual Ch. Hewlett Girl Pebbles and Field Ch. Williams Blue Bonnet. Dual Ch. Baron Fritz of Hohen Tann is another able to prove out versatility in terms of field and show get. Ch. Fliegen Meister Gunner, with a list of show champions that reads like a telephone book for length, has also his Dual—Fritz v. Ziguener, CD, Can.Sh.Ch. But far out and ahead of the whole field is the show-producing stud, Ch. Adam v. Fuehrerheim. He has—to time of writing—still to welcome his Dual, but last count available showed his production nudging the century mark.

One would wish to have been able to spell out the produce of many more than the limitations of this work permit in times of space and general reader interest. The obligation to compile a properly comprehensive Stud Book still rests with the Parent Club and seems even now as far distant in prospect as when this present work went into its first edition in 1963. Under no circumstances can any breed definitive work double as a stud book.

Miss Betty Eschen of Carmel, Calif., with a four-generation team in hand.

Breeder-owner, Mieneke Mills de Hoog of Kent, England, keeps her "Wittekinds" busy. She is pictured at left at a trial with Sh. Ch. Wittekind Erica, whose barbed-wire scar has not hurt her show career (1972).

Below, two photos of Irus v.d. Saaner Mark, 1970 Dutch import to Australia. Detained en route in England for 18 months during a rabies scare, Irus sired three litters for "Wittekind" and had other congenial enjoyments as well. The cooling off photo at bottom clearly demonstrates whence daughter Erica gained her head and shoulder excellences. Irus is owned by J. Thomson, Melbourne.

16

Picking Shorthair Pups

THE litter safely in the nest, check first for abnormalities, happily rare in this breed. Salvage attempts are usually ill-advised. If the litter is very large, at least consider reduction. Six or so, sharing the cafeteria, do fine, make no trouble for anyone; twelve or so can be an intolerable burden to the novice with no facilities. It is also one of the facts of dog-breeding life that novices unknown in the dog world often have trouble selling their pups. Big kennels can cope—what's a few more pups when you're already feeding fifty? The one-bitch owner, of moderate means, working at something else all day, can find a large litter expensive, and unrewarding, too.

When picking over whelps it helps to know the background of your strain. For example, some strains are male-producing, some produce better bitches. Why? No one seems to have the answer. In such cases, it is usually better to work with, rather than against, Nature. If you own a dam from a strongly bitch-producing line, say, don't set your heart beforehand on getting from her a male to set the show world afire. The chances are you won't get him.

Sorting whelps by size alone can also lead you into steel-jawed traps for young players. The snap decision to eliminate all little ones or all big ones could be costly. If you are inexperienced, you could use the help of a breeder who knows the score. Size is trickily comparative. Not long ago, in another breed, we were shown a litter of four. One was tiny; two, medium-sized, were a pair; the fourth looked like the cuckoo in the nest. Now the litter is grown, the tiny is a freak, and the medium pair are undersized. Only the "cuckoo" is correct for size.

In situations like this, value the help of an experienced breeder, especially one who has kept records, weighed and measured pups at birth, checked figures against the size of the dogs when adult.

Many experienced breeders like to check the litter within 24 hours or so after birth. From then on, pups change almost hourly. A newborn can show a fair preview of eventual conformation. Hold it up in the air between your two hands, supporting the head and the hindquarters. The legs will drop down into what would be standing position. This lets you see shoulder lay that governs length of neck, back, loin. Depth of chest you will see (and perhaps better than you will be able to see it again for many a month), and you can see if the ribs are barrel or desirably curved. Out-turned "Charlie Chaplin" feet will show, and a wide forechest, and tail-set.

One of the finest breeders of my acquaintance schooled me in this method. Plucking a new pup from its dam she'd hold it out: "See? See that back, loin, shoulder? If they're not there now, Sister, believe me, they're NEVER going to be!"

German Shorthaired Pointer heads are inclined to be less informative at the new pup stage than are the heads of some other breeds. Yet, all things being equal, the big coarse head on the whelp can be expected to sit, later on, in front of a big coarse dog. Head tendency seems always to be towards more in growth rather than less.

At a later stage, good bone is a must, always remembering that pups "grow up" to their legs and feet. Skin can be difficult for a novice, saggy all over and draped under the chin; but apart from plainly throaty ones, most German Shorthaired Pointers seem to grow into their skins.

The stages-of-growth frights that bedevil all who rear pups come a little later on. Pups never seem to grow all over at the same time, but push up first one end, then the other. These heavings-aloft cancel each other out by maturity, but in the meantime they can give an inexperienced owner fits.

German Shorthaired Pointer pups are smart. Here is 5-month-old Raus v. Schlesweg. Owners: Pioneer breeders, Mangold and Rojem, Nebraska.

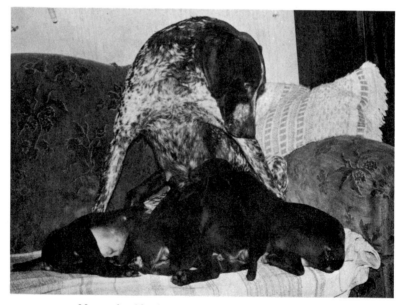

Maternal pride. Owner: Frau Maria Seydel, Germany.

It's a lucky dog breeder that goes along without letting a flyer pup slip through his fingers. Many have the bad luck to sell the litter pick. Many have the good luck to buy it back again. Picking pups successfully calls for luck and the wind with you, as the sailors say. But even if it is your incredible luck to pick out the best one, don't forget that that's just the starting point. The transient world of dog showing is full of people who expect their untrained, unshaped, unpolished dog to do great things just because he is well-born.

In picking an older pup—say in another kennel, with a view to purchase—make your first measure temperament. No matter how good the conformation, how *pretty* the dog, how fast or how stylish, if his temperament isn't good, you are buying only frustration. If he comes to you bouncing, with tail wagging, that's at least one guarantee that temperament is right. If he runs off with his tail tucked, you'd best remember an engagement somewhere else.

If you have mastered your Standard and looked over some good dogs, you should have at least a good idea what to look for. You want bone and balance, a head with a big nose and flared nostrils. You'll turn from a snipy muzzle—*that's* not for picking up fine fat pheasants! You'll look at the bite, remembering that a pup's mouth is not an adult's. Very *slightly* overshot—time will usually fix that. Undershot, *no matter how slightly*, reject. Eyes? Don't take a pup with greeny-yellow eyes. Honey-yellow—yes. Up-ended quarters shouldn't worry you much in adolescence, if the rear-end assembly angulation is right. But if his hocks are overlong and his thighs straight sticks, you won't like what he has later on. Wide chests remain wide chests (they get wider!). Barrel ribs remain barrel ribs. Feet? You can't overlook feet. Pups' feet in these big sporting breeds are *big* feet. But *good* big feet have thick pads in a compact foot, high-arched toes, not spread toes, wide like a duck's.

His parents will be your safest guide. Contrary to the fairy tales, no-goods produce no-goods. One good pup in a mess of rubbish is not for you, either. If that's the one you take home, somewhere along the line the law of averages will catch up with you.

TRAINING THE PUP: The training of your German Shorthaired Pointer is not within the scope of this book. That a training manual for German Shorthaired Pointers is long overdue is self-evident, and the breed in America has suffered for decades because

285

of it. The necessary use of Pointer and Setter manuals for training instruction has not helped to form the breed ideal correctly in the minds of new German Shorthaired Pointer owners. There are many extremely fine and capable professional trainers operating in the breed, and it would be grand if one (or more) would get down to the job of providing a guide for new owners.

Meanwhile, a few observations: First, it is oftenest most important that the *owner* be trained before he attempts to train the pup. If wholly incompetent, especially in terms of a hasty temper—don't try. If you do have the temperament, and you *do* try, and you make a good hunting or field trial dog out of your pride and joy, it will prove one of the most satisfying achievements of your life. If you don't feel competent, shop around before committing yourself to a trainer. There are lots of good ones—and a few bad ones, too!

If you plan to train your bird dog, remember, a first essential is *birds*. If you plan to make him your duck dog, introduce him to water at an early age. It must be wide water, running water; the pan in his run won't do. In the same way, planted birds are poor substitutes for wild ones—but that is often a local problem. You may live where there *are* no wild birds—most of us do. Then you have to settle for the next best.

Don't be sold on fancy methods to get him used to gunfire. The way that is as good as any is to fire off your lighter artillery while he's chasing around, having fun—he'll be too preoccupied to be scared. It is important to protect him from hoodlum mischance. A thrown firecracker has ruined many a young sporting dog forever. And if you're a sucker for gadgets, wait a bit, wait till you've properly learned the score in respect to elementary training practice before you load up on the electronics. There are some ruined dogs to show for those, too. You're in the kindergarten class, right? Well, leave the college stuff till you've graduated.

17

Gait

I N no sphere of dog interest is more errant, utter nonsense talked around the show rings than in connection with dog gait. By and large, it would seem, undesirable gait is the gait that the other fellow's dog employs. This is the more damnable in that the gait of a fast-moving big dog, especially (in which category place the German Shorthaired Pointer, of course), is not to be assessed by the human eye at high speed. It is only possible to *deduce* what happens—which is the reason McDowell Lyon had to employ his slow-motion camera tactics to catch what goes on. In the same way, it long since became apparent to me that my eye could not serve me well enough either. I took to collecting *still* pictures of gaiting dogs in various free-moving breeds of the sporting, working and hound groups. This proved better than using movies, as the movie, like the human eye, moves too rapidly for accurate comprehension.

The stills freeze action so that the exact placings of the legs can be seen. It quickly became apparent to me that the best-moving dogs are those that are balanced—whose hind and front quarters are in tune in terms of substance and angulation. It also became obvious that the major factor in smooth fast going is forehand assembly which permits reach. A dog with a correct forehand, having a long upper arm (as the Standard asks for) set at an angle to permit freedom, can take a stride as much as three times as long as that of a straight-shouldered dog with a short upper arm. This means that a straight-shouldered animal has to work three times as hard and take three times as many steps to cover the same distance. Additionally, his construction produces a short, high step—a prance that looks well in the hackney horse ring, and that has been known to delight the dog show galleries and judges of lesser knowledge, but which imposes restraint and weariness of muscle on the dog.

The use of the long upper arm for which the GSP Standard asks (and too few people take the trouble to find out why it does!) may be better understood by the novice by noting its like employment in fast-moving horses, both trotters (standard breds) and gallopers requiring a construction that permits extended forward reach. Only insofar as a horse is not a dog is there any real difference. The operating principle is exactly the same, and dog owners could do worse than clip out and study newspaper action pictures of great race horses. It's all there to see, fore and aft. Don't expect to see this kind of picture at horse show rings, either. There the showy action is secured not only by breeding for such short, high-stepping construction of the forehand as would literally cripple a dog, but by "mechanical" aids under which dogs would lie down and die.

In regard to forehand construction in the dog, it is very important to understand that this is something a dog is born with. Exercise won't develop it nor prayer command it. It is apparent in the baby puppy as soon as it gets up on its legs—for better or for worse. And it stays with the dog for as long as it lives, even into such fantastic old age as was granted Columbia River Tillie.

The camera can also tell us a great deal about the way a dog uses its rear assembly in free and fast going. Too many people "learn" gait from standing around dog show rings or standing up with the gallery, half-a-mile away, watching field trial dogs run. Here again we need the camera's eye, as our own only produces confusion. There has been great recent interest in gait in England where sporting dog judges are demanding that an end be put to the too-common "rear-end movement." Pointer expert, Mr. John Garnett, describes this as "hind legs swinging from the hips like pendulums." It is, of course, the typical and always ugly, stilted action of a straight-stifled dog. This is all he can do—swing his straight legs

like broomhandles. Mr. Garnett calls for insistence on the requirement that a "dog shall bring his hocks well up behind him," an
action that must surely astonish the many who have only watched
at ringside where dogs may be moved by sluggish, often aged,
handlers within a small area. To see a dog that brings up his
hocks stupefies them. It must be wrong, they comfort each other.
The others don't do it! In this connection we have another il-
luminating comment from a great international judge, Leo C.
Wilson: "Any dog that is expected to work over rough terrain should
be able to pick up his hocks behind him, but too many of our current crop would trip over a candy wrapper left lying in the ring!"

With camera in hand, I found that indeed, the majority of our
best Shorthairs *do* pick up their hocks, if only they can get the
chance. The "chance" means a ring large enough to get going, and
a handler who can step. Some very interesting pictures illustrate
this truth, of which the excellent ones of the East Coast dog,
Ch. Gunhill's Mesa Maverick, are as graphic as any. This is a good
dog, well put together, and blessed with an agile handler. Forward
striding, and usefully picking up his hocks after him as he goes,
Maverick pleases knowledgeable judges with his smooth and fast
gait.

The novice GSP owner should be thoroughly on his guard against
the lofty briefings that are delivered on the subject of gait by self-
proclaimed "experts." The most destructive words are: "It wouldn't
do in the field." For this statement, the novice should have a good
laugh ready. A dog in the field, whatever breed, has no special
gait. He just goes the way he is built, using the same levers that he
was born with for faster or slower. Many fine field trial dogs of
exceptional performance, go in spite of their construction, not because of it. Handicapped by imbalance or faulty construction fore
and-or aft, they go on heart and will-to-please to get from A to B.
But dearly do they often pay for the extra exertion imposed by the
faulty construction. The number of "practical" field trial dogs
that fold with heart trouble is not to be disregarded by those with
breed interest at heart. Such dogs are not found commonly among
the long-lasters, nor do they shine in the sphere of production. A
dog must be correctly equipped in his body for what we ask him to
do, and the death of a dog from heart strain is a reflection on the
owner's lack of discernment in working a deficient animal.

Kelso, taking the International, Laurel, Md.—caught in the full extension of his forehand stride. Compare with Moonshine (below) and Magnet (opposite).

Wide World Photos

Ch. Gretchenhof Moonshine, whose background contains the influence of both dogs on the opposite page, demonstrates reach and balance at speed.

Photo: C. Bede Maxwell

Columbia River Tillie, at age 16, exhibits correct slope of (long) shoulder and a well-angled (long) upper arm which set the dog's forelegs well beneath her. In Shorthairs, the good ones are forever.   *Photo: C. Bede Maxwell*

Kurzhaar-Sieger Magnet v. Ockerbach, famed German stud with great influence on the breed. His forehand construction and balance are illustrated here.

It cannot be too often or too clearly stated that the novice should at all times be leary of the person who tries to sell him the idea that it is of minor importance how a dog is built. It is of primary importance, indeed. The poorly constructed dog of good performance does show up continually, but his glory is often short-lived and his fate not always enviable. Nor is there any reason to doubt that he would have been an even better performer if his construction had matched his great heart, his burning will to hunt, his good nose, or his desire to please.

In the show ring, it is impossible for a big sporting dog's gait to be accurately measured during a brief sally across a small enclosure. Seldom is there scope for such a dog to get into his stride before he and his handler are falling into the ropes across the way. It is certain that a big sporting dog cannot demonstrate gait properly in a constricted area where he has to hold himself against the chance of landing right out of the auditorium, into the street. That the judging of gait (sound or unsound) under such conditions is little better than farcical could be one of the reasons why so many show dogs get by with such poor movement. Not until the big rings are cleared for Group judging does a naturally fast-moving dog in any breed get a chance to display his true gait.

Around the ringsides, some amazing interpretations appear to be read into the brief reference made to gait in the Standard of the German Shorthaired Pointer, in which even the adjective employed is merely "desirable," and in no way obligatory. Strangely enough, these appear to be directed not at the dogs with the ugly, stilted gait imposed by undesirable hind member assembly, but rather at the dogs able to demonstrate a fast, smooth going with such a flexible hock movement as delights the judges.

How a dog places his legs in movement, as opposed to how some folk *think* he does, is not the whole story of sporting dog gait, either. If a dog has not been reared right, fed right, and properly exercised over the important periods of his growth, he is likely to do all manner of peculiar and undesirable things with his legs in adulthood. The several breed Standards directing that hocks shall "turn neither in nor out" refer to a disability that is perhaps the most common of all in the sporting dog rings—hocks that sag, one way or the other, for lack of muscle to support them; no thighs, certainly no second thighs. The long legs of the taller sporting breeds,

Ch. Gunhill's Mesa Maverick, illustrating the necessary picking-up of hock in fast sporting dog gaiting. This movement cannot be seen in straight-stifled dogs.

especially, are no better engineered to stand unbraced than is a tent pole. Fortunately, the German Shorthaired Pointer, with his accepted status as a utility dog, gets rather more running and for this reason, this type of unsoundness is far less prevalent with him than in some other breeds within the Group.

Correct conformation is present from birth. This Irish Setter puppy shows good forehand assembly.

Ch. Sorgeville's Happy Holiday, whose owner, Mrs. Earle Dapper, has an eye for the "fun" photograph.

18

German Titles, Vocabulary, etc.

EVEN with a working knowledge of German, and the help of a dictionary, it can prove hard work translating pedigree information and the show and performance ratings on the papers of imported dogs. The German dog world, like the English or American, has its own language, and words do not always carry the exact dictionary meanings. Abbreviations, much used, make the job even tougher. Names of dogs, as a rule, translate easily, helped by the tendency of German breeders to use their home locality as a strain name. Awards are more complicated, especially in abbreviation. The historically-minded, too, can blunder into confusion because of a re-organization of the canine government that was enforced after 1934 by the Nazi government.

The pre-1934 governing body was the *Deutsches Kartell Für Hundewesen* (DKH). Dogs imported before that time were so sponsored. After 1934, the re-organization brought the body into new being as the *Reichsverband Für Das Deutsche Hundewesen* (RDH), which translates as the Reichs Organization (or Club) for German Dog Affairs. The new body created some confusion by making a retrospective re-issue of pedigrees originally issued by the DKH. Some early-day American imports have certificates from both. The first Nebraska imports (Claus v. Schleswig-Konigsweg and Jane v. grünen Adler) arrived in 1931, were American-registered in 1932. Both have German pedigrees under RDH headings that are dated in Stuttgart (Germany) in 1936. The second brace to Nebraska, several years later, had RDH pedigrees dated 1934. Researchers who have wondered whether there were *two* German canine governing bodies seemingly did not know about the re-organization.

With the establishment of RDH, Specialist clubs catering to various breeds were absorbed as *Fachschafts* (Sections). Each was required to keep a stud book for its breed under the strict supervision of the RDH. In 1937, there came into being the *Reichsverband. Deutscher Kleintier Züchter* (Reichs Organization of German Small Animal Breeders), which sponsored the rule that breeding should be permitted only from dogs rated "excellent" or "very good" by approved judges.

Working breeds were required also to have at least one parent possessed of a Training Certificate—an *Ausbildungkennzeichen*—to ensure that the desired working qualities for the individual breeds were within the gift of sire or dam, preferably both. Along with all the re-organization, most of the Specialist Clubs went along as they had been doing, in individual strength. This was and is true of the *Fachschaft Deutsch Kurzhaar* (Klub Kurzhaar), the Parent Club of the German Shorthaired Pointer, with headquarters in Berlin.

Awards are fairly well understood by most importers. *Sieger* and its feminine counterpart, *Siegerin,* denotes champions that have fulfilled the requirements for the title. At first it was sufficient for a dog to have won three First Prizes with a rating of *Vorzüglich,* (Excellent) under three different approved judges at recognized shows. Later it became necessary for sporting or working breeds to qualify by performance as well as conformation.

Early day dogs earned a *Klub Sieger* (K.S.) title, as many of them as could qualify, with a *Jahressieger* (Champion of the Year) to the winner of the annual Specialist show, provided it had the necessary Vorzüglich rating. After the 1934 re-organization, *Fachschaftsieger* became useable for *Klub Sieger,* and the *Jahressieger* title became *Reichssieger* (R.S.) with, of course, the feminine equivalent where the rule of gender applied. Further, at a designated European show, annually, was made the award of *Welt Sieger* (W.S.)—World Champion—to be won in competition with breed representatives from other countries.

ABBREVIATIONS:

D1 or D1A	*Dienst,* or *Dienstsuch Hund* with a rating of 1 or 1A in performance. (*Working Dog or Working Search Dog.*)
S1 or S11	*Such Hund* with a rating of 1 or 11. (*Search Dog.*)
G.H.St.B	*Gebrauchshund Stammbuch.* The general studbook for Field and Working breeds. It was originated in 1902 as the *Gebrauchsund-Luxushunde* (*Utility and Toy Dog*): *Stammbuch,* catering for the 17 breed specialist clubs then publishing their own studbooks.
Z.K.	*Zuchtbuch Kurzhaar,* the Studbook of the German Shorthaired Pointer breed in Germany.
m.S.	Sharpness Test (killing a cat or a fox under the inspection of two judges.)
F.W.	*Formwert.* (*Conformation marks.*)

Adult imports usually bring the record of their field performances as abbreviations entered on their registrations, and often as separate sheets of performance rating, signed by the judges. Each aspect of the dog's work is separately rated as shown on page 272, the *Zensuren-Vordrück fur Verbands-Jugend-Prufüngen* (Assessment Sheet for Club Youth Search).

To comply with the rules of the *Jagdebrauchshundverband* (Hunting Dog Club), performance is assessed, as in the top left-hand corner, by numbers:

0	*Ungenügend*	Insufficient
1	*Genügend*	Sufficient
2	*Ziemlich Gut*	Fairly Good
3	*Gut*	Good
4	*Sehr Gut*	Very Good
4h	*Hervorragend*	Distinguished/Outstanding

297

A. *Fährtenarbeit*

B. *Feldprüfung* ratings are for *Nase* (Nose), *Suche* (Search), *Vorstehen* (pointing), and *Gehorsam* (Obedience), in all of which this particular young dog (later imported to America) did very well. In *Hasenhetzen* (coursing—hare-chasing) he was marked on voice—*spurlaut* (trail-loud), *sichtlaut* (sight-loud), or *stumm* (silent—dumb). Cosak's combined markings earned him his *Erteilter Preis* (awarded Prize) of 1 d and 4th place in his Prize-class (*Preisklasse*).

Club Utility Search work is assessed on the *Zensurenformblatt für Verbands-Gebrauchsprufüngen* (Assessment Sheet for Club Utility Search). This is divided into four sections: *Waldarbeit* (Forest work), *Wasserarbeit* (Water Work), *Feldarbeit* (Field Work) and *Bringen* (Retrieving). These sections are subdivided and separately marked. *Waldarbeit* alone totals 10 sub-sections, later to be totaled as the *Summe der Urteilsziffer von Sec. I* (Total of Judges' Markings for Sec. 1). *Wasserarbeit* totals 3 sub-sections: Search, Search for Duck in the Reeds, and Retrieving from Deep Water. *Feldarbeit* totals 9 sub-sections, including Nose, Search, Staunch Pointing, Obedience, Steady to Shot, Hare-clean. *Bringen* includes retrieving fur and feather, dealing with beasts of prey (fox or cat), and a final retrieve over an obstacle carrying a fox.

By the time all these separate exercises have been assessed and marked, the judges have compiled a very thorough record of an individual dog's work. What is more, the sheets on which the markings are made are available to the owners, who can take them home to study. There is education as well as satisfaction in such records of performance. However, judges who must so commit themselves to a written record that anyone may scan must be highly competent.

ABBREVIATIONS used in other countries:

F.C.I.   *Federation Cynologique Internationale* (The International European Canine Governing Body).

CACIB   Int. Bench Champion Award made by the F.C.I. Requirement is 3 firsts with the mark of Excellent under 3 different judges. This is the only true "International Championship." This title is often applied to dogs that have won in both America and

Canada, but is not recognized as an International Award by the A.K.C. or elsewhere.

SH. CH. A British award, applied by the English K.C. to Sporting Dogs that have won the titles on the Bench by accumulating 3 Challenge Certificates under 3 different judges at recognized Championship shows. To gain a full championship title a Sporting dog in this country must first gain his "qualifier" under approved Field Trial judges, proving that he possesses the basic qualities of nose, search, steady to shot, etc.

ABBREVIATIONS used in America:

FIELD CH. Field Champion.
CH. Show Champion.
DUAL CH. Field and Show Champion.
C.D. Companion Dog (Obedience—1st Stage).
C.D.X. Companion Dog Excellent (Obedience—2nd Stage).
U.D. Utility Dog (Obedience—Final Stage).
T. Tracking Dog.

The first Sporting Dog to hold all the above Titles, and for long the only one, is an Irish Setter, Dual Ch. Red Arrow Show Girl, U.D.T., owned by L. Heist, of Fontana, California. The feat was matched in 1961 by a Weimaraner.

A brief vocabulary, covering much of the information likely to come with dogs from Germany:

Ahnentafel	Pedigree
Ausbildungskennzeichen	Training Qualifications
Ausstellung	Show (Exhibition)
Ausstellung von Hunden Aller Rassen	All-Breed Show
Beachtung	Notice
Besitzer	Owner
Besitzwechsel	Change of Ownership
Beglaubigungen	Certifications
Bewertung	Rating
Bewertungs-karte	Qualifications Card
Breit	Broad
Decken	To cover—to mate
Decktag	Date of Service
Deckurkunde	Certificate of Mating
Dienstssuchhund	Police Tracking Dog
Dienstssuchhundprüfung	Police Tracking Trial
Eintragen (im Stammbuch)	Registered (in Stud Book)

Eltern	Parents
Farbe und Abzeichen (als unter)	Color and Markings (as under)
Braun	Brown
Braunschimmel	Brown-ticked
Dreifarbig	Tri-color (lit. Three-colored)
Dunkel (Augen)	Dark (eyes)
Gelb	Yellow
Schwartz	Black
Weiss	White
Führer	Handler
Geschlect	Sex
Gebrauchshund	Utility (Working) Dog
Gewörfen	Whelped (Thrown)
Glaathaar	Smooth (or Short) Hair
Grosseltern	Grandparents
Haar	Hair
Hals	Neck
Hund	Dog (any dog, not specifically Hound)
Hundin	Bitch
Kupiert	Cut
Kurz	Short
Lang	Long
Laufen	Running
Mangelhaft	Mediocre (in Performance, etc.)
Ohren	Ears
Ohrbehang	Ear Carriage
Paarsuche	Brace (in Trials)
Platten	Patches (body color)
Quittung	Receipt
Rassekennzeichen	Breed Standard (Characteristics)
Reichsverband für Deutsche Hundewesen (RDH) (Auslandstelle)	Foreign Dept. of the German Kennel Governing Body
Richtig	Correct
Rüde	Male Dog (Stud)
Rute (Schwanz)	Tail (both words)
Schweisshund	Scenting Dog, Trail Dog—ANY Breed
"Schweisshund"	Bloodhound—when specifically used to describe this breed
Sekundierte	Backed (on a Point)
Siegeraustellung	Championship Show
Stammbuch-Führer	Keeper of the Stud Book
Suchhundprüfung	Tracking Test
Urgrosseltern	Great-grandparents
Wurftag (Wurfdatum)	Whelping Date
Wurfmeldung	Litter Registration
Wurfstärke	Size of litter (number of whelp)
Zimmerrein (also Stubenrein)	Housebroken (lit. Room-clean)
Zuchtbuch	Stud Book
Züchter	Breeder
Zuchtbuch No.	Studbook Number
Zuchtbuch Führer	Studbook Keeper
Zuchthundin (Stammmutter)	Foundation bitch

Zuchtbuchstelle	....	Club Pedigree Register
Zuchtverein	....	Specialty Club
Zwinger	....	Strain (Strain Name)

Some of the old-style documentation that came in with the earliest imports included an observer's word-picture of the dog. Such a description survives among the Forwarding Documents of Treu v. Saxony, the big dog imported by Dr. Thornton in 1926. As the examining veterinarian, Dr. Albrecht, saw Treu, he was:

"In schöner weiss und braun gefleckter Farbe, kurz und knapp edel im Haar, mit edlen, ausdruckvollen Kopf, langen breiten Ohrbehang und vorschriftsmässig kupierter Rute, gut auf den Läufen gestellt, kräftig entwickelt."

(*Trans.:* "Handsome white and brown flecked color, coat short and excellently close of hair, with an excellent, expressive head, long and broad ear-hang, tail cut according to regulation requirements, well established on his running-gear, strongly developed.")

FOREIGN BREED CLUBS DEVOTED TO THE
GERMAN SHORTHAIRED POINTER (as of 1962)
Affiliated with the KURZHAAR VERBANDES (Berlin) (KLUB KURZHAAR)

AUSTRIA: Dr. Otto Fischer, Wien XIV, Hellmersberger Gasse 4.

LUXEMBURG: Dr. (med.) E. Franck, Luxemburg, Neutor 3.

SWITZERLAND: Walter Uhlig, Zürich, Sumastrastr. 28.

ENGLAND: A. W. Mongor, Brighton, 6, Sussex, 91 Stanford Avenue.

FRANCE: R. Ohl, Strassburg-Neuhof, rue des Sports 25.

There appears to be no affiliation mentioned by Klub Kurzhaar official publications with respect to any Scandinavian Kurzhaar Clubs, and, of course, the very newly-formed club in Ireland may not yet have found its place on the list. However, the address of the Irish Club is:

IRELAND: German Pointer Club of Ireland, 40 Sth. Avenue, Mount Merrion, Dublin.

The Klub Kurzhaar (Berlin) also lists a separate address for its *Pedigree Stud Register (Zuchtbuchstelle)*—Berlin-Charlottenburg, Lohmeyerstr. 6.

These purely Klub institutions are separate from the German

301

A head study of three Dual Champion sisters. Owner: E. E. Harden, California.

Am.-Can. Field Ch. Arrak von Heisterholz (imp. Germany) was named Northwest Shooting Dog of the Year in 1963 and 1964. Owner: Ralph Park, Sr., Wash.

Backing a bracemate is a very important part of a Field Trial dog's skills. Show Champions Fritz Braunjager and Nixe v. Braun are also practical hunters. Owned by Commander A. G. Brown, Oklahoma.

Kennel Club (*Verband für Deutsche Hundewesen*) that caters for all breeds. The address is: Dorstfelder Hellweg 13, Dortmund.

The International Canine Governing Body (F.C.I.) is to be addressed in care of the Secrétariat-General, 12 Rue Léopold II, Thuin, Belgium.

Ch. Adam v. Fuehrerheim, a very prepotent producer of show champion stock. Owner, Robert McKowan, Pennsylvania.

BIBLIOGRAPHY

ALL OWNERS of pure-bred dogs will benefit themselves and their dogs by enriching their knowledge of breeds and of canine care, training, breeding, psychology and other important aspects of dog management. The following list of books covers further reading recommended by judges, veterinarians, breeders, trainers and other authorities. Books may be obtained at the finer book stores and pet shops, or through Howell Book House Inc., publishers, New York.

Breed Books

AFGHAN HOUND, Complete	Miller & Gilbert
AIREDALE, New Complete	Edwards
ALASKAN MALAMUTE, Complete	Riddle & Seeley
BASSET HOUND, Complete	Braun
BEAGLE, Complete	Noted Authorities
BLOODHOUND, Complete	Brey & Reed
BOXER, Complete	Denlinger
BRITTANY SPANIEL, Complete	Riddle
BULLDOG, New Complete	Hanes
BULL TERRIER, New Complete	Eberhard
CAIRN TERRIER, Complete	Marvin
CHIHUAHUA, Complete	Noted Authorities
COCKER SPANIEL, New	Kraeuchi
COLLIE, Complete	Official Publication of the Collie Club of America
DACHSHUND, The New	Meistrell
DOBERMAN PINSCHER, New	Walker
ENGLISH SETTER, New Complete	Tuck & Howell
ENGLISH SPRINGER SPANIEL, New	Goodall & Gasow
FOX TERRIER, New Complete	Silvernail
GERMAN SHEPHERD DOG, Complete	Bennett
GERMAN SHORTHAIRED POINTER, New	Maxwell
GOLDEN RETRIEVER, Complete	Fischer
GREAT DANE, New Complete	Noted Authorities
GREAT PYRENEES, Complete	Strang & Giffin
IRISH SETTER, New	Thompson
IRISH WOLFHOUND, Complete	Starbuck
KEESHOND, Complete	Peterson
LABRADOR RETRIEVER, Complete	Warwick
LHASA APSO, Complete	Herbel
MINIATURE SCHNAUZER, Complete	Eskrigge
NEWFOUNDLAND, New Complete	Chern
NORWEGIAN ELKHOUND, New Complete	Wallo
OLD ENGLISH SHEEPDOG, Complete	Mandeville
PEKINGESE, Quigley Book of	Quigley
POMERANIAN, New Complete	Ricketts
POODLE, New Complete	Hopkins & Irick
POODLE CLIPPING AND GROOMING BOOK, Complete	Kalstone
PUG, Complete	Trullinger
PULI, Complete	Owen
ST. BERNARD, New Complete	Noted Authorities, rev. Raulston
SAMOYED, Complete	Ward
SCHIPPERKE, Official Book of	Root, Martin, Kent
SCOTTISH TERRIER, Complete	Marvin
SHETLAND SHEEPDOG, New	Riddle
SHIH TZU, The (English)	Dadds
SIBERIAN HUSKY, Complete	Demidoff
TERRIERS, The Book of All	Marvin
TOY DOGS, Kalstone Guide to Grooming All	Kalstone
TOY DOGS, All About	Ricketts
WEST HIGHLAND WHITE TERRIER, Complete	Marvin
WHIPPET, Complete	Pegram
YORKSHIRE TERRIER, Complete	Gordon & Bennett

Care and Training

DOG OBEDIENCE, Complete Book of	Saunders
NOVICE, OPEN AND UTILITY COURSES	Saunders
DOG CARE AND TRAINING, Howell Book of	Howell, Denlinger, Merrick
DOG CARE AND TRAINING FOR BOYS AND GIRLS	Saunders
DOG TRAINING FOR KIDS	Benjamin
DOG TRAINING, Koehler Method of	Koehler
GO FIND! Training Your Dog to Track	Davis
GUARD DOG TRAINING, Koehler Method of	Koehler
OPEN OBEDIENCE FOR RING, HOME AND FIELD, Koehler Method of	Koehler
SPANIELS FOR SPORT (English)	Radcliffe
SUCCESSFUL DOG TRAINING, The Pearsall Guide to	Pearsall
TRAIN YOUR OWN GUN DOG, How to	Goodall
TRAINING THE RETRIEVER	Kersley
TRAINING YOUR DOG TO WIN OBEDIENCE TITLES	Morsell
UTILITY DOG TRAINING, Koehler Method of	Koehler

Breeding

ART OF BREEDING BETTER DOGS, New	Onstott
HOW TO BREED DOGS	Whitney
HOW PUPPIES ARE BORN	Prine
INHERITANCE OF COAT COLOR IN DOGS	Little

General

COMPLETE DOG BOOK, The	Official Pub. of American Kennel Club
DISNEY ANIMALS, World of	Koehler
DOG IN ACTION, The	Lyon
DOG BEHAVIOR, New Knowledge of	Pfaffenberger
DOG JUDGING, Nicholas Guide to	Nicholas
DOG NUTRITION, Collins Guide to	Collins
DOG PEOPLE ARE CRAZY	Riddle
DOG PSYCHOLOGY	Whitney
DOG STANDARDS ILLUSTRATED	
DOGSTEPS, Illustrated Gait at a Glance	Elliott
ENCYCLOPEDIA OF DOGS, International	Dangerfield, Howell & Riddle
JUNIOR SHOWMANSHIP HANDBOOK	Brown & Mason
RICHES TO BITCHES	Shattuck
SUCCESSFUL DOG SHOWING, Forsyth Guide to	Forsyth
TRIM, GROOM AND SHOW YOUR DOG, How to	Saunders
WHY DOES YOUR DOG DO THAT?	Bergman
WORLD OF SLED DOGS, From Siberia to Sport Racing	Coppinger
OUR PUPPY'S BABY BOOK (blue or pink)	